Always Ready

DIRECTIONS FOR DEFENDING THE FAITH

DR. GREG L. BAHNSEN

Always Ready

DIRECTIONS FOR DEFENDING THE FAITH

edited by Robert R. Booth

CMP
Covenant Media Press
8784 FM 226, Nacogdoches, TX 75961

Eleventh printing, September 2011

Printed in the United States of America

ISBN: 0-915815-28-1

Cover design: James Talmage, JET Studio, Byron, Georgia

Cover image of "St. Paul Preaching at Athens" by Raphael—Victoria & Albert Museum — Art Resource

Dedication

In loving memory of Dr. Greg L. Bahnsen
[September 17, 1948 — December 11, 1995]
Who was "always ready" to defend the faith,
and always ready to meet his Lord.

Contents

EDITOR'S PREFACE

The Apostle Peter instructs believers that they should be "always ready to give a defense [*apologia*] to everyone who asks you a reason for the hope that is in you" (1 Peter 3:15). Dr. Greg Bahnsen was not only "always ready" to make such a defense, he was always ready to teach others how to prepare themselves for this essential work. It pleased God, in the mystery of His providence, to raise up this doubly-gifted man for the benefit of His people in this generation. That same mysterious Providence that gave us Dr. Bahnsen also called him home at the early age of 47—he went to be with his Lord on December 11, 1995. Dr. Bahnsen left in his wake a legacy of apologetic evangelism. Not only was he one of the leading apologists and debaters of this century,[1] taking on prominent atheistic champions, he was also devoted to seeing Christians at all levels equipped and competent to defend the faith themselves.

The defense of the Christian faith [apologetics] is the responsibility of every Christian. This was the heart-felt conviction of Dr. Bahnsen, who devoted much of his ministry to the training of men and women for this important task. He was eminently qualified to offer such training and instruction. First, Dr. Bahnsen was a man who loved and was committed to his Lord Jesus Christ—he was called by God to this task. He received a B.A. (*magna cum laude*, philosophy) from Westmont College, and then simultaneously earned the M.Div. and Th.M. degrees from Westminster Theological Seminary, specializing in systematic theology and ethics. From there he went on to the University of Southern California where he received his Ph.D. in philosophy, specializing in the field of epistemology (the theory of knowledge). His dissertation was on the subject of self-deception, making a significant contribution to this important apologetic issue. While a student at seminary, he was called upon by the renowned apologist, Dr. Cornelius Van Til, to lecture for him in his apologetics course. Dr. Bahnsen has done much toward explaining, applying and even popularizing the work of Dr. Van Til's distinctive presuppositional apologetic.[2]

This volume is a compilation of materials produced by Dr. Bahnsen over several years and is intended to introduce students to important foundational concepts essential to biblical apologetics. The first section, previously published as a syllabus, provides a step-by-step explanation of key issues in Christian apologetics and establishes the biblical support for the presuppositional method. The second section of this volume offers further practical advice on how to approach an apologetic situation and provides specific answers to particular apologetic questions such as "the problem of evil." The book concludes with an appendix giving a detailed exposition of the Apostle Paul's defense of the faith as he delivered it at the Areopagus in Athens, as recorded in Acts 17.

Every believer can profit from this material. It may prove especially useful as a textbook for school and church classes. As we become better equipped to defend the faith we find greater confidence and boldness to carry the message of the gospel to every dark place. No challenge shall intimidate the believer as he gently and respectfully closes the mouth of unbelief. May God bless you in your preparation to be "always ready."

> Your fellow servant,
> Randy Booth
> Director of Covenant Media Foundation

Notes:

[1] This is a point conceded even by many of Dr. Bahnsen's theological opponents. Few, if any, were his equal when it came to intellectual acuity and debating skills. A prime example of his apologetic skills is witnessed in his famous debate at the University of California, Irvine, in 1985, with atheist promoter, Dr. Gordon Stein.

[2] "Presuppositional apologetics" is a distinct school of apologetic method, standing over against the "classical" (Thomistic) and fideistic methods. This book is an explanation and application of the presuppositional apologetic method.

SECTION ONE:

THE LORDSHIP OF CHRIST IN THE REALM OF KNOWLEDGE

Biblical epistemology =
   theory of Knowledge

CHAPTER 1:

THE ROBBERY OF NEUTRALITY

The plea for Christians to surrender to neutrality in their thinking is not an uncommon one. Nevertheless it strikes at the very heart of our faith and of our faithfulness to the Lord.

Sometimes the demand to assume a neutral stance, a non-committal attitude toward the truthfulness of Scripture, is heard in the area of Christian scholarship (whether it be the field of history, science, literature, philosophy, or whatever). Teachers, researchers, and writers are often led to think that honesty demands for them to put aside all distinctly Christian commitments when they study in an area which is not directly related to matters of Sunday worship. They reason that since truth is truth wherever it may be found, one should be able to search for truth under the guidance of the acclaimed thinkers in the field, even if they are secular in their outlook. "Is it really necessary to hold to the teachings of the Bible if you are to understand properly the War of 1812, the chemical composition of water, the plays of Shakespeare, or the rules of logic?" Such is the rhetorical question of those who are disposed to insist on neutrality from Christians working in scholarly areas.

Sometimes the demand for neutrality arises in the realm of apologetics (defense of the faith). We are told by some apologists that they would lose all hearing with the unbelieving world if they were to approach the question of Scripture's truthfulness with a preconceived answer to the question. We must be willing, according to this outlook, to approach the debate with unbelievers with a common attitude of neutrality—a "nobody knows as yet" attitude. We must assume as little as possible at the outset, we are told; and this means that we cannot assume any Christian premises or teachings of the Bible.

Other times the plea for neutrality in the thinking of the believer comes with reference to schools. Some Christians feel that there is no real urgency for Christian schools, that secular education is all right as far as it goes, and that it needs only to be supplemented with Christian prayer and Bible reading in the home. Thus the idea is that one can be neutral when it comes to education; one's Christian faith need not dictate any particular assumptions or way of learning about the world and man. We are told that the facts are the same at state schools as they are at Christian schools; so why insist that your children be taught by committed believers in Jesus Christ?

Well then, in these and many other ways we can see that the Christian is called upon to surrender his distinctive religious beliefs to temporarily "put them on the shelf," to take a neutral attitude in his thinking. Satan would love this to happen. More than anything else, this would prevent the conquest of the world to belief in Jesus Christ as Lord. More than anything else, this would make professing Christians impotent in their witness, aimless in their walk, and disarmed in their battle with the principalities and powers of this world. More than anything else, such neutrality would prevent sanctification in the Christian's life, for Christ said that His followers were "sanctified (set apart) by the truth." Immediately He went on to declare, "Thy word is truth" (John 17:17).

Whatever some people may say with respect to the demand for neutrality in the Christian's thought—the demand that believers not be set apart from other men by their adherence to God's truth—the fact is that Scripture sharply differs with this demand. Contrary to neutrality's demand, God's word demands unreserved allegiance to God and His truth in all our thought and scholarly endeavors. It does so for a good reason.

Paul infallibly declares in Colossians 2:3-8 that "All the treasures of wisdom and knowledge are hid in Christ." Note he says *all* wisdom and knowledge is deposited in the person of Christ—whether it be about the War of 1812, water's chemical composition, the literature of Shakespeare, or the laws of logic! Every academic pursuit and every thought must be related to Jesus Christ, for Jesus is the way, *the truth*, and the life. (John 14:6) To avoid Christ in your thought at any point, then, is to be misled, untruthful, and spiritually dead. To put aside your Christian commitments when it comes to defending the faith or sending your children to school is willfully to steer away from the *only* path to wisdom and truth found *in Christ*. It is not the end or outcome of knowledge to fear the Lord; it is the *beginning* of knowledge to reverence Him (Prov. 1:7; 9:10).

Paul declares that all knowledge must be related to Christ, then, according to Colossians 2. He says this for our protection; it is very dangerous to fail to see the necessity of Christ in all our thinking. So Paul draws to our attention the impossibility of neutrality "in order that no one delude you with crafty speech." Instead we must, as Paul exhorts, be steadfast, confirmed, rooted, and established in the faith as we were taught (v. 7). One must be presuppositionally committed to Christ in the world of thought (rather than neutral) and firmly tied down to the faith which he has been taught, or else the persuasive argumentation of secular thought will delude him. Hence the Christian is obligated to presuppose the word of Christ in every area of knowledge; the alternative is delusion.

In verse 8 of Colossians 2 Paul says "Beware lest any man rob you by means of philosophy and vain deceit." By attempting to be neutral in your thought you are a prime target for being *robbed*—robbed by "vain philosophy" of all the treasures of "wisdom and knowledge" which are deposited in Christ alone (cf. v. 3). Paul explains that vain philosophy is that which follows the world and not Christ; it is thinking which submits to the world's demand for neutrality rather than being presuppositionally committed to Christ in all of our thinking.

Are you *rich* in knowledge because of your commitment to Christ in, scholarship, apologetics, and schooling, or have you been *robbed* by the demands of neutrality?

CHAPTER 2:

THE IMMORALITY OF NEUTRALITY

All the *treasures* of wisdom and knowledge are to be found in Christ; thus if one were to try and arrive at the truth apart from commitment to the epistemic authority of Jesus Christ he would be *robbed* through vain philosophy and deluded by crafty deceit (see Col. 2:3-8). Consequently, when the Christian approaches scholarship, apologetics, or schooling he must staunchly refuse to acquiesce to the mistaken demands of neutrality in his intellectual life; he must never consent to surrender his distinctive religious beliefs "for the time being," as though one might thereby arrive at genuine knowledge "impartially." The *beginning* of knowledge is the fear of the Lord (Prov. 1:7).

Attempting to be neutral in one's intellectual endeavors (whether research, argumentation, reasoning, or teaching) is tantamount to striving to erase the antithesis between the Christian and the unbeliever. Christ declared that the former was set apart from the latter by the truth of God's word (John 17:17). Those who wish to gain dignity in the eyes of the world's intellectuals by wearing the badge of "neutrality" only do so at the expense of refusing to be *set apart* by God's truth. In the intellectual realm they are absorbed into the world so that no one could tell the difference between their thinking and assumptions and apostate thinking and assumptions. The line between believer and unbeliever is obscured.

Such *indiscrimination* in one's intellectual life not only precludes genuine knowledge (cf. Prov. 1:7) and guarantees vain delusion (cf. Col. 2:3-8), it is downright *immoral.*

In Ephesians 4:17-18, Paul commands the followers of Christ that they "no longer walk as the Gentiles also walk, in the vanity of their mind, being darkened in their understanding, alienated from the life of God because of the ignorance in them, because of the hardening of their heart." Christian believers must not walk, must not behave or live, in a way which imitates the behavior of those who are unredeemed; specifically, Paul forbids the Christian from imitating the unbeliever's *vanity of mind.* Christians must refuse to think or reason according to a worldly mind-set or outlook. The culpable agnosticism of the world's intellectuals must not be reproduced in Christians as alleged neutrality; this outlook, this approach to truth, this intellectual method evidences a darkened understanding and hardened heart. It refuses to bow to the Lordship of Jesus Christ over every area of life, including scholarship and the world of thought.

One has to make this basic choice in his thinking: to be set apart by God's truth *or* to be alienated from the life of God. It cannot be two ways. One shall be set apart, set against, or alienated from either the world or from the word of God. He will stand in *contrast* to that intellectual method which he refuses to follow. He either refuses to follow God's word or he refuses to follow the vain mind-set of the Gentiles. He distinguishes himself and his thinking either by contrast to the world or by contrast to God's word. The contrast, the antithesis, the choice is clear: either be set apart by God's truthful word or be alienated from the life of God. Either have "the mind of Christ" (1 Cor. 2:16) or the "vain mind of the Gentiles" (Eph. 4:17). Either "bring every thought into captivity to the obedience of Christ" (2 Cor. 10:5) or continue as "enemies in your mind" (Col. 1:21).

Those who follow the intellectual principle of neutrality and the epistemological method of unbelieving scholarship do not honor the sovereign Lordship of God as they should; as a result their reasoning is made vain (Rom. 1:21). In Ephesians 4, as we have seen, Paul prohibits the Christian from following this vain mind-set. Paul goes on to teach that the believer's thinking is diametrically contrary to the ignorant and darkened thinking of the Gentiles. "But you did not learn Christ after this manner!" (verse 20). While the Gentiles are ignorant, "the truth is in Jesus" (verse 21). Unlike the Gentiles who are alienated from the life of God, the Christian has put away the old man and has been "renewed in the spirit of your mind" (verses 22-23). This *"new man"* is distinctive in virtue of the "holiness of truth" (verse 24). The Christian is completely different from the world when it comes to intellect and scholarship; he does not follow the neutral methods of unbelief, but by God's grace he has new commitments, new presuppositions, in his thinking.

Therefore, the Christian who strives after neutrality in his thought is found actually to be endeavoring to efface the fact that he is a Christian! By denying his distinctive religious commitment he is reduced to apostate thought patterns and absorbed into the world of unbelief. Attempting to find a compromise between the demands of worldly neutrality (agnosticism) and the doctrines of Christ's word results in the rejection of Christ's distinctive Lordship by obliterating the great gulf between the thinking of the old man and that of the new man.

No such compromise is even possible. *"No* man *is able* to serve two lords" (Matt. 6:24). It should come as no surprise that, in a world where all things have been created by Christ (Col. 1:16) and are carried along by the word of His power (Heb. 1:3) and where all knowledge is therefore deposited in Him who is The Truth (Col. 2:3; John 14:6) and who must be Lord over all thinking (2 Cor. 10:5), *neutrality is nothing short of immorality.* "Whosoever therefore would be a friend of the world maketh himself an enemy of God" (James 4:4).

Do you have the courage of your Christian *distinctives* in scholarship, apologetics, and schooling, or have you been trying to wipe out the contrast between Christian thought and apostate thought by following the demands of neutrality? Put in biblical perspective this question can be rephrased in this way: does your thinking operate under the Lordship of Jesus Christ or have you become an enemy of God through neutral, agnostic, unbelieving thought patterns? Choose this day whom you will serve!

CHAPTER 3:

THE NATURE OF
UNBELIEVING THOUGHT

In Parts I and II of the present study a discussion of the demand for neutrality in our scholarly, apologetical, or educational endeavors has shown it to lead to unfortunate results. It robs one of all the treasures of knowledge that there are. Secondly, taking a neutral approach to knowledge has been demonstrated to be immoral in character, allowing one's Christian distinctives to be muffled and finally integrated into the rebellious ways of an unbelieving mind-set. Finally, it has been noted that in reality it is impossible for the genuine Christian to be neutral in his intellectual life, for such neutrality in a Christian would call for a dual commitment: one to secular agnosticism, one to saving faith (i.e., "serving two lords").

Returning to Ephesians 4 and Colossians 2, let us ask what the true character of neutralist thinking is. Just what kind of thinking is it that does not base itself upon the teaching of God's Son, that refrains from presupposing the doctrines of Christ?

Paul tells us in Ephesians 4 that to follow the methods dictated by the intellectual outlook of those who are outside of a saving relationship to God is to have a *vain* mind and a *darkened* understanding (vv. 17-18). Neutralist thinking, then, is characterized by intellectual futility and ignorance. In God's light we are able to see light (cf. Ps. 36:9). To turn away from intellectual dependence upon the light of God, the truth about and from God, is to turn away from knowledge to the darkness of ignorance. Thus if a Christian wishes to begin his scholarly endeavors from a position of neutrality he would, in actuality, be willing to begin his thinking in the dark. He would not allow God's word to be a light unto his path (cf. Ps. 119:105). To walk on in neutrality he would be stumbling along in *darkness*. God is certainly not honored by such thought as He should be, and consequently God makes such reasoning *vain* (Rom. 1:21b). Neutrality amounts to vanity in God's sight.

That "philosophy" which does not find its starting point and direction in Christ is further described by Paul in Colossians 2:8. It has been mistakenly thought from time to time that this passage condemns any and all philosophy, that without qualification the Christian must avoid philosophic thought like the plague. However, a careful reading of the passage will evidence that this is not so. Paul does *not* disapprobate philosophy absolutely, for he delineates certain qualifications. It turns out that there is a *particular kind* of philosophic thinking that Paul scorns. Paul is not against the "love of wisdom" (i.e., "philosophy" from the Greek) *per se*. Philosophy is fine as long as one properly finds *genuine wisdom*—which means, for Paul, finding it in *Christ* (Col. 2:3).

However, there is a kind of "philosophy" which does not begin with the truth of God, the teaching of Christ. Instead this philosophy takes its direction and finds it origin in the accepted principles of the world's intellectuals—in the traditions of men. Such philosophy as this is the subject of Paul's disapprobation in Colossians 2:8. It is instructive for us, especially if we are prone to accept the demands of neutrality in our thinking, to investigate his characterizations of that kind of philosophy.

Paul says that it is "vain deception." What kind of thinking is it that can be characterized as "vain"? A ready answer is found by comparison and contrast in scriptural passages that speak of vanity (e.g., Deut. 32:47; Phil. 2:16; Acts 4:25; 1 Cor. 3:20; 1 Tim. 1:6; 6:20; 2 Tim. 2:15-18; Tit. 1:9-10). Vain thinking is that which is not in accord with God's word. A similar study will demonstrate that "deceptive" thinking is thought which is in opposition to God's word (cf. Heb. 3:12-15; Eph. 4:22; 2 Thess. 2:10-12; 2 Pet. 2:13). The "vain deception" against which Paul warns, then, is philosophy which operates apart from, and against, the truth of Christ. Note the injunction of Ephesians 5:6, "Let no man *deceive* you with *vain* words." In Colossians 2:8 we are told to take care lest we be robbed through "vain deceit."

Paul further characterizes this kind of philosophy as "according to the tradition of men, after the fundamental principles of the world." That is, this philosophy sets aside God's word and makes it void (cf. Mark 7:8-13), and it does so by beginning with the *elements of learning* dictated by the world (i.e., the precepts of men; cf. Col. 2:20, 22). The philosophy which Paul spurns is that reasoning which follows the *presuppositions* (the elementary assumptions) of the world, and thereby is "not according to Christ."

It follows from these points that the Christian who strives for neutrality in the world of thought is (1) not neutral after all, and thus (2) in danger of unwittingly endorsing assumptions that are hostile to his Christian faith. While imagining that his intellectual neutrality is compatible with a Christian profession, such a believer is actually operating in terms of unbelief! If he refuses to presuppose the truth of Christ, he invariably ends up presupposing the outlook of the world instead. All men have their presuppositions; none is neutral. Shall your presuppositions be the teachings of Christ or the vain deception against which Paul warns? Choose this day whom ye shall serve!

CHAPTER 4:

THE MIND OF THE NEW MAN ROOTED IN CHRIST

The believer is directed to avoid philosophy which is rooted in worldly, humanistic, and non-Christian presuppositions (Col. 2:8). Instead he is called to be rooted in Christ and established in the faith (v. 7); his presuppositions must be the precepts and doctrines of Christ, not the futile traditions of men (cf. vv. 3, 4, 22; 3:1-2). This precludes the claim to neutrality and prohibits seeking after it. Neutrality is in actuality veiled agnosticism or unbelief—a failure to walk in Christ, an obscuring of Christian commitment and distinctives, a suppression of the truth (cf. Rom. 1:21, 25).

Thus Paul commands us to be rooted in Christ and to shun the presuppositions of secularism. In verse 6 of Colossians 2 he explains very simply how we should go about having our lives (including our scholarly endeavors) grounded in Christ and thereby insuring that our reasoning is guided by Christian presuppositions. He says, "As therefore you received Christ Jesus the Lord so walk in Him": that is, walk in Christ in the same way that you received Him. If you do this you will be "established in your faith even as you were taught." How then did you become a Christian? After the same fashion you should grow and mature in your Christian walk.

When one becomes a Christian his faith has not been generated by the thought patterns of worldly wisdom. The world in its wisdom knows not God (1 Cor. 1:21) but considers the word of the cross to be foolish (1 Cor. 1:18, 21b). If one keeps the perspective of the world, then, he shall never see the wisdom of God for what it really is; thereby he will never be "in Christ Jesus" who is made unto believers "wisdom from God" (1 Cor. 1:30). Hence *faith*, rather than self-sufficient sight, makes you a Christian, and this trust is directed toward Christ, not your own intellect. This is to say that the way you receive Christ is to turn away from the wisdom of men (the perspective of secular thought with its presuppositions) and gain, by the illumination of the Holy Spirit, the mind of Christ (1 Cor. 2:12-16). When one becomes a Christian his faith stands not in the wisdom of men but in the powerful demonstration of the Spirit (1 Cor. 2:4-5).

Moreover, what the Holy Spirit causes all believers to say is "Jesus is Lord" (1 Cor. 12:3). Jesus was crucified, resurrected, and ascended in order that He might be confessed as Lord (cf. Rom. 14:9; Phil. 2:11). Thus Paul can summarize that message which must be confessed if we are to be saved as "Jesus is Lord" (Rom. 10:9). To become a Christian one submits to the Lordship of Christ; he renounces autonomy and comes under the authority of God's Son. The One whom Paul says we receive, according to Colossians 2:6, is Christ Jesus *the* Lord. As Lord over the believer, Christ requires that the Christian love Him with every faculty he possesses (including his mind, Matt. 22:37); every *thought* must be brought captive to the obedience of Christ (2 Cor. 10:5).

Consequently, when Paul directs us to walk in Christ after the same fashion in which we received Him, we can see at least this much: the Christian walk does not honor the thought patterns of worldly wisdom but submits to the epistemic Lordship of Christ (i.e. His authority in the area of thought and knowledge). In this manner a person comes to faith, and in this manner the believer must continue to live and carry out his calling—even when he is concerned with scholarship, apologetics, or schooling.

If the Christian will evidence commitment to Christ's personal Lordship and presuppose the word of the Lord, then he will be walking in Christ after the manner in which he received Him. Hereby you will be "rooted in Him" rather than rooted in the apostate presuppositions of worldly philosophy, and we shall be able to behold "the steadfastness of your faith in Christ" (Col. 2:5). Such firm, presuppositional faith in Christ will resist the secular world's demand for neutrality and reject the unbeliever's standards of knowledge and truth in favor of the authority of Christ's word. This faith will not be plundered of all the treasures of wisdom and knowledge that are hidden in Christ, and will not be deluded by the crafty speech and vain deceit of secular philosophies (vv. 3-8). Therefore, the unqualified precondition of genuine Christian scholarship is that the believer (along with all his thinking) be "rooted in Christ" (v. 7). Interestingly, the verb tense of the Greek for "rooted" in this verse suggests an action which has been accomplished in the past but continues in force or effect in the present—which is precisely Paul's point in verse 6! The principles which apply to the Christian's walk (inclusive of his thought) are the same which applied to his previous reception of Christ at conversion. The Christian scholar, having been rooted in Christ by renouncing the authority of secular wisdom for the Lordship of Christ, must carry out his scholarly endeavors by continuing to be rooted in Christ in the same fashion.

Therefore, the new man, the believer with a renewed mind that has been taught by Christ, is no more to walk in the intellectual vanity and darkness which characterizes the unbelieving world (read Eph. 4:17-24). The Christian has new commitments, new presuppositions, a new Lord, a new direction and goal—he is a *new* man. That newness is expressed in his thinking and scholarship, for (as in all other areas) *Christ must have the preeminence* in the world of thought (cf. Col. 1:18b). We must concur with Dr. Cornelius Van Til in saying:

> It is Christ as God who speaks in the Bible. Therefore the Bible does not appeal to human reason as ultimate in order to justify what it says. It comes to the human being with absolute authority. Its claim is that human reason must itself be taken in the sense in which Scripture takes it, namely, as created by God and as therefore properly subject to the authority of God... The two systems, that of the non-Christian and that of the Christian, differ because of the fact that their basic assumptions, or presuppositions differ. On the non-Christian

basis man is assumed to be the final reference point in predic-
tion... The Reformed method...begins frankly "from above."
It would "presuppose" God. But in presupposing God it cannot place itself at any point on a neutral basis with the non-
Christian... Believers themselves have not chosen the Christian position because they were wiser than others. What they
have they have by grace alone. But this fact does not mean
that they must accept the problematics of fallen man as right
or even as probably or possibly right. For the essence of the
idea of Scripture is that it *alone* is the criterion of truth. (*A
Christian Theory of Knowledge*, Presbyterian and Reformed
Publishing Co., 1969, pp. 15, 18, 43.)

CHAPTER 5:

REVELATION AS THE FOUNDATION OF KNOWLEDGE

The new man in Christ has new presuppositions and a new Lord over his thoughts. Rather than striving for intellectual neutrality he is "rooted in Him," walking after the manner in which he received Christ: in faith, by the enlightenment of the Holy Spirit, under the supreme authority of Jesus Christ—not according to the thought patterns of worldly wisdom. That is, the Christian *presupposes* the truthful word of God as his *standard* of truth and direction.

God tells us to apply our hearts unto His knowledge if we are to know the certainty of the words of truth (Prov. 22:17-21). It is characteristic of philosophers today that they either deny that there is absolute truth or they deny that one can be certain of knowing the truth; it is either not there, or it is unreachable. However, what God has written to us (i.e., Scripture) can "make you know the certainty of the words of truth" (vv. 20-21). The truth is accessible! However, in order to firmly grasp it one must heed the injunction of verse 17b: "apply your mind to My knowledge." God's knowledge is primary, and whatever man is to know can only be based upon a reception of what God has originally and ultimately known. Man must think God's thoughts after Him, for "in

Thy light shall we see light" (Ps. 36:9).

David's testimony was that "The Lord my God illumines my darkness" (Ps. 18:28). Into the darkness of man's ignorance, the ignorance which results from attempted self-sufficiency, come the words of God, bringing light and understanding (Ps. 119: 130). Thus Augustine correctly said, "I believe *in order* to understand." Understanding and knowledge of the truth are the promised results when man makes God's word (reflecting God's primary knowledge) his presuppositional starting point for all thinking. "Attend unto My wisdom: incline your ear to My understanding in order that you may preserve discretion and in order that your lips may keep knowledge" (Prov. 5:1-2).

To make God's word your presupposition, your standard, your instructor and guide, however, calls for renouncing intellectual self-sufficiency—the attitude that you are autonomous, able to attain unto genuine knowledge independent of God's direction and standards. The man who claims (or pursues) neutrality in his thought does not recognize his complete dependence upon the God of all knowledge for whatever he has come to understand about the world. Such men give the impression (often) that they are Christians only because they, as superior intellects, have figured out or verified (to a large or significant degree) the teachings of Scripture. Instead of beginning with God's sure word as foundational to their studies, they would have us think that they begin with intellectual self-sufficiency and (using this as their starting-point) work up to a "rational" acceptance of Scripture. While Christians may fall into an autonomous spirit while following their scholarly endeavors, still this attitude is not consistent with Christian profession and character. "The *beginning* of knowledge is the fear of Jehovah" (Prov. 1:7). All knowledge begins with God, and thus we who wish to have knowledge must presuppose God's word and renounce intellectual autonomy. "Talk no more proudly: let not arrogance come from your mouth, for Jehovah is a God of knowledge" (1 Sam. 2:3).

Jehovah is the one who teaches man knowledge (Ps. 94:10). So *whatever* we have, even the knowledge which we have about the world, has been given to us from God. "What do you have that you have not received?" (1 Cor. 4:7). Why then should men pride themselves in intellectual self-sufficiency? "According as it stands written, He that glorieth, let him glory in the *Lord* (1 Cor. 1:31). Humble submission to God's word must precede man's every intellectual pursuit. When men do not glorify God as they should (bowing before His Lordship in the world of thought) or give thanks unto Him (even for the knowledge that He grants them), their reasonings become vain and their hearts are darkened (Rom. 1:21). The man who claims "scholarly neutrality" or "philosophic autonomy" incurs God's judgment upon that very area in which the man boasts—his intellect. Those who refuse to presuppose the epistemic Lordship of Christ, the truth of Scripture as the standard of knowledge, and the necessity of God's light before they can see light, are led into futile thoughts and darkness. Just examine the sort of "scholarly" material that is produced by the universities of our land: existential despair, relativism respecting truth, irrelevance in detailed studies, dehumanizing scientific "advances," and a political paper-chase! "Hath not God made foolish the wisdom of the world?" (1 Cor. 1:20). When men are not proper stewards of that which God has given them (e.g., scholarly ability), then God takes away even that which was previously possessed (e.g., making such scholarship vain, that is, "empty").

However, as Christians, we have heard Christ's word, which is able to turn us from darkness to light (Acts 26:18). The only-wise God (Rom. 16:27) who made the world according to wisdom (Ps. 104:24) gives us a spirit of wisdom and enlightens our eyes (Eph. 1:17-18) so that we might both know Him (in salvation) and have knowledge about His world (in truth). The foundation of knowledge is God's revelation. Are you founded there or intellectually adrift?

CHAPTER 6:

SUMMARY AND APPLICATION: GOD'S SELF-ATTESTING AUTHORITY

The material from the past five studies can be arranged into the following topical summary:

1. All knowledge is deposited in Christ; man's knowledge of the truth depends upon God's prior knowledge, begins with the fear of the Lord, and requires submission to God's word.
2. Philosophy which does not presuppose God's word is a vain deception; by suppressing the truth, submitting to human traditions, and reasoning according to the presuppositions of the world instead of Christ, such thinking leads to a darkened mind and futile conclusions. God makes foolish the vaunted wisdom of the world.
3. Endeavoring to take a neutral stance between presupposing God's word and not presupposing it is an immoral attempt to serve two lords.
4. Neutralist thinking would erase the Christian's distinctiveness, blur the antithesis between worldly and believing mind-sets, and ignore the gulf between the "old man" and the "new man." The Chris-

tian who strives for neutrality unwittingly endorses assumptions which are hostile to his faith.

5. The Christian is a "new man," having a renewed mind, new commitments, a new direction and goal, a new Lord, and hence new presuppositions in the world of thought; the believer's thinking ought to be rooted in Christ (after the same manner in which he was converted): submitting to His epistemic Lordship rather than the thought patterns of apostate pseudo-wisdom. The Christian renounces the arrogance of human autonomy and seeks to love God with all his mind and to reason in such a manner that God receives the full glory.

6. The alternatives are then quite clear: either ground all your thought in Christ's word and thereby gain the treasures of wisdom and knowledge, or follow the dictates of autonomous thought and be thereby deluded and robbed of a genuine knowledge of the truth.

7. Therefore, God's word (in Scripture) has absolute authority for us and is the final criterion of truth.

From the fact that God is the sovereign Creator of heaven and earth, from the fact that the world and history are only such as His plan decrees, from the fact that man is the creaturely image of God, we must conclude that all knowledge which man possesses is received from God, who is the originator of all truth and the original Truth. Our knowledge is a reflection, a receptive reconstruction, of the primary, absolute, creative knowledge of God's mind. We must think His thoughts after Him—as the first premise above states. By holding down the truth about God, then, one's thinking and interpretative endeavors will, of necessity, be misdirected into error and foolishness (premise 2). There can be no middle ground; one consciously begins with God in his thoughts or he does not (premise 3). Believers who try to establish such a middle ground must, then, either lose their own solid ground or end up working from the unbeliever's base (which is no ground at all)—as indicated in premise 4. The very nature of what it is to be, become, and live as a Christian sufficiently establishes that the believer must presuppose the truth of God's word and give up any sinful claim to self-sufficiency or neutrality (premise 5). Thus one is faced with an obvious choice to live under the authority of God, or not (premise 6). Reflection upon the Creator/creature distinction (with which this paragraph opened) cannot fail to lead us, then, to the conclusion (premise 7) that the Creator's voice is the voice of absolute, unquestionable authority; His word must be the standard by which we judge all things and the starting point of our thinking. Such is the unavoidable teaching of Scripture (from which the above points have been derived).

Men should notice that when Jesus taught, He taught with self-attesting authority and not as one whose opinions had to be backed with the authority of other considerations or other persons (Matt. 7:29). Thus no man has the prerogative to call the word of Christ into question. If a man will not receive and heed the words of Christ, then not only is he a fool who builds his life upon the destructive sand (Matt. 7:26-27), but he shall be judged by those very same, authoritative words (John 12:48-50). God's word has supreme authority. "Woe to him who strives with his Maker!" (Isa. 45:9).

The standard by which we judge all teachings must be this word of authority from God (1 John 4:11; Deut. 13:1-4): "To the law and to the testimony; if they speak not according to this word surely there is no light for them" (Isa. 8:20). If you fail to submit presuppositionally to God's self-attesting, authoritative word, then you shall be "double-minded" and unstable in all your ways, driven by the wind and tossed about (James 1:5-8). Instead of being driven by the "Wind" of God's "Spirit," you will be carried about by every wind of doctrine through the cunning of humanistic thought and the craftiness of error (Eph. 4:13-14). Therefore, we must *unyieldingly* hold fast to the confession of our Christian hope (Heb. 10:23). Hear God's assertion: "I, Jehovah, speak righteousness; I declare things that are right" (Isa. 45:19). His word, from the very outset, must be accounted as authoritatively true; one must not waver in this regard. God's veracity is the ultimate standard for our thoughts: "let God be found true, but every man a liar!" (Rom. 3:4).

The word of the Lord is self-attestingly true and authoritative. It is the criterion we must use in judging all other words. Thus, God's word is unassailable. It must be the rock-bottom foundation of our thinking and living (Matt. 7:24-25). It is our presuppositional starting-point. All our reasoning must be subordinated to God's word, for no man is in a position to reply against it (Rom. 9:20) and any who contend with God will end up having to answer (Job 40:1-5). It must not be the changing opinions of men but the self-attesting, authoritative, ultimately veracious word from God that has the preeminence in our thoughts, for "canst thou thunder with a voice like Him?" (Job 40:9).

SECTION TWO:

THE CONDITIONS NECESSARY
FOR THE APOLOGETIC TASK

CHAPTER 7:

THREE ARGUMENTS AGAINST PRESUPPOSITIONALISM

God's word has been seen to be foundational to all knowledge. It has absolute epistemic authority and it is the necessary presupposition of all knowledge which man possesses. All our knowledge must be a receptive reconstruction of God's primary thoughts; the Lord is the originator of all truth. God's word must then be taken as the final standard of truth for man. Those who would feign intellectual self-sufficiency and refrain from presupposing the word of Christ in Scripture are led into foolish ignorance. One must *begin* with Christ in the world of thought or else surrender any hope of attaining knowledge—about himself, the world, or God. This has been the testimony of Scripture as we have examined it in our previous studies: "The fear of the Lord is the beginning of knowledge, but the foolish despise wisdom and instruction" (Prov. 1:7); "in Christ are hid all the treasures of wisdom and knowledge" (Col. 2:3).

John Calvin recognized this biblical outlook and made it foundational to his *Institutes of the Christian Religion*:

Nearly all the wisdom we possess, that is to say, true and sound wisdom, consists of two parts: the knowledge of God and of ourselves. But, while joined by many bonds, which one precedes and brings forth the other is not easy to discern. In the first place, no one can look upon himself without immediately turning his thoughts to the contemplation of God, in whom he lives and moves... Again, it is certain that man never achieves a clear knowledge of himself unless he has first looked upon God's face, and then descends from contemplating Him to scrutinize himself (Bk. I, ch. I.1).

With good reason the ancient proverb strongly recommended knowledge of self to man. For it is considered disgraceful for us not to know all that pertains to the business of human life... But since this precept is so valuable, we ought more diligently to avoid applying it perversely. This, we observe, has happened to certain philosophers, who, while urging man to know himself, propose the goal of recognizing his own worth and excellence... But knowledge of ourselves lies first in considering what we were given at creation and how generously God continues his favor toward us...to bear in mind that there is nothing in us of our own, but that we hold on sufferance whatever God has bestowed upon us. Hence we are ever dependent on him... It behooves us to recognize that we have been endowed with reason and understanding so that, by leading a holy and upright life, we may press on to the appointed goal of blessed immortality" (Bk. II, ch. I,1).

These are the opening words of Book I and Book II in the *Institutes*; Calvin considered it necessary to presuppose God's word in *both* "The Knowledge of God the Creator" as well as in "The Knowledge of God the Redeemer." To know about anything pertaining to the business of human life, whether touching upon creation or salvation, one must reject the autonomy promoted by pagan philosophies and submit to the truth of God and admit utter reliance upon Him for the origin, direction, and enabling of our use of reason. In short, Christ must have the preeminence (Col. 1:18)—even in the world of thought. With such a perspective

Calvin activated the most significant and blessed reform of Western church and culture that modern history has witnessed.

It is not surprising that the biblical and reformed principle of presupposing the word and authority of Christ in the world of thought and making it foundational to all knowledge would strike us as "dogmatic" or "absolutistic." We live in a culture which has for so long been saturated with the claims of intellectual autonomy and the demand for neutrality in scholarship that this ungodly perspective has been ingrained in us: like the supposed "music of the spheres," it is so constant and we are so accustomed to it that we fail to discern it. It is common fare, and we simply expect it.

No wonder, then, that the epistemological position of biblical and reformed thinking stands out in stark contrast! It challenges the *status quo,* demands a reorienting of our lives and thoughts, and threatens to "turn the world upside-down." It appears dogmatic and absolutistic because, it is dogmatic and absolutistic. The Christian should not be ashamed of this fact. He ought to have the humble boldness to tell a lost world that the Christian message is unconditionally true and the necessary presupposition of all thought (absolutistic), that Christ's gospel demands repentance (including a "change of mind"), and that God's word has definite doctrinal content which is authoritatively revealed "directly from above" (dogmatic). Of course the biblical outlook is not "dogmatic and absolutistic" in the derisive sense often attributed to these words. The Christian's claim that all thought requires the presupposition of Christ's word is not arrogant, unreasoning, or unfounded.

Another criticism leveled at the position of biblical presupposition is that, if knowledge can only be attained by first presupposing the authoritative word of God, then unbelievers are deprived of all knowledge; they cannot be said to know anything—even about the most elementary facts of experience or truths of science. And that seems clearly absurd, for surely some of the best scientists in the world have been unbelievers. How then does presuppositionalism explain that non-Christians know certain things?

A third argument advanced against the presuppositional outlook is that it would prevent any meaningful discussion or argumentation with the unbeliever. There would be no "common ground" upon which such argumentation could commence. Being deprived of knowledge, the unbeliever could have nothing to contribute or learn from a discussion with a Christian. That is, until the unbeliever is converted there is no use in talking to him.

Of course all these attacks upon the position of biblical epistemology rest upon either misunderstandings or incomplete information. In the course of the subsequent studies in this series we shall consider the three major criticisms of presuppositionalism from the perspective of scriptural teaching. It will become apparent that the biblical position in epistemology is not unfounded and arrogant, that it guarantees (rather than deprives) the unbeliever of a knowledge of the truth, and that it is the only ground upon which argument with unbelievers can be carried on. A preview of our treatment can be given here in closing from the words of Cornelius Van Til:

> Believers themselves have not chosen the Christian position because they are wiser than others. What they have they have by grace alone. But this does not mean that they accept the problematics of fallen man as right... Fallen man does *in principle* seek to be a law unto himself. But he cannot carry out his own principle to its full degree. He is restrained from doing so... In spite of what he does against God, he can and *must* work for God; thus he is able to make a "positive contribution" to human culture. (*A Christian Theory of Knowledge*, New Jersey: Presbyterian and Reformed, 1969, pp. 43, 44).

CHAPTER 8:

HUMBLE BOLDNESS,
NOT OBSCURANTIST ARROGANCE

It is a shame that Christian scholars, apologists, and philosophers have so often neglected a detailed study of the book of Proverbs in their attempts to exposit and work from a biblical epistemology (theory of knowledge). The book abounds in allusions and insights to wisdom, instruction, foolishness, understanding, etc. Proverbs can certainly aid us in the development and elaboration of the presuppositional approach to knowledge which has been discussed in our series previously.

In the last study we heard three common arguments which are directed against the position of biblical presuppositionalism. The first was that it amounted to arrogance and intellectual pride. It demands that every single thought be brought under subjection to Christ, for otherwise foolish ignorance will result. It teaches that men who will not begin with a fear of God cannot attain genuine knowledge of anything. It criticizes the attitude of scholarly neutrality toward God's word. In the battle with unbelief it demands *unconditional* surrender by the non-Christian and deprecates compromise in Christian thinkers who wish to take a more "reasonable" or "enlightened" approach. Now, it is asked, what could generate such a stringent outlook except undue commendation of one's own thoughts and abilities? Overwhelming self-esteem!

How is the presuppositionalist to respond? Should he defend obscurantist arrogance? Or should he confess that he had become dangerously close to the vertigo of self-aggrandizement? Both approaches have been variously pursued in Christian circles in past years. Both have done disservice to the Christian witness, one failing to evidence requisite and appropriate Spiritual fruit, the other failing to set forth the full and appropriate rigor of scriptural thinking. The wisdom of Proverbs can guide us between these unhappy extremes. We read in Proverbs 15:32-33,

> He that refuseth correction despiseth his own soul: But he that hearkeneth to reproof getteth understanding.

> The fear of Jehovah is the instruction of wisdom. And before honor goeth humility.

We need to concentrate upon both thrusts of this passage.

First, the Christian must indeed be bold in his challenge to unbelieving and compromising epistemologies. (The man who will not heed correction in having his thinking required to submit to Christ's Lordship in the world of thought, that man is doing despite to his own soul.) The Christian should consistently witness to such a thinker that understanding is, indeed, only possible when the reproof of the gospel challenge is heeded. To compromise with unbelieving standards or methods in the world of thought is to do grave disservice to the needs of those with whom we speak: to be willing to assume a position of neutrality would be conducive to anything *but* spiritual health in our hearers. The facts must be presented without wavering: reasoning which is not built upon the presupposed word of Christ is geared toward intellectual foolishness and spiritual death. The correction and reproof of Scripture cannot be watered down.

The Christian scholar, just as much as any believer in the redemptive work and lordship of Christ, must communicate to those whom he contacts that repentance and faith are commanded by God. The Christian scholar must be bold here, "casting down reasonings and every high thing that is exalted against the knowledge of God" (2 Cor 10:5). In defending the faith he must be firm in proclaiming "let God be found true, but every man a liar!" (Rom. 3:4). He must point out to those who do not presuppose the truth of God's word that their minds need to be renewed (Eph. 4:23). Because they live in *ignorance*, such men must *repent* (Acts 17:30)—must show "change of mind" (as the Greek word for "repent" suggests) and redirection. Repentance is *unto belief* (e.g., Matt.

21:32) and belief or *faith precedes knowledge* (2 Peter 1:5). The path from ignorance to knowledge is traversed by repentant faith. Indeed, presuppositionalism should be *boldly* presented in the world of thought, without apologies for the rigor of its demands.

Yet there is a second thrust in the Proverbs passage cited above. Not only must the non-presuppositionalist receive the correction and reproof of God's word (namely, that the beginning of wisdom is the fear of the Lord), but the Christian scholar who presupposes the truth of Scripture in his intellectual endeavors must be fully aware that his wisdom is *not inherently his own* but rests completely upon the fear of the Lord. Without that reverence, the Christian scholar would be as foolish as all other men. His wisdom is not due to superior mental ability and profundity of insight; instead it has been given by God. We noted above that repentance and faith are requisite for knowledge. The Christian, who possesses a knowledge of the truth, does so only because faith has been given him as a gift (Eph. 2:8-9) and repentance has been granted from the Lord (Acts 5:31; 11:18). In order to have faith you must be *born of God* (1 John 5:1) who gives repentance unto a genuine knowledge of the truth (2 Tim. 2:25). The Christian is in a position of knowledge only because of the grace of God. His spiritual rebirth is not of himself but solely the result of God's mercy (Ezek. 11:19-20; John 1:13; Rom. 9:16). This gracious regeneration has brought him a new mind.

Indeed, as Paul teaches, the Christian receives the things of the Spirit only by being transformed from natural hostility to glad submission. The believer has now the "mind of Christ" instead of the foolish mind of the natural man (1 Cor. 2:16 in context). This is the source of his wisdom and knowledge; the honor of knowing the truth stems from the undeserved grace of God. Therefore, humility is befitting the Christian scholar. In Philippians 2, where Paul exhorts us to have "the mind of Christ," he goes on to characterize this Christ as one who "humbled himself." Thus Proverbs teaches us that before such honor as attends the instruction of wisdom—before such wisdom as rests upon fear of the Lord—there goes *humility*. The Christian scholar has nothing to boast of in himself. He must be humble before the world, acknowledging that his knowledge depends upon the gracious work of God in him.

Therefore, presuppositional epistemology demands two attitudes. Both attitudes are inherent in the very position. First, the presuppositionalist must be *bold*, for knowledge is impossible aside from presupposing God's truth. Second, he must be *humble*, for the reason why he presupposes God's truth (and the only way any man can come to such a presupposition) resides in the grace of God alone. The fear of the Lord is foundational to wisdom, and hence the wise must be humble. The Christian scholar, then, must evidence a *humble boldness* in his confrontation with others in the world of thought.

> Walk in wisdom toward them that are without, buying up the opportunity. Let your speech be always with grace, seasoned with salt, that ye may know how ye ought to answer each one (Col. 4:5-6).

CHAPTER 9:

INESCAPABLE REVELATION, INESCAPABLE KNOWLEDGE

Having dismissed the taunting accusation of obscurantist arrogance in presuppositional epistemology, we go on to consider a second kind of criticism that is commonly leveled at the position. A biblical theory of knowledge proclaims the absolute requirement of God's revealed truth as the tacit foundation of understanding and knowledge.

Against such an outlook it has been urged that the unbeliever would be reduced to the level of inescapable stupidity—deprived of any knowledge whatsoever. If Christian presuppositions are necessary to understanding, then allegedly the non-Christian cannot understand anything at all! Yet from what we see in the world around us and from what we read of history, it is clear that unbelievers have attained knowledge of many things. Thus it would appear that presuppositional epistemology implies something that is patently false, in which case presuppositionalism is itself false.

But does presuppositionalism really imply any such thing? No, far from it. In fact, the presuppositionalist claims that only his epistemological position *guarantees* that unbelievers *can* make positive contributions to the edifice of knowledge! What the critic has erroneously inferred is that, if revealed presuppositions are necessary to understanding of the world, then non-Christians are totally ignorant *since they do not admit to revealed presuppositions.*

However, the presuppositionalist maintains that the unbeliever *can* come to know certain things (*despite* his espoused rejection of God's truth) for the simple reason that he *does* have revealed presuppositions—and *cannot but have them* as a creature made as God's image and living in God's created world. Although he outwardly and vehemently denies the truth of God, no unbeliever is inwardly and sincerely devoid of a knowledge of God. It is not a *saving* knowledge of God to be sure, but even as condemning knowledge natural revelation still provides a knowledge of God. Thus, according to biblical epistemology, while men deny their Creator they nevertheless possess an inescapable knowledge of Him; and because they know God (even though they know Him in curse and reprobation) they are able to attain a limited understanding of the world.

You see, the unbeliever is actually double-minded. At base all men know God as His *creatures*, but as *sinners* all men refuse to acknowledge their Creator and live by His revelation. Hence we can say that men *both* know and do not know God; they *know* Him in judgment and in virtue of natural revelation, but they do *not* know Him in blessing unless it is in virtue of supernatural revelation and saving grace. Though hampered by his moral condition, the unbeliever's scholarship is not completely defunct. He can attain knowledge *despite* himself. *In principle* his unbelief would preclude understanding of anything, for (as Augustine said) one must believe in order to understand. However, *in practice* the unbeliever is restrained from a consistent, self-destructive following of his unbelieving profession.

If the unbeliever were a total idiot he would be free from guilt. But Paul's point in Romans 1 is that the unbeliever's rebellion is willful and knowledgeable; he sins against his better knowledge and is thus "without excuse" (vv. 20-21). And while he suppresses this better knowledge in unrighteousness (v. 18), that knowledge provides a foundation of his (limited, but real) understanding of God's world.

Central to the position of biblical presuppositionalism is an affirmation of the clarity and inescapability of natural revelation. The world was created by the word of God (Gen. 1:3; John 1:3; Col. 1:16; Heb. 1:2) and thereby reflects the mind and character of God (Rom. 1:20). Man was created as the image of God (Gen. 1:16-27) and thus cannot escape the face of God. There is no environment where man can flee to escape the revelational presence of God (Ps. 139:8). God's natural revelation goes out to the end of the world (Ps. 19:1-4) and all people see His glory (Ps. 97:6). Therefore, even when living in open (idolatrous) rebellion, men are in the condition of "knowing God" (Rom. 1:21)—*the* living and true God, not merely "a god." Christ enlightens every man (John 1:9), and so Calvin declares:

> For we know that men have this unique quality above the other animals, that they are endowed with reason and intelligence and that they bear the distinction between right and wrong engraved in their conscience. Thus there is no man to whom some awareness of the eternal light does not penetrate...the common light of nature, a far lowlier thing than faith (*Calvin's Commentaries*, tr. T.H.L. Parker; Grand Rapids: Eerdmans 1959).

Because the unbeliever is inconsistent in his adherence to a denial of God's truth, because he and the world are not what he professes them to be, the unbeliever is afforded some knowledge. Thus the antithesis between believer and unbeliever is absolute only *in principle* at this time. Van Til rightly observes:

> The absolute contrast between the Christian and the non-Christian in the field of knowledge is said to be that of principle. Full recognition is made of the fact that in spite of this absolute contrast of principle, there is relative good in those who are evil... So far as men self-consciously work from this principle they have no notion in common with the believer... But in the course of history the natural man is not fully self-conscious of his own position... He has within him the knowledge of God by virtue of his creation in the image of God. But this idea of God is suppressed by his false principle, the principle of autonomy. This principle of autonomy is, in turn, suppressed by the restraining power of God's common grace... And by the striving of the Spirit...their hostility is curbed in some measure... And as such they can *cooperate* by virtue of the ethical restraint of common grace (*The Defense of the Faith*; Presbyterian and Reformed, 1955, pp. 67, 189-190, 194).

Hereby the challenge of presuppositionalism is strengthened further.

All knowledge, even the knowledge possessed by the unbeliever in unrighteousness, must be founded upon the accepted truth about God. Therefore, both the unbeliever's knowledge and God's common grace should be used, *not to encourage neutrality*, but to press home the demands of God at every point. Van Til says,

> Common grace is not a gift of God whereby his own challenge to repentance unto men who have sinned against him is temporarily being blurred. Common grace must rather serve the challenge of God to repentance. It must be a tool by means of which the believer as the servant of Christ can challenge the unbeliever to repentance. Believers can objectively show to unbelievers that unity of science can be attained only on the Christian theistic basis (*ibid.*, p. 195).

We see then that the criticism laid down at the beginning of this study does no damage to, but rather serves to point up even more the strength and necessity of, presuppositional epistemology.

CHAPTER 10:

COMMON GROUND
WHICH IS NOT NEUTRAL

In the previous two studies we have seen that the necessity of presupposing God's revealed truth in order to attain to knowledge of anything—from the chemical composition of water to the way of salvation—does not (1) generate unreasoning arrogance, or (2) deprive unbelievers of a knowledge of the world. A third charge against the epistemological position of Christian presuppositionalism is that it precludes meaningful discussion and successful argumentation with non-Christians. Allegedly a presuppositionalist denies that there is any common ground between believers and unbelievers, and thus the apologist would have no point of contact with the unbeliever and no basis upon which he could communicate ideas.

A proper response to this line of attack requires that we take account of (1) the God whom we represent, (2) the sinner to whom we speak, and (3) the context in which we reason with him.

The Lord God is *Creator* of heaven and earth (Gen. 1:1); our understanding should begin here. He has made *everything* (Ex. 20:11; Neh. 9:6, Ps. 104:24; Isa.44:24); "in Him were all things created, in the heavens and upon the earth, things visible and things invisible (Col. 1:16a). All men are His creations, the rich and the poor (Prov. 22:2). And "the Lord has made all things *for Himself*" (Prov. 16:4): "all things have been created through Him and unto Him" (Col. 1:16b). His sovereign dominion extends over every single thing in the world. He works all things according to His counsel (Eph. 1:11), and every minute of the day belongs to Him

(Ps. 74:16). He owns everything in creation, and every facet of life should serve Him. "The earth is the Lord's and the fullness thereof, the world and they that dwell therein" (Ps. 24:1); God declares "whatsoever is under the whole heaven is mine" (Job 41:11; cf. Gen. 14:19; Ex. 9:29; Deut. 4:39; 10:14; etc.). As Rahab confessed "The Lord your God, he is God in heaven above and in earth beneath" (Josh. 2:11); thus the greatness, power, glory, victory and majesty are His, for *all* that are in heaven and earth are His possession (1 Chron. 29:11). God's sovereign rule extends to the ends of the earth (Ps. 59:13), over every soul (Ezek. 18:4), unto all generations (Ex. 15:18; Ps. 10:16; 145:13; 146:10). Therefore, the God who created all things rules over all (Ps. 103:19).

In this case everything in the created realm must serve, and be used to serve, the Lord Creator: "*of* Him, and *through* Him, and *unto* Him are *all* things" (Rom. 11:36). There is not a square inch of the world, not a split second of time, that is not dependent upon, controlled by, and subservient to God. Hence man is commanded to do *everything* he does to God's glory (1 Cor. 10:31); our bodies are required to be living sacrifices in God's service (Rom. 12:1). Indeed, everything we do, whether in word or deed, comes under this command (Col. 3:17). Even the use of our reason or minds must be according to God's direction and for His glory (2 Cor. 10:5), for His sovereign rule is inclusive of the areas of wisdom and knowledge (Col. 2:3). So we see that quite literally *in all things* God is to be glorified (1 Peter 4:11). Because everything and every area is created and ruled by God nothing is exempted from the requirement to be consecrated, or set apart, unto Him—we must be holy in "all manner of living" (1 Peter 1:15).

The conclusion of this line of thought is forcefully evident: there can be *no neutral ground* between believer and unbeliever, between obedience and rebellion, between respecting and abusing that which belongs to God (i.e., everything). "No man can serve two masters" (Matt. 6:24); "He that is not with me is against me" (Matt. 12:30). Therefore, there is no area in the world, in thought, in word, or in deed which is irrelevant, indifferent, or neutral toward God and His demands. The Christian must recognize this fact as he deals with the unbeliever. There is no subject matter that he can discuss which is devoid of bearing upon the religious question or which is free of religious commitment. No "demilitarized" zone exists between the camp of unbelief and the forces obedient to Christ.

God owns everything or nothing. Every area of life and every fact are what they are because of God's sovereign decree, and so there is no place a man can flee in order to escape the influence, control, and requirements of God. In God's world neutrality is impossible.

Furthermore, not only has God created all things for Himself, and not only does He rule over every area, but He persistently and universally reveals Himself to all men. God has never left Himself without a witness (Acts 14:17). No man can claim ignorance of his Creator, for God himself has made what can be known of Him manifest to every man (Rom. 1:19). Indeed His invisible attributes are clearly perceived through the created world (Rom. 1:20). Here again, then, we must conclude that there can be *no neutral ground*, no area which fails to exert revelational pressure upon the sinner. Wherever he looks the sinner finds himself confronted by the God with whom he has to do. There cannot be a safety zone where the sinner can flee for refuge. If there were, the sinner would stay there permanently to escape his Maker. But there is no escape from God (Ps. 139:7-8).

Thus the Christian should be striving to bring unbelieving thinkers to a full realization of God's extensive claim upon them. The universally sustaining, universally reigning, universally revealing God of the universe has not, and cannot, afford the creation of even the slightest area of neutrality. Consequently, the believer is wrong to seek (and presume to find) a subject matter that will not challenge the unbeliever with the presuppositional demands we have discussed in previous studies. The hope that such a neutral topic or fact could become the starting point for an argument which progressively convinces the unbeliever of the truth of God's word (by inches) is futile. Christ is the Lord, even in the world of thought. No fact, no area of knowledge or wisdom, fails to drive home His requirements and manifest His sovereign control. The starting point for understanding is not neutrality but reverence for the Lord.

The foregoing considerations not only establish that there is *no neutral ground* between the believers and unbelievers, but also that there is *ever present common gound* between the believer and the unbeliever. What must be kept in mind is that this common ground is *God's ground*. All men have in common the world created by God, controlled by God, and constantly revealing God. In this case, *any* area of life or *any* fact can be used as a point of contact. The denial of neutrality secures, rather than destroys, commonality.

CHAPTER 11:

WHERE POINT OF CONTACT IS,
AND IS NOT, FOUND

Coming to the question of common ground with the unbeliever, we have first considered the God whom we represent. Since God is the creator of all things, since He sovereignly controls every event, and since He clearly reveals Himself in every fact of the created order, it is utterly *impossible* that there should be any *neutral* ground, any territory or facet of reality where man is not confronted with the claims of God, any area of knowledge where the theological issue is inconsequential. Yet this perspective guarantees that there is *common ground* between the believer and the unbeliever—common ground of a metaphysical nature. The whole world, the created realm and public history, constitute commonality between the Christian and the non-Christian. But this common ground is not neutral ground; it is God's ground. There is nowhere to stand in the world—even the world of thought—that is not God's territory.

In addition to considering the God whom we represent, we must take cognizance of the person to whom we speak. In particular we must recognize the noetic effects of sin. The fall of man had drastic results in the world of thought; even the use of man's reasoning ability becomes depraved and frustrating. The whole creation was made subject to vanity (Rom. 8:20), thus bringing confusion, inefficiency, and skeptical despair into the epistemic realm. Even more, moral corruption overcame man's thoughts (Gen. 6:5), so that the evil use of man's mind became exhaustive, continual, and inescapable. Man unrighteously suppresses the truth in order to embrace the lie (Rom. 1:18, 25). In its pseudo-wisdom the world refuses to know God (1 Cor. 1:21), for Satan has blinded the minds of men (2 Cor. 4:4). Man uses his reason, not to glorify God and advance His kingdom, but to rise up in arrogant opposition to the knowledge of God (2 Cor. 10:5).

> When we say that sin is ethical we do not mean, however, that sin involved only the will of man and not also his intellect. Sin involved every aspect of man's personality. All of man's reactions in every relation in which God had set him were ethical and not merely intellectual; the intellectual itself is ethical. (Cornelius Van Til, *The Defense of the Faith*. Philadelphia: Presbyterian and Reformed,1955, p. 63).

In his *Institutes of the Christian Religion* John Calvin very pointedly remarked that *philosophers* need to see that man is corrupt in every aspect of his being—that the fall pertains to man's mental operations as much as to his volition and emotions.

Of course, this points up why we cannot aim to find common ground in the unbeliever's interpretation or self-conscious understanding of things, whether they be the laws of logic, the facts of history, or the experiences of human personality. The non-Christian seeks to suppress the truth, to distort it into a naturalistic scheme, to preclude the interpretation of the God who makes things and events what they are (determining the end from the beginning, Isa. 46:10). The Christian scholar cannot find anything beyond *formal* agreement, he cannot locate a genuinely common understanding, in the unbeliever's words and opinions. Specifically, and very much at the heart of disagreements with unbelieving scholars or thinkers, we should see that the unbeliever has an incorrect diagnosis of his situation and of his own person. The non-Christian thinks that his thinking process is normal. He thinks that his mind is the final court of appeal in all matters of knowledge. He takes himself to be the reference point for all interpretation of the facts. That is, he has epistemologically become a law unto himself: *autonomous*.

Consequently, the depravity and alleged autonomy of man's thinking prevent the regenerate Christian from seeking common ground in the unbeliever's self-conscious and admitted outlook on anything. Rather than agreeing with the sinner's conception, ordering, or evaluation of his experience, the Christian seeks his repentance—repentance in the world of thought. Our approach should be that of Isaiah 55:7, "Let the wicked forsake his way, and the unrighteous man his thoughts: and let him return unto the Lord." A dying patient may require surgery and yet dread it, thereby self-deluding himself into thinking that his condition only calls for a band-aid. A doctor who accepted his patient's conception of himself and his condition would not only be a quack, he would show absolutely no concern for the patient's true health and recovery. So also, the Christian scholar who genuinely desires the spiritual reclamation of the unregenerate thinker must not allow the unbeliever to diagnose his own condition and thoughts and then prescribe an insufficient cure. The unregenerate thinker does not merely need a band-aid of additional information; he needs the major internal surgery of regeneration. He needs to forsake his thoughts and be renewed in knowledge after the image of his creator (Col. 3:10).

However, in denying common ground in the area of the non-Christian's autonomous interpretation of experience, the presuppositionalist does *not* teach that he has *no point of contact* with the unbeliever. The fact that the unbeliever is wrong in his self-conscious interpretative efforts does not mean that he and the Christian are (epistemologically speaking) like ships passing in the dark. For there is something of great significance in common between the believer and unbeliever; they are both, irrespective of their saved and lost conditions, both the creaturely *image of God*. While the unregenerate needs to be renewed with respect to it, the image of God remains his. Man cannot cease being man, and to be man is to be God's image. Man is the finite replica of God, being like Him in every respect that is appropriate for the creature to resemble his Creator. Hereby no man can escape the face of God, for God's image is carried along with man wherever he goes—even into Hades. Therefore, the believer can find point of contact in his discussion with unbelievers deep down inside them. Creation establishes forever that no man is beyond the touch of God's revelation; men have been created with the capacity to understand and recognize their Maker's voice. Van Til says that we are:

> ....assured of a point of contact in the fact that every man is
> made in the image of God and has impressed upon him the

law of God. In that fact alone (we) may rest secure with respect to the point of contact problem. For that fact makes men always accessible to God... Only by thus finding the point of contact in man's sense of deity that lies underneath his own conception of self-consciousness as ultimate can we be both true to Scripture and effective in reasoning with the natural man (*ibid.*, pp. 111, 112).

We have seen, then, thus far that presuppositionalism takes seriously doctrines of creation, God's sovereignty, natural revelation, man's creation as God's image, and total depravity. Presuppositionalism holds that there is very definitely a realm of common ground between believers and unbelievers (ground which is metaphysical in nature), but that common ground is not neutral ground. Moreover, that ground is not found in the natural man's autonomous conception and interpretation of his experience or the facts of the world. The Christian does not have a point of contact there, but rather in the actual condition of man as the image of God. Hence it is clear that the third criticism of presuppositionalism which was rehearsed in an earlier part of this series is thoroughly groundless. Far from isolating men in mutually inaccessible towers of thought, presuppositionalism secures both common ground and point of contact between Christian and non-Christian. It is all a matter of finding them in the right place!

CHAPTER 12:

OVERALL SUMMARY
CHAPTERS 1-11

It will be convenient to pause at this point and summarize our discussion in the past studies in order that we gain a concise overview of our pattern of thought.

The first part of this series set forth the *Lordship* of Christ in the realm of knowledge and applied that truth to the *exercise* of man's reason. We concluded with Calvin that God's word must be presupposed in order to have knowledge in *either* the realm of creation or redemption; however, because our culture has been saturated with the contrary demands of *autonomy and neutrality*, there is a pressing need for reformation in the world of thought. *Three basic objections* to presuppositionalism in the theory of knowledge arise from an unreformed culture; these three complaints were subsequently considered in order to demonstrate their *invalidity*, to exhibit the *strength* of presuppositionalism, and expound *further aspects* of that position.

CHRIST'S EPISTEMIC LORDSHIP

1. God's knowledge is *original, comprehensive,* and *creative.* There are no higher principles or standards of truth to which He looks and attempts to bring His thoughts into conformity. There is no mystery surrounding His understanding, for it is infinite. God's mind gives both diversity and order to all things, thus guarantying the reality of particulars (multiplicity) and yet assuring that they are intelligible (unity).

2. All knowledge and wisdom have been deposited *in Christ*, the source, standard, and embodiment of truth.
3. God's word thus has supreme, absolute, and unquestionable *authority* in the realm of *knowledge* as well as morality.
4. This also means that God's word must be the *final standard of truth* for man, in which case it cannot be challenged by some more ultimate criterion.
5. Consequently, the teaching of Christ in Scripture has *self-attesting* authority; Christ clearly speaks with the authority of God, is the repository of knowledge, and is subject to no authority or standard more basic than Himself as "the way, the truth, and the life." He alone is adequate to witness to Himself and His word.

MAN'S EXERCISE OF REASON

1. There is *absolute truth*, the knowledge of which is *accessible* to man; while he may not know exhaustively, he does have adequate knowledge.
2. Man's knowledge must be a *receptive reconstruction* of God's original and creative knowledge; to come to a knowledge of the truth man must "think God's thoughts after Him."
   a. The *starting point* of knowledge is therefore God; the beginning of knowledge is the fear of the Lord—thus requiring respect and submission.
   b. In particular one must submit to the truth of *God's revealed word*.
   c. Man must be *grateful* to God for whatever he possesses, including his knowledge and understanding; all that we have comes from God.
   d. Thus belief precedes understanding, and revelation undergirds reason; theology is *foundational* to every area of study.
   e. So also, man does *not* have the *prerogative* to call God's word into question.
3. Philosophy which *suppresses* rather than presupposing the truth of God evidences the darkness of a sinful mind—that is, it is in both *epistemological and moral rebellion* against God.
   a. Such thinking is *made foolish* by God and leads to futile conclusions; it makes the use of reason impossible.
   b. Thinking which submits to the elementary principles (the

presuppositions) of worldly philosophy and the traditions of men *deludes* men with crafty speech; it misleads them into spiritual destruction.

4. Neutrality in scholarship, apologetics, or schooling is both *impossible and immoral.*

   a. No man can serve two masters, and thus one must choose to ground his intellectual efforts in Christ or in his own autonomous reason; there *is no middle ground* between these two authorities.

   b. Neutrality would erase the *distinctiveness* of the Christian's position and muffle the *antithesis* between godly and ungodly thinking.

   c. A Christian who strives to be neutral not only denies the Lordship of Christ in knowledge and loses his solid ground in reasoning, he also *unwittingly* endorses assumptions which are *hostile* to his faith.

5. The believer is a "new man" in Christ, being *renewed in mind.*

   a. Conversion requires *repentance* ("change of mind") from attempted autonomy.

   b. The Christian walks *by faith,* in the regenerating and illuminating power of the Holy Spirit, rather than by self-sufficient intellect.

   c. His every thought is made captive to, and rooted in, Christ as his new Lord. Hence he *presupposes* the truth of God's word and *applies* it to every aspect of life (including intellectual activity).

   d. The believer must love the Lord his God with *all his mind,* seeking in all things to glorify Him—even in the world of thought.

Further Crucial Aspects of Presuppositionalism

1. Men come to presuppose the truth of God *only by the grace of God.*

   a. Because it is the truth and grace *of God* which has transformed us, we must be *bold* in our challenge to intellectual belief.

   b. Since it is *the grace* of God (not our own wisdom) which accounts for our change of mind, *humility* is befitting the Christian scholar; we have nothing in ourselves of which to boast.

   C. THEREFORE, IT MUST BE HUMBLE BOLDNESS—NOT COMPROMISE, NOT obscurantism, not arrogance—which characterizes our scholarship.

2. All men are "without excuse" for rebellion against the Lord, for *all men know* the living and true God by means of his common revelation.

   a. Despite his contrary profession, even the unbeliever knows what may be known about God from nature and conscience; *God has clearly revealed Himself* to every man.

   b. All men *attempt to suppress* this knowledge of God, as is manifest in the various, multiform, and profuse schemes of anti-Christian thought and philosophy.

   c. But because the unbeliever cannot rid himself of a knowledge of God, because he continues to use the "borrowed capital" of theistic truths, he is *enabled* to come to a *limited understanding* of the truth about the world and himself—despite, not because of, his attempted autonomy.

3. God has *created* all things for Himself, *directs* them to His own sovereign ends, and *owns* everything—in which case, everything in the created realm must serve Him.

   a. This *precludes* the possibility of any *neutral ground* between the believer and unbeliever, but it assures us that there is *abundant common ground* (metaphysically speaking) between them, since all men are God's creatures and live in God's world.

   b. As God's creature, created in God's image, and living in an environment which constantly brings the revelation of God to bear upon him, the unbeliever is always accessible to the gospel. The believer always has *a point of* contact with the unbeliever: (1) his being the *image of God*, and (2) the *suppressed truth* deep inside him.

SECTION THREE:

HOW TO DEFEND THE FAITH

CHAPTER 13:

THE FOOLISHNESS OF UNBELIEF

The central declaration and challenge of Christian apologetics is expressed by Paul's rhetorical question, "Hath not God made foolish the wisdom of the world?" (1 Cor. 1:20). Critical attacks which are leveled against the Christian faith in the world of thought cannot be met by piece-meal replies and appeals to emotion. In the long run the believer must respond to the onslaught of the unbeliever by attacking the unbeliever's position at its foundations. He must challenge the unbeliever's presuppositions, asking whether knowledge is even possible, given the non-Christian's assumptions and perspective. The Christian cannot forever be defensively constructing atomistic answers to the endless variety of unbelieving criticisms; he must take the offensive and show the unbeliever that he has no intelligible place to stand, no consistent epistemology, no justification for meaningful discourse, predication, or argumentation. The pseudo-wisdom of the world must be reduced to foolishness—in which case none of the unbeliever's criticisms have any force.

If we are to understand how to answer the *fool*, if we are to be able to demonstrate that God has made the pseudo-wisdom of the world *foolish*, then we must first study the *biblical* conception of the fool and his foolishness.

In scriptural perspective the fool is not basically a shallow-minded or illiterate ignoramus; he can be quite educated and sophisticated in social reckoning. However, he is a fool because he has forsaken the source of true wisdom in God in order to rely on his own (allegedly), self-sufficient, intellectual powers. He is unteachable (Prov. 10:8) and despises instruction (Prov. 15:5); whereas the wise man heeds counsel given to him, "The way of a fool is right in his own eyes" (Prov. 12:15). The fool has utter self-confidence and imagines himself to be intellectually autonomous. "He that trusteth in his own heart is a fool" (Prov. 28:26). A fool cannot think of himself as mistaken (Prov. 17:10). He judges matters according to his own pre-established standards of truth and right, and thus his own thoughts always turn out in the long run to be correct. The fool is sure that he can rely on his own rational authority and intellectual scrutiny. "The fool beareth himself insolently and is confident" (Prov. 14:16), and therefore he utters his own mind (Prov. 29:11).

In actuality, this autonomous man is dull, stubborn, boorish, obstinate and stupid. He professes himself to be wise, but from the opening of his mouth it is clear that he is (in the biblical sense) "a fool"—his only wisdom would consist in keeping silent (Prov. 17:28). "The heart of fools proclaimeth foolishness" (Prov. 12:23), and the fool flaunts his folly (Prov. 13:16). He eats up folly unreflectingly (Prov. 15:14), pours it out (Prov. 15:2), and returns to it like a dog to his vomit (Prov. 26:11). He is so in love with his folly and so dedicated to its preservation that "It is better for a man to meet a bear robbed of her whelps, than a fool in his folly" (Prov. 17:12). The fool does not really want to find the truth; he only wants to be self-justified in his own imaginations. While he may feign objectivity, "A fool hath no delight in understanding, but only that his heart may reveal itself" (Prov. 18:2). He is committed to his own presuppositions and wishes to guard his autonomy. Thus he will not depart from evil (Prov. 13:19), and thus all his knowledgeable talk reveals nothing but perverse and lying lips (Prov. 10:18; 19:1). He may talk proudly, but "A fool's mouth is his destruction, and his lips are the snare of his soul" (Prov. 18:7). He shall not endure the judgment of God (Ps. 5:5).

How does a man become such a self-deluded, allegedly autonomous, fool? A fool despises wisdom and instruction, *refusing to begin his thinking with reverence toward the Lord* (Prov. 1:7). He rejects God's commandments (Prov. 10:8) and even dares to reproach the Almighty (Ps. 74:22; Job 1:22). "The thought of foolishness is sin" (Prov. 24:9). The fool will not be governed by God's word; he is lawless, just as his thinking is lawless (i.e., sinful, 1 John. 3:4). Rejecting God's law or word, the fool respects his own word and law instead (that is, he is *auto*-nomous). Scripture describes people who do not know God, His ways, and His judgments as foolish (cf. Jer. 5:4). The fool lives in practical ignorance of

God, for in his heart (out of which are the issues of life, Prov. 4:23) the fool says there is no God (Ps. 14:1; cf. Isa. 32:6). He lives and reasons in an atheistic manner—as though he were his own lord. Rather than being Spiritually directed, the fool's vision is earth-bound (Prov. 17:24). He serves the creature (e.g., the authority of his own mind) rather than the Creator (Rom. 1:25).

The man who hears Christ's words and yet builds his life on a rejection of that revelation is a fool (Matt. 7:26), and the man who suppresses God's general revelation in the created realm is also described as a fool (Rom. 1:18). It is quite clear, then, that *a fool is one who does not make God and His revelation the starting point* (the presupposition) *of his thinking*. Fools despise the preaching of the cross, refuse to know God, and cannot receive God's word (1 Cor. 1-2). The self-proclaimed autonomous man, the unbeliever, will not submit to the word of God or build his life and thinking upon it. Disbelief and ignorance of God's will, therefore, produce foolishness (1 Cor. 15:36; Eph. 5:17).

As a result, the fool does not have the concentration necessary to find wisdom; he vainly thinks that it is easily dispensed or gained (Prov. 17:16, 24). By glorying in man, the fool's thinking becomes futile and shameful (1 Cor. 3); his heart is darkened, and his mind is vain (Rom. 1:21). Because of his unbelief and rebellion against God's word, the fool does *not* have *knowledgeable* lips (Prov. 14:7). Indeed, because he does not choose to reverence the Lord, the fool *hates knowledge* (Prov. 1:29). The unbeliever who criticizes the Christian faith is this fool which we have been describing above. In answering the fool a Christian apologist must aim to demonstrate that unbelief is, in the final analysis, destructive of all knowledge. The fool must be shown that his autonomy is hostile to knowledge—that *God makes foolish* the "wisdom" of the world.

CHAPTER 14:

A TWO-FOLD APOLOGETIC PROCEDURE

"Where is the wise? where is the scribe? where is the disputer of this world? Hath not God made foolish the wisdom of the world?"

Paul could stake his apologetic for Christian faith on this set of rhetorical questions (1 Cor. 1:20), knowing that the word of the cross destroys the world's wisdom and brings its discernment to nothing (v. 19). The unregenerate heart, with its darkened mind, evaluates the gospel as weakness and folly (vv. 18, 23), but in actual fact it expresses God's saving power and true wisdom (vv. 18, 21, 24).

What the world calls "foolish" is in reality wisdom. Conversely, what the world deems "wise" is actually foolish. The unbeliever has his standards all turned around, and thus he mocks the Christian faith or views it as intellectually dishonorable. But Paul knew that God could unmask the arrogance of unbelief and display its pitiable pretense of knowledge: "the foolishness of God is wiser than men, and the weakness of God is stronger than men" (v. 25). Although the unbeliever sees the Christian faith as foolish and weak, that faith has the strength and intellectual resources to expose "worldly wisdom" for what it truly is: utter foolishness. God has chosen the (so called) foolish things of the world in order that He might *put to shame* those who boast of their (so called) wisdom (v. 27).

In the face of God's revelation the unbeliever is "without an apologetic" (cf. Rom. 1:20, in the Greek). His intellectual position has no worthwhile credentials in the long run. When he comes up against the intellectual challenge of the gospel as Paul would present it, the unregenerate is left with no place to stand. The outcome of the encounter is summarily expressed by Paul when he declares, "*Where* is the *wise? Where* is the disputer of *this world?*" The fact is that God *makes foolish* the wisdom of this world, and thus the genuinely wise unbeliever is not to be found. The man who can adequately debate and defend the outlook of this world (i.e., unbelief) has never lived. Rejection of the Christian faith cannot be justified, and the intellectual position of the unbeliever cannot be genuinely defended in the world of thought. The Spiritual weapons of the Christian apologist are mighty before God unto the *casting down* of every high imagination that is exalted against the knowledge of God (2 Cor. 10:4-5). The unbeliever, as we saw in the last study, is a fool in the scriptural perspective, and as such his position amounts to a *hatred of knowledge* (Prov. 1:22, 29); his intellectual attack on the gospel stems from "knowledge" which *is falsely so called* (1 Tim. 6:20).

The apologist should aim to put this pretense of knowledge (which is, at base, a hatred of knowledge) to shame; he should manifest the foolishness of this world's "wisdom." This calls for much more than a piecemeal attempt to adduce vague probabilities of isolated evidences for the reasonableness of Christianity. It requires, instead, the full scale demonstration of the *unreasonableness* of anti-Christianity in contrast to the *certainty* of truth to be found in God's word. Dr. Van Til writes:

> The struggle between Christian theism and its opponents covers the whole field of knowledge... Christian theism's fundamental contention is just this, that nothing whatsoever can be known unless God can be and is known... The important thing to note is this fundamental difference between theism and antitheism on the question of epistemology. There is not a spot in heaven or on earth about which there is no dispute between the two opposing parties *(A Survey of Christian Epistemology*, den Dulk Christian Foundation, 1969, p.116).

> The method of reasoning by presupposition may be said to be indirect rather than direct. The issue between believers and non-believers in Christian theism cannot be settled by a direct

appeal to "facts" or "laws" whose nature and significance is already agreed upon by both parties to the debate... The Christian apologist must place himself upon the position of his opponent, assuming the correctness of his method merely for argument's sake, in order to show him that on such a position the "facts" are not facts and the "laws" are not laws. He must also ask the non-Christian to place himself upon the Christian position for argument's sake in order that he may be shown that only upon such a basis do "facts" and "laws" appear intelligible...

Therefore the claim must be made that Christianity alone is reasonable for men to hold. And it is utterly reasonable. It is wholly irrational to hold to any other position than that of Christianity. Christianity alone does not crucify reason itself... The best, the only, the absolutely certain proof of the truth of Christianity is that unless its truth be presupposed there is no proof of anything. Christianity is proved as being the very foundation of the idea of proof itself (*The Defense of the Faith*, Philadelphia: Presbyterian and Reformed, 1955, pp. 117-118, 396).

The fool must be answered by showing him his foolishness and the necessity of Christianity as the precondition of intelligibility.

In Proverbs 26:4-5 we are instructed as to how we should answer the foolish unbeliever—how we should demonstrate that God makes foolish the so called "wisdom" of this world. "Answer not a fool according to his folly, lest thou be like unto him. Answer a fool according to his folly lest he be wise in his own conceit." The two-fold apologetic procedure mentioned by Van Til above is here described. In the first place, the unbeliever should not be answered in terms of his own misguided presuppositions; the apologist should defend his faith by working within his own presuppositions. If he surrenders to the assumptions of the unbeliever, the believer will never effectively set forth a reason for the hope that is in him. He will have lost the battle from the outset, constantly being trapped behind enemy lines. Hence Christianity's intellectual strength and challenge will not be set forth.

But then in the second place the apologist should answer the fool according to his self-proclaimed presuppositions (i.e., according to his folly). In so doing he aims to show the unbeliever the outcome of those assumptions. Pursued to their consistent end presuppositions of unbelief render man's reasoning vacuous and his experience unintelligible; in short, they lead to the destruction of knowledge, the dead-end of epistemological futility, to utter foolishness. By placing himself on the unbeliever's position and pursuing it to its foolish undermining of facts and laws, the Christian apologist prevents the fool from being wise in his own conceit. He can conclude, "Where then *is* the wise disputer of this world?!" There is none, for as the history of humanistic philosophy so clearly illustrates, God has made foolish the wisdom of the world. It is confounded by the "foolish" preaching of the cross.

CHAPTER 15:

ANSWERING THE FOOL

In the last two studies we have begun to look at apologetics from the biblical point of view. It has been observed that (1) the intellectual outlook of the unbeliever is that of a "fool" (in the scriptural sense), (2) the unbeliever proclaims a pseudo-wisdom which is in reality a hatred, and destruction, of knowledge, (3) God makes foolish the wisdom of the world and puts it to shame through His people, who are enabled to cast down every high imagination exalted against a knowledge of Him, and (4) in order to give an answer to the fool, the believer should follow a two-fold procedure: (a) *refusing* to answer in terms of the fool's presuppositions, for they undermine the Christian position, and then (b) *answering* in terms of the fool's presuppositions in order to show where they lead, namely, to epistemological futility.

Here we find the prescribed course for giving an answer to every man who asks a reason for the hope that is in us (cf. 1 Peter 3:15). The apologetic strategy rehearsed above meets the precondition laid down by Peter for defending the faith, that we "set apart Christ *as Lord* in your hearts." By refusing to suspend the presupposed truth of God's word when we argue with those who criticize the Christian faith, we acknowledge the lordship of Christ over our thinking. His word is our ultimate authority. If we were to reason with the unbeliever in such a way that we trusted our own intellectual powers or the teachings of the (so-called) experts (in science, or history, or logic, or whatever) more than we trusted the veracity of God's revelation, we would end up the argument (if consistent) by agreeing with the unbeliever. In the language of Proverbs 26, we would answer the fool and end up being *like him*.

Also, by employing the apologetic procedure laid out above we can arrive at the same conclusion as did Paul in 1 Corinthians 1, that the intellectual outlook of the unbeliever is at base foolishness. Consequently, we can rhetorically ask "Where is the wise? Where is the disputer of this world?" The fact of the matter will be abundantly manifest: God makes foolish the wisdom of the world, and He does it by the word of the cross. By demonstrating to the fool that his presuppositions can produce only *falsely called* knowledge, the believer answers him in such a way that he cannot be wise in his own conceits. Thereby this two-fold procedure in presuppositional apologetics aims at argumentative success without compromising spiritual fidelity. It renders a reasoned account of the Christian hope as well as reducing all contrary and critical positions to impotence. It is to be remembered at this point, of course, that the apologist must do this destructive work "with humility and reverence" (1 Peter 3:15b).

A useful and instructive summary of the presuppositional approach to apologetics is given in 2 Timothy 2:23-25.

> Avoid foolish and undisciplined questions, knowing that they produce quarrels, and a servant of the Lord must not quarrel, but must be gentle toward all, skillful in teaching, patient, one who courteously instructs those who oppose themselves, if perhaps God may grant to them conversion unto a genuine knowledge of truth.

First, this passage makes it very clear that the apologist simply must not have an arrogant attitude in dealing with unbelievers. He must be gentle, patient, courteous, and unquarrelsome. These attributes come hard to most people who hold to strong doctrinal positions and who are diligent to defend those positions. It is easy to become headstrong and zealous to dominate your opponent. However, it is the opposite attitude, which is peaceable and gentle, that demonstrates that our wisdom is *from above* (James 3:13-17).

Second, this passage teaches that those who are challenged to defend their faith must not consent to answer in terms of foolish unbelief. Paul commands us to *reject* foolish questions—that is, questions given from the fool's point of view. We are not to submit to the autonomous outlook which suppresses the truth of God; we are not to comply with the demand for agnostic neutrality in our discussions. The fool-oriented question is to be put aside. However, the avoidance of foolish questions does not take the form of silence, for the passage above indicates *that we are to educate* the questioner. An answer is to be given, but not an answer which conforms to the foolish presuppositions behind the question. Otherwise contention rather than education will result.

Third, it is revealed that the unbeliever "opposes himself." By his foolish presuppositions the unbeliever actually works against himself. He suppresses the clear truth about God which is foundational to an understanding of the world and of oneself, and he affirms a position which is contrary to his better knowledge. He is intellectually schizophrenic. This must be made clear to him.

Fourth, Paul indicates that what the unbeliever needs is not simply additional information. Instead he needs to have his thinking completely *turned around*; he must undergo a conversion unto a genuine knowledge of the truth. Until this turn-about takes place the unbeliever will have a knowledge of God which *condemns* him (cf. Rom. 1:18ff), but a genuine or sincere knowledge of the truth—a *saving* knowledge—can *only* come with conversion. The unbeliever must be taught to renounce his feigned autonomy and submit to God's clear word of authority.

Finally, the passage quoted above leaves no doubt as to what the source of apologetic success must be: God's sovereign will. A man will be converted only if it is *granted* to him from God. Since it is He who determines the destinies of all men (cf. Eph. 1:1-11), He it is who also determines whether our apologetic witness will be fruitful or not. Thus it behooves us to avoid any attempt to "improve" upon the scriptural approach to apologetics. Our duty is to be faithful to the Lord's instructions. He will bless obedience to His will; success cannot come by circumventing it.

CHAPTER 16:

WORLDVIEWS IN COLLISION

In terms of theoretical principle and eventual out-working, the unbeliever opposes the Christian faith with a whole, antithetical *system* of thought—not simply with piecemeal criticisms. His attack is aimed, not merely at certain random points of Christian teaching, but at its foundation. The particular criticisms utilized by the unbeliever rest upon basic, key assumptions which unify and inform his thinking. It is this presuppositional root which the apologist must aim to eradicate if his defense of the faith is to be effective.

Because the unbeliever has such an implicit system of thought directing his attack on the faith the Christian can never be satisfied to defend the hope that is in him by merely stringing together isolated evidences which offer a slight probability of the Bible's veracity. Each particular item of evidence will be evaluated (as to both its truthfulness and degree of probability) by the unbeliever's tacit assumptions; his general world-and-life view will provide the context in which the evidential claim is understood and weighed. What one presupposes as to possibility will even determine how he rates "probability."

For this reason the apologetic strategy we see illustrated in Scripture calls for argumentation at the *presuppositional* level. For instance, when Paul stood before Agrippa and offered his defense for the hope in him (Acts 26:2, 6-7; cf. 1 Peter 3:15) he declared the public fact of Christ's resurrection (v. 26); however, one must note the presuppositional groundwork and context which Paul provided for this appeal to fact. The very first point Paul endeavored to make in his defense of the faith was a pre-observational, transcendental matter: what is *possible* (v. 8). God was taken as the sovereign determiner of what can and cannot happen. Paul then proceeded to explain that the termination of hostility to the message of the resurrection requires submission to the *Lordship* of Christ (vv. 9-15). One must understand who the genuine and ultimate authority is. Paul went on to explain that the message he declared called for a radical *"change of mind"* (repentance), turning from darkness to true light and from the domination of Satan to God (vv. 18-20). The unbeliever must renounce his antagonistic reasoning and embrace a new system of thought; thus his presuppositional commitments must be altered. Finally, Paul placed his appeal to the fact within the context of *Scripture's* authority to pronounce and interpret what happens in history (vv. 22-23, 27). The ultimate ground of the Christian's certainty and the authority backing up his argumentation must be the word of God. Paul could go to the facts, then, only in terms of an undergirding *philosophy of fact* and in accordance with the foundational axioms of *Biblical epistemology*.

Consequently the apologist needs to recognize that the debate between believer and unbeliever is fundamentally a dispute or clash between two complete worldviews—between ultimate commitments and assumptions which are contrary to each other. An unbeliever is not simply an unbeliever at separate points; his antagonism is rooted in an overall philosophy (Col. 2:8) which is according to the world's tradition; thus he is an enemy of God in his mind (Col. 1:21; James 4:4) and uses his mind to nullify or obviate God's word (Mark 7:8-13). Because he cannot receive or know the things of the Spirit (1 Cor. 2:14), the unbeliever suppresses the truth (Rom. 1:18) and exalts his reasoning against the knowledge of God (2 Cor. 10:5).

Two philosophies or systems of thought are in collision: one submits to the authority of God's word as a matter of presuppositional commitment and one does not. Appeals to fact will be arbitrated in terms of the conflicting presuppositions held by the two philosophies; the debate between the two perspectives will thus eventually work down to the level of one's ultimate authority. Does this bring the argument to end in a stalemate, each person arbitrarily choosing a starting point to his own subjective liking? Not at all. Rather, this situation points up the great need for a presuppositional method of defending the faith. The presuppositionalist realizes that every argument chain must end in a self-authenticating starting point; every worldview has its unquestioned and unquestionable assumptions, its primitive commitments. All religious debate will develop into a question of ultimate authority. In principle the two options will stand in full, stark contrast to each other. At this point only a presuppositional argument can resolve the tension.

As discussed in recent studies in this series, the presuppositional procedure has been seen to involve two steps: (1) an internal critique of the unbeliever's system, demonstrating that his outlook is a foolish destruction of knowledge, and (2) a humble yet bold presentation of the reason for the hope in us, communicated in terms of the believer's presuppositional commitment to God's true word. Such a procedure can resolve the tension between competing authorities and conflicting starting points because it asks which position provides the preconditions for observation, reason, and meaningful discourse.

The apologetic discussion does not end in a stalemate because the Christian, by placing himself on the unbeliever's position, can show how it results in the destruction of intelligible experience and discursive thought. If the unbeliever were correct in his presuppositions, then nothing whatever could be understood or known. The philosophy of the unbeliever has been afflicted with vanity (Rom. 1:21) so that his "knowledge" is (in terms of his own assumptions) falsely so-called (1 Tim. 6:20) and he opposes himself by it (2 Tim. 2:25). By pitting his foolish thinking (in the name of "wisdom") against the wisdom of the gospel (which he labels "foolish") the unbeliever must be unmasked of his pretensions (1 Cor. 1:18-21) and shown that he has no apologetic for his viewpoint (Rom. 1:20) but has been left with a vain, darkened, ignorant mind which needs renewal (Eph. 4:17-24).

The Christian can then teach the unbeliever that all wisdom and knowledge must take Jesus Christ as its reference point (Col. 2:3). The believer's thinking, just as the unbeliever's is grounded in a self-validating starting-point. This ultimate truth must be an expression of God's mind; He alone speaks with unquestionable authority and self-attesting veracity. Thus Jesus categorically claimed to be *the truth* (John 14:6); there is no standard higher than His divine person and word. Christ demonstrated that God and His word must be the self-authenticating, indisputable starting point for all thought when He, unlike Adam, refused to put the Lord to a test (Matt. 4:7), rendering implicit obedience to God's authoritative law (Deut. 6:16). The Christian's starting point, it should then be observed, provides the precondition for intelligible experience and meaningful thought rather than destroying the epistemological enterprise, for it teaches that man was created to think God's thoughts after Him and thereby know the truth.

We have briefly seen, then, that apologetics must eventually bring in *presuppositional* argumentation: the destruction of the unbeliever's philosophy at its epistemological base and the presentation of the only workable foundation for knowledge—God's self-attesting, authoritative revelation.

CHAPTER 17:

THE ULTIMATE STARTING POINT: GOD'S WORD

The disagreement between the believer and the unbeliever which gives rise to the need for apologetics, as we saw in the last study, is not merely over particular, isolated points. In principle two complete philosophic systems or perspectives come into conflict when the veracity of the Christian faith is debated. It is for that reason that the apologist cannot be satisfied to argue merely about certain facts (even those very special facts known as "miracles," like Christ's resurrection). Factual argumentation may become necessary, but it is never sufficient. What one takes to *be* factual, as well as the *interpretation* of accepted facts, will be governed by his underlying *philosophy of fact*—that is, by more basic, all-pervasive, value-oriented, categorizing, possibility-determining, probability-rating, supra-experiential, religiously-motivated *presuppositions*. It is at this presuppositional level that the crucial work in defending the faith must thus be done.

This is also manifest in a somewhat different way. All argumentation about ultimate issues eventually *comes to rest* at the level of the disputant's presuppositions. If a man has come to the conclusion, and is committed to the truth of a certain view, P, when he is challenged as to P, he will offer supporting argumentation for it, Q and R. But of course, as his opponent will be quick to point out, this simply shifts the argument to Q and R. Why accept them? The proponent of P is now called upon to offer S, T, U, and V as arguments for Q and R. And on and on the process goes. The process is complicated by the fact that *both* the believer and unbeliever will be involved in such chains of argumentation. But all argument chains must come to an *end* somewhere. One's conclusions could never be demonstrated if they were dependent upon an infinite regress of argumentative justifications, for under those circumstances the demonstration could never be completed. And an incomplete demonstration demonstrates nothing at all.

Eventually all argumentation terminates in some logically primitive starting point, a view or premise held as unquestionable. Apologetics traces back to such ultimate starting points or *pre*suppositions. In the nature of the case these presuppositions are held to be *self-evidencing*: they are the ultimate authority in one's viewpoint, an authority for which no greater authorization can be given. So then, all apologetic argumentation will require such a final foundation, an ultimate and self-validating presupposition or starting point for thought and commitment. The conscientious apologist should be aware of just what his actual starting point is.

But now a problem obviously arises. If argument chains must eventually terminate, and if the believer and unbeliever have conflicting starting points how can apologetic debate ever be resolved? Since there are different primitive authorities in the realm of thought, does apologetics reduce to a blind, voluntaristic "will to believe"? Is the decision for or against the faith a mere matter of personal taste eventually? Well, the answer would have to be yes if the apologist contented himself merely with arguments and evidences for selected, isolated facts. But the answer is no if the Christian carries his argument *beyond* "the facts and nothing but the facts" to the level of self-evidencing presuppositions—the ultimate assumptions which select and interpret the facts.

At this level of conflict with the unbeliever the Christian must ask, what actually is the *unquestionable* and *self*-evidencing presupposition? Between believer and unbeliever, who *actually* has the most certain starting point for reasoning and experience? What is that presuppositional starting point? Here the Christian apologist, defending his ultimate presuppositions, must be prepared to argue the *impossibility of the contrary*—that is, to argue that the philosophic perspective of the unbeliever *destroys* meaning, intelligence, and the very possibility of knowledge, while the Christian faith provides the only framework and conditions for intelligible experience and rational certainty. The apologist must contend that the true starting point of thought *cannot be other than* God and His revealed word, for no reasoning is possible apart from that ultimate authority. Here and only here does one find the genuinely unquestionable starting point.

It should be clear that this is the perspective of Scripture. It is God's word which must be our ultimate and indisputable presupposition in thought and argumentation, rather than independently supported "brute facts." Christ demonstrated that God's word (and thus His own teaching) had highest authority in the world of thought; it was the firm starting point, self-validating foundation, and final standard of the truth. As such, nothing was more ultimate than it or could call it into question. Thus Christ would never consent to put the Lord God to a test (Matt. 4:7). So also, Christ designated Himself as "the truth" (John 14:6). Christ and His word stand *firm* as the most ultimately established, trustworthy, point of truth; He alone can designate Himself "the Amen" (Rev. 3:14; cf. Isa. 65:16) and preface His pronouncements with "Amen, amen I say unto you..." (John 3:3, 5, 11, etc.). Christ and His word are *self-attestingly* true.

As the very standard of truth against which all other claims must be measured, Christ did not rely upon the backing or evidence of others for His teaching: He taught with *self*-sufficient authority (Matt. 7:29). Should anyone refuse to receive His words, *those very words* would stand in judgment over *him* (John 12:48-50); they had ultimate authority as coming from *the Lord*, thus not being subject to challenge (cf. Matt. 20:1-15). Christ declared that it would be more tolerable for Sodom than for that city which would not receive the apostolic proclamation for (as He explained to the apostles) "he that heareth you, heareth me" (Luke 10:10-16). The divine word is authoritative in itself, carrying its own evidence inherently. Consequently, no man has the prerogative to call it into question (Rom. 9:20); instead, those who contend with God are required to answer (cf. Job 38:1-3; 40:1-5). God's veracity is to be *automatically* presupposed (Rom. 3:1), for He *speaks* with *unmistakable* clarity (Rom. 1:19-20; Ps. 119:130).

Christ disdained those who sought signs beyond the authority of His words (Matt. 12:39; 16:4); mindful of that, Luke prefaced such an incident with the words "Blessed are they that hear the word of God and keep it" (Luke 11:28). Apologists should keep in mind that Christ needs not the witness and glory of man (John 5:31, 41); His greatest witness comes from the Father, speaking in the *Scripture* (John 5:37, 39). The refusal of men to believe Christ's word is *not* attributed to a lack of *factual evidence*, but rather to their *not abiding in* that self-evidencing *word of God* (John 5:36-38). Scripture is authoritative *in itself* to testify of Christ, for God's word is *more sure* than any eye-witness experience of the facts (2 Peter 1:16-19). If men will not submit to the self-evidencing, ultimate starting point of God's word, neither will the fact of an historical resurrection convince them (Luke 16:31). Hence, when certain disciples were reluctant to believe the fact of Christ's resurrection, He rebuked them, not for failure to attend to the experienced evidence, but for their hesitance to believe *the Scriptures* (Luke 24:24-27).

So we see that, in terms of a Biblically guided method, the crux of Christian apologetics is not mere experienced facts (necessary though they may be), but God's revelation in its self-attesting truthfulness. As defenders of the faith, we are obligated to "test the spirits, whether they are from God" (1 John 4:1); that discernment and defense is required at the level of starting point and presupposition, just as at every higher level. The final standard by which all religious claims (affirmative or negative) are to be tried is the *apostolic teaching* (1 John 4:2-3)—which means that it is itself tried by nothing more ultimate; there is no "higher authority" than God's own self-evidencing word.

Therefore, when the apologetic debate centers (eventually) on the issue of conflicting presuppositions, the believer must defend *God's word* as the ultimate starting point, the unquestionable authority, the self-attesting foundation of all thought and commitment. At the level where there are conflicting claims as to the true, self-evident starting point, our apologetic argumentation must require all or nothing: either complete surrender to the epistemic Lordship of Christ (Col. 2:3) or utter intellectual vanity and striving after wind (Eccl. 1:13-17). We must argue from the impossibility of the contrary. The fundamental truth of the Christian faith cannot be given a more ultimate or rigorous defense than this. Simple evidences from nature, personality, logic, or history cannot suffice when the debate reaches the presuppositional level: they cannot cast down every high reasoning which exalts itself against the knowledge of God and demand that *every thought* be made captive to the obedience of Christ (cf. 2 Cor. 10:4-5).

The unbeliever should not be left with false pretensions: such as, that his problem is merely a lack of information, or that he simply needs to correct some of his syllogisms, or that his experience and thinking are all right as far as they go. In actuality, the unbeliever's espoused principles of thought, reason, and reality would lead to utter intellectual foolishness and destruction (1 Cor. 1:20; Matt. 7:26-27). This is what must be pointed out, thus witnessing that the *contrary* of Christianity is *impossible*, while on the other hand the dogmas of the faith provide the necessary pre-conditions of intelligibility and meaning. Such is the Scriptural perspective and method.

The source of the unbeliever's moral and epistemological problem is that he has the *wrong* (allegedly self-evidencing), authoritative starting point in his thought. It should be obvious, then, that the apologist can help the unbeliever *only* if the apologist is conscientiously aware of the *correct*, genuinely self-evidencing, ultimate authority in the realm of thought, and is faithful in arguing in such a way that his defense is *rooted* in that presupposition (Matt. 15:14; cf. 2 Cor. 4:4; Eph. 4:18 with John 9:39; Acts 26:18; Ps. 119:18).

Indeed, it is the case, as many will be quick to point out, that this presuppositional method of apologetics *assumes* the truth of Scripture in order to *argue for* the truth of Scripture. Such is unavoidable when ultimate truths are being debated. However, such is not damaging, for it is not a flat circle in which one reasons (i.e., "the Bible is true because the Bible is true"). Rather, the Christian apologist simply recognizes that the *ultimate* truth—that which is more pervasive, fundamental, and necessary—is such that it cannot be argued *independently* of the preconditions inherent in it. One must presuppose the truth of God's revelation *in order to reason at all*—even when reasoning about God's revelation. The fact that the apologist presupposes the word of God in order to carry on a discussion or debate about the veracity of that word does *not nullify* his argument, but rather *illustrates* it.

CHAPTER 18:

SUMMARY ON APOLOGETIC METHOD: CHAPTERS 13-17

From the preceding section of studies on apologetic procedure we can now *summarize* the *way* in which we ought to go about defending the Christian hope within us:

The Nature of the Apologetic Situation:
1. The controversy between the believer and unbeliever is in principle an *antithesis* between two *complete systems* of thought involving ultimate commitments and assumptions.
2. Even laws of thought and method, along with factual evidence, will be accepted and evaluated in light of one's governing presuppositions.
3. All chains of argumentation, especially over matters of ultimate personal importance, trace back to and depend upon starting points which are taken to be self-evidencing; thus circularity in debate will be unavoidable. However, not all circles are intelligible or valid.
4. Thus appeals to logic, fact, and personality may be necessary, but they are not apologetically adequate; what is needed is not piecemeal replies, probabilities, or isolated evidences but rather an attack upon the underlying presuppositions of the unbeliever's system of thought.
5. The unbeliever's way of thinking is characterized as follows:
    a. By nature the unbeliever is the image of God and, therefore,

inescapably religious; his heart testifies continually, as does also the clear revelation of God around him, to God's existence and character.

b. But the unbeliever exchanges the truth for a lie. He is a fool who refuses to begin his thinking with reverence for the Lord; he will not build upon Christ's self-evidencing words and suppresses the unavoidable revelation of God in nature.

c. Because he delights not in understanding but chooses to serve the creature rather than the Creator, the unbeliever is self-confidently committed to his own ways of thought; being convinced that he could not be fundamentally wrong, he flaunts perverse thinking and challenges the self-attesting word of God.

d. Consequently, the unbeliever's thinking results in ignorance; in his darkened futile mind he actually hates knowledge and can gain only a "knowledge" falsely so-called.

e. To the extent that he actually knows anything, it is due to his unacknowledged dependence upon the suppressed truth about God within him. This renders the unbeliever intellectually schizophrenic: by his espoused way of thinking he actually "opposes himself" and shows a need for a radical "change of mind" (repentance) unto a genuine knowledge of the truth.

f. The unbeliever's ignorance is culpable because he is without excuse for his rebellion against God's revelation; hence he is "without an apologetic" for his thoughts.

g. His unbelief does not stem from a lack of factual evidence but from his refusal to submit to the authoritative word of God from the beginning of his thinking.

The Requirements of the Apologist:

1. The apologist must have the proper attitude; he must not be arrogant or quarrelsome, but with humility and respect he must argue in a gentle and peaceable manner.

2. The apologist must have the proper starting point; he must take God's word as his self-evidencing presupposition, thinking God's thoughts after Him (rather than attempting to be neutral), and viewing God's word as more sure than even his personal experience of the facts.

3. The apologist must have the proper method; working on the

unbeliever's unacknowledged presuppositions and being firmly grounded in his own, the apologist must aim to cast down every high imagination exalted against the knowledge of God by aiming to bring every thought (his own, as well as his opponent's) captive to the obedience of Christ.

4. The apologist must have the proper goal: securing the unbeliever's unconditional surrender without compromising one's own fidelity.

   a. The word of the cross must be used to expose the utter pseudo-wisdom of the world as destructive foolishness.

   b. Christ must be set apart as Lord in one's heart, thus acknowledging no higher authority than God's word and refusing to suspend intellectual commitment to its truth.

The Procedure for Defending the Faith:

1. Realizing that the unbeliever is holding back the truth in unrighteousness, the apologist should reject the foolish presuppositions implicit in critical questions and attempt to educate his opponent.

2. This involves presenting the facts within the context of the Biblical philosophy of fact:

   a. God is the sovereign determiner of possibility and impossibility.

   b. A proper reception and understanding of the facts requires submission to the Lordship of Christ.

   c. Thus the facts will be significant to the unbeliever only if he has a presuppositional change of mind from darkness to light.

   d. Scripture has authority to declare what has happened in history and to interpret it correctly.

3. The unbeliever's espoused presuppositions should be forcefully attacked, asking whether knowledge is possible, given them:

   a. In order to show that God has made foolish the wisdom of the world the believer can place himself on the unbeliever's position and answer him according to his folly, lest he be wise in his own conceits; that is, demonstrate the outcome of unbelieving thought with its assumptions.

   b. The unbeliever's claims should be reduced to impotence and impossibility by an internal critique of his system; that is, demonstrate the ignorance of unbelief by arguing from the impossibility of anything contrary to Christianity.

4. The apologist should appeal to the unbeliever as the image of God who has God's clear and inescapable revelation, thus giving him an ineradicable knowledge of God; this knowledge can be exposed by indicating unwitting expressions or by pointing to the "borrowed capital" (un-admitted presuppositions) which can be found in the unbeliever's position.

5. The apologist should declare the self-evidencing and authoritative truth of God as the precondition of intelligibility and man's only way of salvation (from all the effects of sin, including ignorance and intellectual vanity):

   a. Lest the apologist become like the unbeliever, he should not answer him according to his folly but according to God's word.

   b. The unbeliever can be invited to put himself on the Christian position in order to see that it provides the necessary grounds for intelligible experience and factual knowledge—thereby concluding that it alone is reasonable to hold and the very foundation for proving anything whatsoever.

   c. The apologist can also explain that Scripture accounts for the unbeliever's state of mind (hostility) and the failure of men to acknowledge the necessary truth of God's revelation; moreover, Scripture provides the only escape from the effects of this hostility and failure (futility and damnation).

SECTION FOUR:

THE CONDITIONS NECESSARY
FOR APOLOGETIC SUCCESS

CHAPTER 19:

GOD MUST SOVEREIGNLY
GRANT UNDERSTANDING

If the Christian is to have success in defending the faith he must be prepared to call into question the competence of the unbeliever's thinking. Even if the believer does not have the impressive credentials of educated scholarship possessed by the unbeliever, he is able to do this. The so-called educated "experts" criticized our Lord with respect to His educational credentials (John 7:14-15), but Jesus countered by challenging the competence of His opponents. Because they refused to follow the will of God they were in no position to judge His teaching (vv. 17, 19). The Christian, being indwelt by the Holy Spirit (John 14:17) and dwelling in Christ's word (John 8:31-32), knows the truth. *All* things pertaining to life are granted through a *knowledge of God* (2 Peter 1:3), and thus those who refuse to acknowledge God and the truth about Him will be led into futility and error in all fields of thought (Rom. 1:18-21). Their unrighteousness blinds them, and accordingly the enlightened Christian can challenge his opponent's reasoning. Even Christianity's cultured and educated despisers can be presented an effective apologetic by any believer: "God chose the foolish things of this world that He might put to shame them that are wise" (1 Cor. 1:27). Apologetic success begins with this confidence.

Such confidence, however, must be followed by a properly guided method. In particular the apologist must refrain from appealing to the autonomous principles of secular thought in his attempt to bring understanding to the unbeliever, for the unbeliever's method, standard, and starting point are inherently contrary to that saving understanding at which the apologist aims. Autonomy and understanding are mutually exclusive. Apologetic success will be precluded if the believer rests his case on unbelieving presuppositions or the attitude of autonomy; since these are the *source* of the unbeliever's lack of understanding, *a fortiori* they cannot provide the path to understanding.

The entire human race is dead in trespasses and sin, falling short of God's glory (Eph. 2:1, 5; Rom. 3:23; 5:15); as a result, *no one seeks* after God or *has understanding* (Rom. 3:10-12). Sin has led the unbeliever to exalt his own imaginations and to ignore the revelation of God, and thereby the unbeliever's reason is always deflected into futile, erroneous, and unrighteous conclusions. In his heart (out of which are the issues of life) the foolish unbeliever says that there is no God, and thus he *has no knowledge or understanding* (Ps. 53:1-4; Rom. 3:10-12). The man with whom the apologist argues, then, lacks understanding, and his reasoning is unprofitable. In his mind he is a child of wrath (Eph. 2:3); his mind is at enmity with God and he is unable to do God's will (Rom. 8:7). It is the sinner's intellectual assumptions, operation, and competence which are on trial in an apologetical encounter, not the revelation of Christ. The rebel thinker walks according to his own thoughts and is thus locked into the foolishness which proceeds from his heart (Isa. 65:2; Mark 7:21-22). Since he departs from the faith he unavoidably speaks falsehood and teaches demonic lies (cf. 1 Tim. 4:1-2; Rom. 1:25).

These are harsh and unpopular words to modern ears. Because contemporary apologists so often share the autonomy of secular thought they are unwilling to indict its root foolishness. The thoroughgoing defectiveness and unrighteousness of non-Christian epistemology is overlooked by many in an attempt to gain a hearing and to show that compromise between intellectual self-sufficiency and soteriological dependence on God is possible. However, it is impossible to evade the Bible's stringent indictment of unbelieving thought and its exposure of the unbeliever's foolishness. The principal antithesis between Christian epistemology and apostate epistemology must be underscored. In contrast to the man whose thoughts are vain stands the man who is instructed out of God's law (Ps. 94:11-12; cf. 1 Cor. 3:20). The Christian rejoices that he operates, not according to fleshly wisdom, but (in diametric contrast) according to God's grace (2 Cor. 1:12).

What kind of apologetic, if it is not to share the autonomy of unbelieving thought, can be successful in bringing the unbeliever to an understanding of the truth? The answer is that, like faithful preaching, faithful defense of the gospel must be rooted in the *Word* and the *Spirit*. God can only be known by a voluntary revelation by the Son and Spirit of God (Matt. 11:27; 1 Cor. 2:10); together they deal with man's ethical hostility to God's revelation and enable him to have a saving knowledge of his Creator.

The understanding which the unbeliever lacks can only be provided when his *mind* has been *opened* (e.g., Luke 24:45) and he has been *convicted* by the Spirit of Truth (John 16:8). This Spirit continually witnesses to Christ, conducting His case before the world as Christ's legal representative for the defense (i.e., the "Advocate"; John 15:26). That is, the success of our apologetic depends on the work of the Holy Spirit (cf. John 3:3, 8). Moreover, only if the unbeliever comes to abide in Christ's word can he have God and know the truth (John 8:31-32; 2 John 9). Until he gains the mind of Christ he is completely unable to know Spiritual things (1 Cor. 2:14, 16). Having the mind of Christ requires humility (cf. Phil. 2:5, 8), and thus renunciation of self-sufficiency in order to obey the truth of God. One can only come to a knowledge of Him who is Truth (John 14:6) when the Son *grants him the understanding* which is lacking (1 John 5:20).

Therefore, the apologist is called upon to give a faithful witness to the truth, rather than to attempt to improve on the Lord's wisdom by autonomous arguments. Being confident of his ability to challenge apostate thought, the believer must reason, not according to the principles of secular thought, but on the presupposed truth of Christ's word, and looking to the power of His Spirit to bring conviction, conversion, and understanding. A successful apologetic, being given according to Christ's *Word* and *Spirit*, is a function of the grace of God, not human cleverness and wisdom.

CHAPTER 20:

ONE MUST BELIEVE
IN ORDER TO UNDERSTAND

The testimony of Scripture is clear in teaching that man cannot come to an understanding of God (and thereby of God's world) by means of his independently exercised reason. One does not first satisfy his intellect with certain autonomous proofs that God exists and has a particular nature, and then after gaining this understanding place his faith in the Lord. Rather, reverence and faith precede one's understanding or knowledge of God and all that He has made. To know God in salvation and approach unto Him has definite preconditions or requirements. The motto of the Wisdom literature is that "The beginning (i.e., the first and controlling principle) of knowledge is the fear (or reverent submission) of the Lord" (Prov. 1:7). About this verse Matthew Henry aptly comments: "In order to the attaining of all useful knowledge this is most necessary, that we fear God; we are not qualified to profit by the instructions that are given us unless our minds be possessed with a holy reverence of God, and every thought within us be brought into obedience to him."

The book of Hebrews repeatedly touches on the theme of drawing unto or coming to God (e.g., 4:16; 7:25; 10:22; 12:22), which has been made possible by the perfect ministry and accomplishment of redemption by Jesus Christ (cf. 8:1-13). This benefit of the New Covenant is summarily designated "*knowing* the Lord" (v. 11; cf. John 17:3). The unavoidable prerequisite of coming to the Lord in saving knowledge is laid down in Hebrews 11:6 as faith; without this it is impossible to please Him. Faith enables us to draw near unto God and know Him.

That which God demands of men is that they have faith in His Messianic Son (John 6:28-29), and Jesus declared that doing the will of God was necessary if one were to gain the knowledge of God's true revelation (John 7:17). From this it is evident that autonomous knowledge does not first pick out the genuine revelation of God, and then savingly trust the Savior who is revealed therein. Faith is the precondition of a proper understanding. Augustine drew the inference with clarity: "Understanding is the reward of faith; therefore, do not seek to understand in order to believe, but believe that thou mayest understand" (*Homilies on the Gospel of John* 29.6). Virtue or personal rectitude (i.e., the discipline despised by fools who hate knowledge, Prov. 1:7b-8, 29) is the necessary support for knowledge; if a man's heart is wrong, his thinking will correspondingly be futile. Just as knowledge is supported by virtue, so also virtue is supported by faith (2 Peter 1:5). Thus we must conclude that faith precedes knowledgeable understanding.

Since this is the case, and since repentance is unto faith (Matt. 21:32), the apologist must aim to bring those who live in ignorance to repentance (Acts 17:30). Knowledge can only be gained when the unbeliever repents and comes to faith in Christ: aside from this radical "change of mind" and confident submission to the truth of God, knowledge would be automatically excluded. Therefore, apologetical success depends on the sinner's conversion: his thinking must be completely turned around, not simply supplemented with autonomous arguments. Faith and repentance, which produce reverence for the Lord, are foundational to knowledge, not *vice versa*. Understanding is not gained in the wisdom of man, but only when such pseudo-wisdom is abandoned for the truth of God. The apologetic method of the believer must take this fact into account at all times: if it does, the apologist will be faithful and bold to present the full challenge of presuppositional argumentation rather than the piecemeal attempts of those approaches which fail to call the sinner to abandon his system of thought with its autonomous assumptions and futile methodology. The opponent of the gospel will not come to knowledge until he renounces his sinful pride and alleged intellectual self-sufficiency—that is, until he epistemologically bows before the Lord in repentant faith.

But if repentant faith is necessary for the unbeliever to see the truth of the gospel which we defend, then the success of our apologetic is in the hands of our sovereign Creator and Redeemer. Our polemic will be convincing only to the extent that our unbelieving hearers are renewed in their minds and recreated by God's Spirit in the holiness of the truth (Eph. 4:23-24). Only then will they stop walking in the vanity of their minds with darkened understanding and ignorance (cf. vv. 17-18). Knowledge requires repentance and faith, and thus knowledge depends on the grace of God who gives faith as a gift (Eph. 2:8) and grants repentance (Acts 5:31; 11:18). When the sinner is benefited in these ways by God's mercy and love, then he "puts on the new man who is *renewed unto genuine knowledge* according to the image of his Creator" (Col. 3:10). Faith requires that one be born of God (1 John 5:1) who gives repentance *unto a genuine knowledge* of the truth (2 Tim. 2:25). The apologist's opponent must come to repentant faith if he is to gain understanding and knowledge, and this takes place, not by superior knowledge or clever reasoning on the part of the apologist, but by God's gracious work in the sinner so that he is enabled to know the truth of the apologist's faithful testimony and argument (as they are rooted in Christ's word and are powerful according to Christ's Spirit).

God must give us the success in our apologetic endeavors. Thus we must "walk in wisdom toward them on the outside" (Col. 4:5), not arguing from the foolish presuppositions of unbelief but according to the presupposed authority and truth of God's wise revelation in the gospel. When we do this we will know how to answer every man (v. 6), looking to God in continuing prayer that He might grant apologetical success by opening a door for the word (vv. 2-3). The corrupt communication which characterizes humanistic thought (cf. Matt. 7:17-18) must not proceed from our mouths, but rather good words which represent the mind of God (cf. Matt. 19:17) and can minister grace to our hearers (Eph. 4:29). As Paul, our speech must not be with the enticing words of human wisdom but with the powerful proof (demonstration) of the Spirit (1 Cor. 2:4), knowing that the faith of our opponents must stand in the power of God and not the wisdom of men (v. 5). Such faith is unto understanding. Consequently the apologist must work from the presupposed word of Christ, be constant in prayer, and look to God for the door to be opened to the word (cf. Acts 14:27; 1 Cor. 16:19; 2 Cor. 2:12) and for the granting of wisdom, genuine knowledge, and enlightenment (cf. Eph. 1:16-17).

CHAPTER 21:

STRATEGY GUIDED BY
THE NATURE OF BELIEF

If someone is to have success at some endeavor, it is imperative that he know what the proper end, aim, or goal of that endeavor is. Success at the endeavor does not come accidentally or arbitrarily, and thus you cannot calculate what steps to take without an understanding of where you are going. The fact that the medical profession aims to bring health to its patients has critical significance for determining what methods and procedures it employs. A man does not know what to do in building his house until he learns what is necessary to keep the roof from falling in. Moreover, the goal of one's endeavor delimits the ways in which he can successfully achieve it; for instance, if your aim is to reach Australia, success demands the exclusion of automobile travel.

Therefore, if the apologist is to have success at defending the faith, he should understand the nature of his goal. That at which he aims will dictate the method he should follow. Now unless the apologist is engaged in a proud intellectual game, the goal of his defense and discussion with the unbeliever must be to see the *unbeliever* come to *belief*—that is, to saving faith. And once we grasp what God's word teaches about the nature of saving faith we will be greatly advanced in understanding what method of apologetic argumentation should be followed in order (prayerfully) to achieve success.

There can be no doubt that Scripture sets forth Abraham to us as the paradigm for faith. Hence he is called "the father of all who believe" (Rom. 4:11). We are called upon to walk in his steps of faith (v 12). The kind of faith possessed by Abraham was that which did not walk by sight or intellectual self-sufficiency; the hope which human reasoning and scientific investigation could afford was not Abraham's guiding light. Instead, Abraham believed the incredible (by human standards) promise that, even though he was an old man without a visible heir, his seed would be innumerable (Gen. 15:5-6). He "in hope believed *against hope*" yet "*according to that which had been spoken*" by God that he would be the father of many nations (Rom. 4:18). Contrary to the conclusions which might be drawn by the thinking of man, but according to the spoken word of God—that was the nature of genuine faith. Abraham had to know what was most dependable, what to presuppose, what guiding standards to follow. Thereby he illustrated so well that "faith is the conviction of things *not seen*" (Heb. 11:1). Faith does not rely upon man's autonomous thinking and what it "*sees*" but rather begins with a presuppositional conviction about the veracity of God's word. That which is not seen in human ability is *seen by faith* which submits to the Lord's self-attesting word (Heb. 11:27). The essence of Sarah's faith was that she deemed the Promiser (God) faithful (Heb. 11:11). Full dependence on God's veracity and giving His word epistemic priority over man's excogitation are irradicable elements of genuine faith.

The scope of faith, then, is not the horizon of what human hopes dictate as credible. Rather, the man of faith submits to the *a priori* dependability of God's word—just as Abraham did in obeying the command to sacrifice his only son after he had received him according to the promise. Abraham did this simply accounting God's ability even to raise the dead (Heb. 11:17-19). Abraham did not walk according to self-satisfying sight and demonstrable verification; his was a faith which made God's ability and faithfulness foremost. He trusted that "no word is too hard for Jehovah" (Gen. 18:14) simply on the basis that God Himself had declared it. God's word is its own authentication; it is self-attestingly authoritative. Abraham believed God's word on its own merits. He was fully assured and wavered not in unbelief by concentrating on the promise of God (Rom. 4:20-21). Here indeed is saving faith (v. 22)!

Given this clear example we can understand why Scripture teaches that our trust must be exclusively in God, putting no confidence in the flesh (cf. Phil. 3:3). When a man trusts in himself he departs from the Lord (Jer. 17:5). Thus it is sheer foolishness for men to trust their own self-proclaimed, autonomous, thinking (Prov. 28:26). Faith cannot be planted and grow in the soil of human wisdom; it requires that, instead, one presuppose the word of God. Therefore, Paul declares that his speech was not rooted in the persuasiveness of human wisdom "in order that your faith should not stand in the wisdom of men but in the power of God" (1 Cor. 2:4-5). Faith begins with the Lord and submits wholeheartedly to His wisdom; it is set over against reliance on one's own understanding or reasoning. The book of true wisdom exhorts us: "*Trust in the Lord* with *all* thy heart, and *lean not* upon thine *own* understanding" (Prov. 3:5). When one willingly limits his faith, presuming to question the ability or truth of God based on human intellect or argumentation, it is serious provocation before the Lord (e.g., Ps. 78:18-22). Consequently, faith is obviously not to be grounded in man's self-reliant thinking. God must be taken at His word, for He is Truth itself.

Since this is the end which we hope to achieve in speaking apologetically with the unbeliever, it should be clear that our defense must be rooted in the presupposed word of God rather than guided by clever arguments which rest in assumed intellectual autonomy. We ought not in our apologetic teach the unbeliever to trust himself in *order to* (savingly) rely wholly on the Lord!

CHAPTER 22:

NOT BEING BEGUILED AS WAS EVE

Christ is the very wisdom of God (1 Cor. 1:24) even though the world of unbelief sees Him and His gospel as folly (v. 18). This fact must take hold of the apologist in order that he might remain faithful to his presuppositions as found in God's revealed word, despite the world's demand for signs and philosophical proofs (vv. 22-23) which cater to its own assumptions and presumed autonomy in the realm of epistemology. In consideration of one's own gracious salvation he can see the utter foolishness of infatuation with human wisdom (v. 26). One did not become a believer by listening to the world and its self-professed intellectual autonomy, but by submitting wholeheartedly to the Lordship of Jesus Christ in his thinking and behavior. The Christian must surely *reason* with those who are outside the faith, but he must ever remember that such reasoning does *not* require that he abandon his presuppositions so as to play the deceptive part of a "neutral man" who can self-sufficiently adjudicate all claims of revelation from whatever gods there may be.

When the believer encounters the unbeliever, he must do so with the wisdom of God, not the worldly wisdom which is confounded by God (v.27). Hence Paul did not come from Athens to Corinth with the elaborate language or philosophical subtlety of the thinkers he encountered there (2:1). He did not utilize Athenian intellectual wares. Instead, his proclamation and defense were rooted in the sure word of God (2:2-5). Without this word or revelation from God there can be no theoretical basis for logic, science, or history; one's thought has no meaningful content, dependable use, or objective referent and certainty apart from thinking God's thoughts after Him. Apologetical success hinges on this realization. With it, the Christian can be bold in challenging unbelieving presuppositions and be faithful in adhering to his own (thus remaining loyal to Christ's lordship in the realm of thought). The unbeliever can fight against the gospel only by ruining the foundation of his intellectual efforts. To avoid the same plight the defender of the faith must stay true to the sovereign word of God as his most basic presupposition and guideline. He needs to argue from within that perspective, not in a way which is extraneous or contrary to it, giving in to the assumptions of his opponent not even for a moment (cf. Gal. 2:5).

The moment one abandons his sure footing in the presupposed word of God his apologetic becomes unfaithful and precarious. A vivid confrontation of that fact can be taken from the account of man's fall into sin according to Genesis 3. Even in the garden man was responsible to submit without question to God's revelation given by special word to him. Satan's strategy then (as now) was to work toward undermining man's presuppositional submission to this authoritative word from God. He began by calling the word into question (v. 1) and then contradicting it openly (v. 4). The epistemological situation was thrown into upheaval when Eve began thinking that she could have a meaningful and proper understanding of reality apart from God's revelation. In that case she was free to examine what God had to say and autonomously determine its truth over against the conflicting hypothesis of Satan. She suspended thinking God's thoughts after Him in order to become the prime authority in the world of thought. Specifically, she abandoned loyalty to her Creator so as to make herself His equal (v. 5), determining good and evil for herself. She took her stand as a "neutral" judge over God's hypothesis, thereby exalting her "autonomous" reason over God's epistemologically necessary word. By thus usurping the epistemic prerogatives of the Lord, she plunged the human race into the lawlessness we see ever about us in thought and behavior.

Jesus Christ came to atone for such sins (even intellectual transgressions against God's word) and to call men back to unswerving loyalty to His revealed word. The apologist cannot turn a deaf ear to that call and demand, thinking that he nevertheless defends the Lord of glory. Paul, the apostle of Christ, makes it very clear that we must learn the lesson of Adam and Eve in the garden. In 2 Corinthians 11:3 he says, "But I fear, lest by any means, as the serpent deceived Eve in his craftiness, your minds should be corrupted so as to turn from the single-mindedness and purity that is toward Christ." The epistemological implications of the narrative about man's fall into sin were only too obvious to Paul. Thus he dreaded that the church might, like Eve, be seduced away from absolute loyalty to Jesus Christ. What is required of the Christian is undivided devotion or single-hearted adherence to Christ the Lord; we must be free from duplicity in our thinking. The double-minded man (attempting to follow two lords) is unstable in all his ways (James 1:8), being blown about by every wind of doctrine (cf. v. 6). Thus, we must be *purified* from double-mindedness (James 4:8). As Paul indicates in 2 Corinthians 11, if we are not thus purified, we shall be beguiled by the deceptive thinking of Satan (the father of all lying, John 8:44) and his ministers (v. 15). No extraneous corruptions can be allowed in our thinking, for it shall become debauched when we deviate even slightly from the word of Christ. Genesis 3 must drive home the need for a presuppositional method in apologetics.

By taking such a stand in the argument with unbelief, we may very well be ridiculed as lacking the oratory, eloquence and cunning rhetoric of the "sophisticated" academic mind which is trained in the ways of autonomous philosophy (cf. 1 Cor. 1:17; 2:4); when you do not reason in a way pleasing to your hearer, he will take you for a *layman* in matters of intellect. However, the fact remains that only by resisting the deception to which Eve submitted can we salvage the epistemic enterprise; we speak a wisdom which is discerned when the Spirit frees men's minds from bondage (cf. 1 Cor. 2:6-16). As Paul declared, subsequent to his warning about Eve's deception, "though I be rude in speech, *yet am I not in knowledge* (2 Cor. 11:6).

CHAPTER 23:

NOT LYING TO DEFEND THE TRUTH

A source of great disappointment to the Christian scholar in the present day is the refusal of many apologists to reckon with certain hard but indisputable facts taught in God's word. The impression is often given that these men as *theologians* want to admit what Scripture says about the nature of fallen man and the utmost and necessary authority of God's revelation in any field of knowledge; however, *as apologists* they want to act in oblivion or temporary suppression of these truths. Such duplicity is dishonoring to the Christian's calling.

Saving faith cannot be grounded in human wisdom or secular presuppositions: it must be generated in the power of God (1 Cor. 2:4-5). Accordingly the apologist does not speak the wisdom of this world (which is brought to nothing) but the wisdom of God (1 Cor. 2:6-7). Recognition of Christ as the wisdom of God stems not from presuppositions which deny, ignore, or undermine this fact; instead, such recognition results from the inward work of the Holy Spirit (1 Cor. 2:10) Who alone can enable us to gain a knowledge of the things of God (v. 12). Because only the Spirit of God knows these things (v. 11), the Christian does not speak or rely upon autonomous philosophy, history, or science as the world teaches (v. 13). To follow secular presuppositions incapacitates one from discerning the truth about God (v. 14), for they can be understood only by the enlightenment of the Spirit (vv. 15-16). The pseudo-wisdom of the world, then, is most unsuitable as a foundation or standard for the defender of Christian faith; it cannot improve upon the mind of the Lord

(v. 16) but instead leads one inevitably to challenge the truth of God's revelation. Apologetic success is precluded, then, by dependence upon or catering to unauthoritative human foolishness which is unalterably inclined to crucify the Lord of glory rather than bowing before His sovereign demands (cf. v8).

It is the regenerated and enlightened believer, converted from his old manner of disobedient living, who gains wisdom, understanding, and knowledge; right thinking is correlated with right living. Hence the unbeliever's form of life is an unsuitable framework for the apologist to operate within. If one continues in intellectual sin—refusing to submit every thought to the Lordship of Christ in the realm of knowledge—he will never come to saving belief. "To *depart* from evil is understanding" (Job 28:28), and "a good understanding have all they that do His commandments" (Ps. 111:10). Consequently, the apologist cannot attempt to persuade the unbeliever by using the unbeliever's style of thought or standards of evidence and truth, etc. Such a procedure simply will not woo him to Christ but encourage him to assert his own autonomous authority over Christ's claims. However, God's sure word declares that we can know God only if we keep His commandments (1 John 2:3-5), and those commandments include our obligation to refrain from putting God to a test (Deut. 6:16) and to bring every thought captive to the obedience of Christ (2 Cor. 10:5). Our wisdom and understanding are not found in the "cleverness" of autonomous thinking, but in obeying the law of God (Deut. 4:6). Genuine knowledge and stability in the face of false opinion are correlated with spiritual maturity in the stature of Christ (Eph. 4:13-14); it is a pleasing walk and morally worthy life which lead to genuine knowledge (Col. 1:9-11).

Now then, it is frankly immoral for the theologian who sees the above truths to use a double standard, admitting these things as a dogmatician but giving a completely opposite impression in his apologetic procedure. The apologist must not let the unbeliever assume that knowledge is possible given autonomous presuppositions and a disobedient life; God's word is never verified in such a context. In his attempt to bring about the good situation of an unbeliever accepting the word of Scripture, the apologist makes use of an unjustifiable lie if he assumes or leads the unbeliever to think that knowledge is to be gained apart from God or while one persists in a rebellious way of living and thinking. It cannot be ignored that repentance and faith are necessary for a knowledge of the truth; it must not be suggested that the unbeliever needs nothing more than intellectual proof of God's veracity according to standards dictated by secular philosophy and science. The worthy end of converting the unbeliever cannot be realized by, nor can it justify, making apologetical use of a means which operates in disagreement with (or opposition to) the teaching of Scripture. "If the truth of God abounded by my lie unto His glory, why am I still judged as a sinner? And not rather (as we are blasphemed and some allege that we say), Let us do evil in order that good may come? The damnation of whom is just" (Rom. 3:7-8).

Apologists are prohibited from using a non-presuppositional method in defending the faith under the excuse that thereby truth might abound. The obedient Christian does not lay aside the authority of Christ in the realm in order to argue on the basis of autonomous "scholarship." To do so would be to operate with a *lie* (namely, the Satanic lie that knowledge can be determined apart from God: Gen. 3:5; cf. Rom. 1:25) in order to defend the *truth*! The faithful witness to Christ will not behave *as an unbeliever* (denying Christ's Lordship) in order *to make him a believer*.

Evil men cannot speak good things (Matt. 12:34); the evil treasure of the unbeliever's thought is where his heart is (Matt. 6:21; Luke 6:45), from which proceeds evil, deceitful, foolish thoughts (Matt. 15:18-19; Rom. 1:21; Jer. 17:9). Hence his tongue is full of iniquity and an unruly evil (James 3:5-8); with it he uses deadly deceit (Rom. 3:13-14). He thinks that he alone is lord over the use of his lips (Ps. 12:4), leading him to speak falsehood (v. 2). Obviously, then, the apologist must not think and speak after the manner of the unbeliever. Instead his thoughts and words must be rooted in God's word which is pure and eternally valuable (Ps. 12:6-7). It is this word which alone stops every mouth (Rom. 3:19) and leaves men speechless (e.g., Job 40:4). We must guard the apostolic deposit (Scripture) by *turning away from* the vain claims of pseudo-knowledge (1 Tim. 6:3-5, 20; cf. 2 Tim. 2:14-18). Before God and His word all the world must be silent (Isa. 6:5; Dan. 10:15; Hab. 2:20; Zeph. 1:7, Zech. 2:13). We, then, must rely upon God and not our own wisdom (Isa. 50:4-9); only then will we see apologetic success as He enables us not to be confounded and makes none able to contend with our message (Isa. 50:4-9). Therefore, we conclude that the apologist must be transformed by a renewed mind and not fashion his thinking according to the world (Rom. 12:2). He must not lie or abandon God's presupposed truth in order to bring acceptance of that truth by evil speakers.

CHAPTER 24:

EFFECTIVELY ENCOUNTERING
THE VARIETIES OF OPPOSITION

OVERALL SUMMARY (CHAPTERS 1-23) AND APPLICATION:

Situations constantly arise which provide occasion for the Christian to defend his faith. Opposition to biblical Christianity comes to practical expression in a great variety of ways: popular media and entertainment, propaganda from cults and false religions, teaching in schools and colleges, remarks made by colleagues, neighbors, and friends, not to mention modern trends in psychology, politics, medicine, society—and the list could be easily multiplied. The opinions, assumptions, and behavior of the people who come into contact with our lives are for the most part grounded in hostility (active and passive) to the teaching of Scripture. The believer is apologetically challenged on every side. Of course, his need to defend his beliefs is greatly increased to the extent that he initiates an evangelistic witness with those around him. Thus, there is no lack of opportunity to engage in apologetics.

Nor is there a shortage of the kinds of criticisms and problems encountered by the Christian apologist. First, there are direct *attacks* on Christian tenets. Some reject *God* (atheists, agnostics, skeptics). Some reject the possibility of *revelation*; others reject the *Bible* as being God's revelation. The latter group allegedly base their response on *logic* (supposing to find contradictions in the Bible's *system* of doctrine or between its recorded *accounts*), or *factual* matters (rejecting the *textual* accuracy, the *historical* veracity, or possibility of *miracles* in Scripture), or *ethical* concerns (criticizing God's *actions or commandments*), or finally on *personal* considerations (saying the Bible is not to their *liking*, does not meet their *needs*, or being *indifferent* and *relativistic*). Secondly, there are systems in *competition* with evangelical Christianity. Some accept the wrong *god* (deism, pantheism, or the various world religions). Some accept the wrong *revelation* (internal intuition or personal feeling, social opinion or human tradition, or other sacred writings). And others accept the wrong *interpretation* or improperly understand the *Bible* (as less than it claims for itself—modern unorthodoxy, or as teaching an incorrect theology and *soteriology*—the cults).

Therefore, opposition to biblical Christianity is of *many kinds* and comes in *many ways*. When you stand back and get an idea of the intensity and scope of the attacks on the Christian world and life view, you could easily be tempted to give up all hope of being an effective apologist, exclaiming "who is sufficient for these things?"—especially if you do not have advanced training in these matters. However, such a despairing attitude, such a lack of confidence, would tend wrongly to release you from your clear and unavoidable responsibility to be *prepared* to give an answer to *any* man who asks for a reasoned defense of the hope (confidence) that is in you (1 Peter 3:15). Well, then, how can any Christian fulfill this apologetical task?

The answer lies in recognizing that, despite the variety of criticisms and the many modes in which they are expressed, there is a common, basic, set of circumstances and principles that are embodied in each and every apologetic encounter. All critics have a fundamental and identical problem; Christianity is always and only the answer to this problem. That is why the preceding studies in this series have focused on *central themes* and *general guidelines* for apologetics. If the believer can penetrate to the heart of the matter and grasp the basic principles that come to play in apologetic interaction, he will be prepared for every sort of challenge to the faith. At bottom, the issue is always a matter of recognizing the sovereign Creator who has clearly revealed Himself, as well as your total dependence on Him even in the realm of thought and knowledge. The previous parts of this series have elaborated and built upon these points.

A quick synopsis of those studies will hopefully bring everything together in capsulated form. We began with the fundamental principle which must guide all thinking: *the lordship of Christ in the realm of knowl-*

edge. God speaks with self-attesting authority, and His revelation is the necessary foundation of man's knowledge. The attempt to take a neutral stance with respect to God's revelation, then, is immoral and unavoidably leads (in principle) to the disintegration of knowledge. Consequently, the Bible characterizes the unbeliever's thoughts as vain and foolish, and it requires the believer (who is renewed in mind) to be set apart from the world by submission to Christ's word of truth as the ultimate authority. The Christian, then, is rescued from epistemic futility by presupposing God's word over all contrary claims.

Certain conditions were then seen to characterize apologetical situations and *make fruitful argumentation* (in humble boldness) *possible* with the unbeliever. Due to God's inescapable revelation every unbeliever nevertheless knows God and thereby (contrary to his espoused principles) knows himself and the world in some measure; knowing God, all men are then without an apologetic for their rebellion against His truth. The whole created realm constantly reveals the living and true God, thus providing abundant common ground between the believer and unbeliever. Since the latter is always the image of God, and since he possesses the truth of God (though suppressed), the apologist always has a point of contact with him.

How should the Christian go about *defending the faith*, given the above truths? First, he must firmly acknowledge that unbelief results in intellectual foolishness. Given that conviction and understanding, the believer can repudiate the unbeliever's presuppositions, present the absolute claims of Christ (even in the realm of thought), and do an internal critique of the unbeliever's thought—showing him where its assumptions inevitably lead. The unbeliever must be shown that he actually opposes himself. This presuppositional approach is required since two full worldviews are being set against each other—not simply a few alleged facts and applications of logic. The very possibility of knowledge outside of God's revelation (savingly presented in Christ) must be undermined. Since all argumentation over fundamental issues of life and belief reduce to a question of one's starting point, the Christian apologist must stand firmly on the word of God, setting forth its self-attesting nature over against the destructive assumptions of unbelief for epistemology.

By understanding and operating upon these central principles, the apologist can have full confidence in his ability to answer all varieties of opposition to Christianity. Finally, then, the *conditions of a successful apologetic treatment* of unbelief can be rehearsed. First, the apologist must be true to his presuppositions and remember the nature of saving faith; working toward unconditional submission to the word of God on its own merits, the believer will not move to a neutral position or give the deceptive impression that autonomy can lead to meaningful and true conclusions. Second, the unbeliever must see that belief is the foundation of understanding; submission to Christ must ground one's use of reasoning. Finally, success is possible only if God himself sovereignly grants the unbeliever an understanding of the truth, enlightening his mind, converting his heart, and giving him the gift of faith.

The principles summarized above prepare the believer to answer any and all opposition to the faith, irrespective of the form or circumstance in which it appears. Every apologetical situation is characterized by these facts: God's revelation is at base necessary for knowledge of any kind, all unbelievers are without excuse since they possess and suppress the knowledge of God, and the Christian is characterized by unconditional surrender to Christ in all things. These facts not only guide us as to how we should defend the faith, they also *guarantee* that we can drive to the heart of any variety of opposition, unmask it, and set forth the sterling claims of Christ (2 Cor. 10:4-5). With Christ "set apart as Lord in your heart," the believer is "prepared" for any challenge to the faith; he can have genuine hope or *confidence* in looking ahead to the defense of "the hope that is in you." As Scripture declares, "He that believeth on him shall *not be confounded*"—will not have occasion to be ashamed of his confidence and flee in disappointment (Rom. 9:33, 1 Peter 2:6).

SECTION FIVE:

ANSWERS TO APOLOGETIC CHALLENGES

CHAPTER 25

READY TO REASON

Is it Necessary?

A surge of pious agreement overcame me the first time I heard someone confidently assert that "The word of God no more needs defense than does a lion in a cage. Just let the lion loose, and it will take care of itself!" There seemed something very right about that sentiment. It almost appeared irreverent to disagree with it.

Well, something about that assertion is indeed right. God is certainly not in *need* of *anything*—much less the puny efforts of any particular man or woman to defend His word. He is the Creator of heaven and earth, almighty in power, and sovereign in controlling all things. The Apostle Paul, when reasoning with the Athenian philosophers, made that very point: he declared that God is not worshipped with men's hands "as though He needed any thing, seeing that He gives to all life and breath and all things" (Acts 17:24). If God were ever to hunger, for instance, He would not need to tell us since the fullness of all creation is His (Ps. 50:12)! He depends upon nothing outside Himself, and everything outside of Him depends upon Him for its existence, qualities, abilities, accomplishments, and blessings. "In Him we live, and move, and have our being" (Acts 17:28).

So it is obvious that God does not *need* our inadequate reasoning and our feeble attempts to defend His word. Nevertheless, the pious-sounding remark with which we began is still mistaken. It suggests that we should not concern ourselves with efforts at apologetics because God will directly take care of such matters Himself. The remark is just as mistaken as saying that God does not need us as evangelists (He could even make the stones to cry out, couldn't He?)—and therefore efforts at evangelistic witness are unimportant. Or, a person might misguidedly think that, because God has the power and ability to provide his family with food and clothing without "help from us," he does not need to go to work tomorrow.

Thinking like this is unbiblical. It confuses what God Himself needs from us and what God requires of us. It assumes that God ordains ends, but not means to those ends (or at least not the instrumentality of created means). There is no need for God to use our evangelistic witness, our daily work for a paycheck, or our defense of the faith—but He chooses to do so, and He calls us to apply ourselves to them. The Bible directs us to work, although God *could* provide for our families in other ways. The Bible directs us to evangelize, even though God *could* use other means to call sinners to Himself. And the Bible also directs us to defend the faith—not because God would be helpless without us, but because this is one of His ordained *means* of glorifying Himself and vindicating His truth.

Christ speaks to the church as a whole through Jude, commanding us to "contend earnestly for the faith which was once for all delivered to the saints" (Jude 3). False and heretical teaching was threatening the church and its grasp of gospel truth. Jude very well knew that God was in sovereign control, and indeed that God would in time directly deal with wicked teachers, consigning them to everlasting condemnation. Still Jude *also* urged his readers themselves to contend with the error of false teaching, not sitting back and expecting that God would simply take care of it Himself.

Paul wrote to Titus that overseers (pastors and elders) in the church are required to be especially adept at refuting those who oppose the truth of God (Titus 1:9). However this is not merely the assigned task of ordained men. *All* believers are commanded to engage in it as well. Addressing himself to all members of the congregation, Peter penned the following command: "sanctify Christ as Lord in your hearts, always being ready to give an answer to anyone who asks from you a reason for the hope that is within you, yet with gentleness and respect" (1 Peter 3:15). It is God Himself, speaking through Peter's inspired words, who calls upon us as believers—each and every one of us—to be prepared to defend the faith in the face of challenges and questions which come from unbelievers—any one of them.

The necessity of apologetics is not a divine necessity: God can surely do His work without us. The necessity of apologetics is a moral necessity: God has chosen to do His work through us and has called us to it. Apologetics is the special talent of some believers, and the interested hobby of others; but it is the God-ordained responsibility of all believers.

What It Isn't

We should look at 1 Peter 3:15 again and notice a few things that it does not say.

(1) It does not say that believers are supposed to take the initiative and start arrogant arguments with unbelievers, telling them that we have all the answers. We do not have to go out looking for a fight. We certainly should not sport or encourage a "I'll prove it to you" spirit, an attitude which relishes refutation. The text indicates that we offer a reasoned defense in answer to those who ask for such from us, whether they do so as an opening challenge to the integrity of God's word or as the natural response to our evangelistic witness.

The text also indicates that the spirit in which we offer our apologetic answer is one of "gentleness and respect." It is not pugnacious and defensive. It is not a spirit of intellectual one-up-manship. The task of apologetics begins with humility. After all, the fear of the Lord is the starting point of all knowledge (Prov. 1:7). Moreover, apologetics is pursued in service to the Lord, and "the Lord's servant must not strive, but be gentle toward all, apt to teach" (2 Tim. 2:24). Apologetics is not a place for vain flexing of our intellectual muscles.

(2) Another thing that 1 Peter 3:15 does not say is that believers are responsible to *persuade* anybody who challenges or questions their faith. We can offer sound reasons to the unbeliever, but we cannot make him or her subjectively believe those reasons. We can refute the poor argumentation of the unbeliever, but still not persuade them. We can close the mouth of the critic, but only God can open the heart. It is not in our ability, and not our responsibility, to regenerate the dead heart and give sight to the blind eyes of unbelievers. That is God's gracious work.

It is God who must enlighten the eyes of one's understanding (Eph. 1:18). "The natural man receives not the things of the Spirit of God, for they are foolishness to him; and he cannot know them because they are Spiritually discerned" (1 Cor. 2:14). Until God in His sovereign grace changes the sinner from within, he will not see the kingdom of God or submit to the King. Jesus taught this to Nicodemus, reminding him that "the wind [same Greek word as "Spirit"] blows where it will... So is every one who is born of the Spirit" (John 3:8). Our task is to present a faithful and sound witness and defense. The task of persuasion is God's. That is why apologists should not evaluate their success or adjust their message on the basis of whether the unbeliever finally comes to agree with them or not.

(3) Yet another thing that 1 Peter 3:15 does not say is that defending the faith has a different ultimate authority than does the task of expounding the faith. It is a common mistake among evangelicals to imagine that the authority of God and His word is the basis for their theology and preaching, but the authority for defending this faith must be something other than God and His word—or else we would be begging the question raised by unbelievers. Accordingly, believers will sometimes be misled into thinking that whatever they take as the ultimate standard in apologetical thinking must be neutral and agreed upon by believer and unbeliever alike; and from here they go on to make the second mistake of thinking that something like "reason" is such a commonly understood and accepted standard.

These ideas are quite obviously out of accord with Biblical teaching, however. Does apologetics have a different epistemological[1] authority than expounding theology? Our theology is founded upon the authority of Christ, speaking by His Spirit in the words of Scripture. 1 Peter 3:15 teaches us that the precondition of presenting a defense of the faith (apologetics) is *also* that we "sanctify [set apart] Christ as Lord in your hearts." It would be a mistake to imagine that Peter is speaking of the "heart" here as though it is our center of emotions over against the mind with which we think. In Biblical terminology the "heart" is the location of our reasoning (Rom. 1:21), meditation (Ps. 19:14), understanding (Prov. 8:5), thinking (Deut. 7:17; 8:5) and believing (Rom. 10:10). It is just here—in the center of our thinking and reasoning—that Christ is to be consecrated as Lord, when we engage in apologetical discussion with inquiring unbelievers. Thus theology and apologetics have the same epistemological authority—the same Lord over all.

Reason and Reasoning

Believers who aim to defend their faith make a serious mistake when they imagine, then, that something like "reason" should displace Christ as the ultimate authority (Lord) in their thinking and argumentation. They also fall into very sloppy and confused thinking due to misunderstanding over the word "reason."

Christians are often befuddled about "reason," not knowing whether it is something to embrace or to eschew. This is usually because they do not pinpoint the precise way in which the word is being used. It may very well be the most ambiguous and obscure word in the field of philosophy. On the one hand, reason can be thought of as a *tool*—man's intellectual or mental capacity. Taken in this sense, reason is a gift of God to man, indeed part of the divine image. When God bids His people "Come let us reason together" (Isa. 1:18), we see that we, like God, are capable of rational thought and communication. God has given us our mental abilities to serve and glorify Him. It is part of the greatest commandment of the law that we should "love the Lord thy God... with all thy mind" (Matt. 22:37).

Reason Not Ultimate

On the other hand, reason can be thought of as an ultimate and independent authority or *standard* by which man judges all claims to truth, even God's. In this sense, reason is a law unto itself, as though man's mind were self-sufficient, not in need of divine revelation. This attitude commonly leads people to think that they are in a position to think independently, to govern their own lives, and to judge the credibility of God's word based on their own insight and authority; more dramatically, this attitude deified Reason as the goddess of the French Revolution. "Professing themselves to be wise, they became fools," as Paul said (Rom. 1:22). This view of reason does not recognize that God is the source and precondition of man's intellectual abilities—that reason does not make sense apart from the perspective of God's revelation. It does not recognize the sovereign and transcendent character of God's thought: "For as the heavens are higher than the earth, so are. . . My thoughts higher than your thoughts" (Isa. 55:9).

Reason as God's Gift

Should Christians endorse the use of reason? Two equal but opposite mistakes are possible in answering that question. (1) Believers can
recognize the appropriateness of using reason, taken as their intellectual
faculty, but then slide into endorsing reason as intellectual *autonomy*. (2)
Believers can recognize the inappropriateness of reason as intellectual *autonomy*, but then mistakenly think this entails rejecting reason as an intellectual *faculty*. The first group honors God's gift to man of reasoning
ability, but dishonors God through its rationalism. The second group
honors God's ultimate authority and the need for obedience in all aspects
of man's life, but it dishonors God through anti-intellectual pietism.

Paul counterbalances both of these errors in Colossians 2. He writes
that "all treasures of wisdom and knowledge are deposited in Christ" (v.
3). Accordingly we must "beware lest anyone rob you through philosophy, even vain deceit, which is after the tradition of men, after the elementary principles of the world, and not after Christ" (v. 8). This ex-
hortation is not a diatribe against the use of reason or the study of philosophy.

Paul makes it clear that believers have the advantage of the best reasoning and philosophy because Christ is the source of all knowledge—*all*
knowledge, not simply religious matters or sentiment. Moreover, if there
are many philosophies which are not "after Christ," there is also that
philosophy which is. Anti-intellectualism throws the baby out with the
bath. It destroys true wisdom in the name of resisting foolishness.

On the other hand, it is equally plain from Colossians 2 that Paul
does not endorse reasoning and philosophy which refuse to honor the
ultimate authority of the Lord Jesus Christ. It is in Christ that wisdom
and knowledge must be found. Any alleged wisdom which follows the
traditions of men and elementary principles of the world—rather than
Christ—is to be rejected as dangerous and deceitful.

The Bible teaches us, therefore, that "reason" is not to be taken as
some neutral authority in man's thinking. It is rather the intellectual
capacity with which God created man, a tool to be used in serving and
glorifying the ultimate authority of God Himself.

Sharpening the Tool

Reason properly understood (reasoning) is to be endorsed by believers in Christ. In particular it is to be employed in defending the Christian faith. This is one of the things which Peter communicates to us when he wrote that we should always be "ready to give a defense to anyone who asks from you a reason for the hope within you" (1 Peter 3:15). A word of explanation and defense is to be offered to those who challenge the truth of our Christian faith. We are not to obscure the glory and veracity of God by answering unbelievers with appeals to "blind faith" or thoughtless commitment. We are to "cast down reasonings and every high thing exalted against the knowledge of God" (2 Cor. 10:5), realizing all along that we cannot do so unless we ourselves "bring every thought captive to the obedience of Christ."

In 1 Peter 3:15 Peter uses the expression "always ready." This is significant for those who wish to honor the Biblical necessity of engaging in apologetics. What the Lord asks of us is that we be *prepared* to offer an answer in defense of our faith, whenever anybody asks us for a reason. We are to be "ready" to do this—indeed, "always ready." And that means that it is imperative that we reflect on the questions that unbelievers are likely to ask and challenges which are commonly laid down to Christianity. We should study and prepare to give reasons for our faith when the faithless ask.

Christians need to sharpen the tool of their reasoning ability so as to glorify God and vindicate the claims of the gospel. We should all give our best efforts in the service of our Savior, who termed Himself "the Truth" (John 14:6). Every believer wants to see the truth of Christ believed and honored by others. And that is why we need to be "ready to reason" with unbelievers. This study and those which follow are intended to help us become better prepared for that necessary task.

Notes:

[1] "Epistemology" refers to one's theory of knowledge (its nature, sources, limits). When we ask "How do you know that to be true? (or how could you justify that claim?)," we are asking an epistemological question.

CHAPTER 26:

THE HEART OF THE MATTER

Knowing and Believing

Christians are often called "believers," while non-Christians are termed "unbelievers." Scripture itself speaks this way: we read that "believers were the more added to the Lord" (Acts 5:14), and that they should not be "unequally yoked together with unbelievers" (2 Cor. 6:14). There are obviously two classes of people distinguished by whether they believe or not. It can rightly be said that what separates Christians from non-Christians is the matter of faith.

Christians believe certain things which non-Christians do not. Christians believe the claims of Christ and the teachings of the Bible to be true, but non-Christians disbelieve them. Christians have faith in Christ and trust His promises; non-Christians do not believe in Him and doubt His word. It is quite natural, then, that the gospel can be called "the word of faith" (Rom. 10:8). Becoming a Christian entails that you "believe in your heart that God raised Him [Christ] from the dead" (v. 9); likewise, "he who comes to God must believe that He is, and that He is the rewarder of them who diligently seek Him" (Heb. 11:6). Examples could be multiplied. What sets Christians apart from non-Christians is the matter of belief or faith.

However, the difference between them is more than that in an important sense, and we need to understand this if we are going to do a faithful job in defending the faith. The Christian claims to "believe" the teachings of Scripture or to have "faith" in the person of Christ[1] because the element of trust is so prominent in our relationship with the Savior. But the Christian actually claims more than simply to believe Christ's claims to be true. The Christian also affirms that he or she "knows" those claims to be true. What is involved in saving faith is more than hope (although that is present) and more than a commitment of will (although that too is present). Job confidently asserted, "I know my Redeemer lives" (Job 19:25). John indicated that he wrote his first epistle so that those "who believe on the name of the Son of God" "may know that you have eternal life" (1 John 5:13). Paul declared that God "has furnished proof" that Jesus will judge the world (Acts 17:31). Jesus promised His disciples that they would "know the truth, and the truth shall set you free" (John 8:32).

In what way does knowledge go beyond belief? Knowledge includes having justification or good reason to support whatever it is you believe. Imagine that I believe there are thirty-seven square miles in a particular city, and imagine also that it just so happens that this claim is accurate— but imagine as well that I simply got this answer by guessing (rather than doing measurements, mathematics, or checking an almanac, etc.). I believed something which happened to be true, but we would not say that I had "knowledge" in this case because I had no *justification* for what I believed. When we claim to know that something is true, we are thereby claiming to have adequate evidence, proof or good reason for it.

The difference between the Christian and the non-Christian is not simply that one believes the Bible and the other does not. People's beliefs can be frivolous, random, or silly. The Christian also claims that there is justification for believing what the Bible says. The non-Christian says, to the contrary, that there is no justification (or adequate justification) for believing the Bible's claims—or, in stronger cases, says that there is justification for disbelieving the Bible's claims. Apologetics amounts to an inquiry into and debate over who is correct on this matter. It involves giving reasons, offering refutations, and answering objections.

Conflicting Worldviews

Whose perspective is intellectually justified, the Christian's or the non-Christian's? Many budding Christian apologists approach the answer to this question in a very simplistic and naive fashion, thinking that all we have to do is go look at the observable evidence and see whose hypothesis is verified. "After all," it is thought, "this is how we resolve disagreements in our ordinary affairs, as well as in science."[2] If a dispute arises over the price of eggs at the store, we can jump in the car, drive down to the market, and go look for ourselves at the price listed on the eggs. If scientists disagree over the claim that smoking causes cancer, they can run tests, do statistical comparisons, etc. In such cases, it seems that what we do, at base, is "look and see" if one hypothesis or its opposite is true. Of course, disagreements such as these can be readily resolved in this fashion only because the two people who disagree nevertheless *agree* with each other regarding *more basic* assumptions—such as the reliability of their senses, the uniformity of natural events, the accuracy of data reporting, the honesty of researchers, etc.

However, when the dispute is over more fundamental issues, as it is between believers and unbelievers, simple appeals to observational evidence need not be decisive at all. The reason is that a person's most fundamental beliefs (or presuppositions) determine what he or she will accept as evidence and determine how that evidence will be interpreted. Let me illustrate. Naturalism and supernaturalism are conflicting outlooks regarding the world in which we live and man's knowledge of it. The naturalist claims that what is studied by empirical science[3] is all that there is to reality, and that every event can (in principle) be explained without resorting to forces outside the scope of man's experience or outside the universe. Christian supernaturalism, on the other hand, believes that there is a transcendent and all-powerful God who can intervene in the universe and perform miracles which cannot be explained by the ordinary principles of man's natural experience. Now then, having well-accredited reports of a "miraculous" event is not in itself sufficient to change the mind of the naturalist—and for good reason. The naturalist's presuppositions will *require* him to dispute the claim that such an event really occurred, or alternatively, will lead him to say that the event is subject to a natural explanation once we learn more about it. Simple evidence need not dislodge his naturalistic approach to all things—any more than simple eye-ball evidence could ever in itself refute the Hindu conviction that everything about man's temporal experience is Maya (illusion). Our presuppositions about the nature of reality and knowledge will control what we accept as evidence and how we view it.[4]

Everybody has what can be called a "worldview," a perspective in terms of which they see everything and understand their perceptions and feelings. A worldview is a network of related presuppositions in terms of which every aspect of man's knowledge and awareness is interpreted. This worldview, as explained above, is not completely derived from human experience, nor can it be verified or refuted by the procedures of natural science. Not everybody reflects explicitly upon the content of his worldview or is consistent in maintaining it, but everybody has one nonetheless. A person's worldview clues him as to the nature, structure and origin of reality. It tells him what are the limits of possibility. It involves a view of the nature, sources and limits of human knowledge. It includes fundamental convictions about right and wrong. One's worldview says something about who man is, his place in the universe, and the meaning of life, etc. Worldviews determine our acceptance and understanding of events in human experience, and thus they play the crucial role in our interpreting of evidence or in disputes over conflicting fundamental beliefs.[5]

We saw above that apologetics, in the nature of the case, involves argumentation over the *justification* of belief or rejection of belief. What we have just observed is that one's treatment of the issue of justification of belief will be governed by his underlying *worldview* or presuppositions. Effective apologetics necessarily leads us to challenge and debate the unbeliever at the level of his most basic commitments or assumptions about reality, knowledge and ethics. Our approach to defending the faith is shallow and ineffective if we think that the unbeliever simply lacks information or needs to be given observational evidence.[6]

The Bible teaches us that the mental and spiritual perspectives of believers and unbelievers differ radically from each other. In *principle*, and according to what they *profess*, the basic worldviews—the fundamental presuppositions—of the Christian and non-Christian conflict with each other at every point.[7] The all-pervading sinful depravity of the unregenerate man touches his intellect as much as anything else. "The mind of the sinful nature is at enmity with God, for it is not subject to the law of God, nor can it be" (Rom. 8:7). Paul's description of the unbelieving mind in Ephesians 4:17-19 is graphic. Unbelievers walk in vanity of mind, with darkened understanding, ignorance and a hardened heart. "Professing themselves to be wise, they became fools" (Rom. 1:22). On the other hand, believers are said to be transformed by the renewing of their minds (Rom. 12:2; cf. Eph. 4:23-24). They now have the mind of Christ (1 Cor. 2:16) and bring every thought captive to Him (2 Cor. 10:5). It is not surprising, therefore, that believers and unbelievers—with their conflicting worldviews and heart conditions—do not really share a common view of knowledge, logic, evidence, language, or truth. Pilate arrogantly asked, "what is truth?" (John 18:38). Agrippa differed with Paul over what is "believable" (Acts 26:8). What unbelievers call "knowledge," believers shun as "pseudo-knowledge" (1 Tim. 6:20). What believers call wisdom, unbelievers call foolishness (1 Cor. 1:18-2:5).

The Impossibility of the Contrary

If the way in which people reason and interpret evidence is determined by their presupposed worldviews, and if the worldviews of the believer and unbeliever are in principle completely at odds with each other, how can the disagreement between them over the justification of Biblical claims be resolved? It might seem that all rational argumentation is precluded since appeals to evidence and logic will be controlled by the respective, conflicting worldviews of the believer and unbeliever. However this is not the case.

Differing worldviews can be compared to each other in terms of the important philosophical question about the "preconditions of intelligibility" for such important assumptions as the universality of logical laws, the uniformity of nature, and the reality of moral absolutes. We can examine a worldview and ask whether its portrayal of nature, man, knowledge, etc., provide an outlook in terms of which logic, science and ethics can make sense. It does not comport with the practices of natural science to believe that all events are random and unpredictable, for instance. It does not comport with the demand for honesty in scientific research, if no moral principle expresses anything but a personal preference or feeling. Moreover, if there are internal contradictions in a person's worldview, it does not provide the preconditions for making sense out of man's experience. For instance, if one's political dogmas respect the dignity of men to make their own choices, while one's psychological theories reject the free will of men, then there is an internal defect in that person's worldview.

It is the Christian's contention that all non-Christian worldviews are beset with internal contradictions, as well as with beliefs which do not render logic, science or ethics intelligible. On the other hand, the Christian worldview (taken from God's self-revelation in Scripture) demands our intellectual commitment because it does provide the preconditions of intelligibility for man's reasoning, experience, and dignity.

In Biblical terms, what the Christian apologist does is demonstrate to unbelievers that because of their rejection of God's revealed truth, they have "become vain in their reasonings" (Rom. 1:21). By means of their foolish perspective they end up "opposing themselves" (2 Tim. 2:25). They follow a conception of knowledge which does not deserve the name (1 Tim. 6:20). Their philosophy and presuppositions rob one of knowledge (Col. 2:3, 8), leaving them in ignorance (Eph. 4:17-18; Acts 17:23). The aim of the apologist is to cast down their reasonings (2 Cor. 10:5) and to challenge them in the spirit of Paul: "Where is the wise? Where is the disputer of this world? Has not God made foolish the wisdom of the world?" (1 Cor. 1:20).

In various forms, the fundamental argument advanced by the Christian apologist is that the Christian worldview is true because of the impossibility of the contrary. When the perspective of God's revelation is rejected, then the unbeliever is left in foolish ignorance because his philosophy does not provide the preconditions of knowledge and meaningful experience. To put it another way: the proof that Christianity is true is that if it were *not*, we would not be able to *prove anything*.

What the unbeliever needs is nothing less than a radical change of mind—repentance (Acts 17:30). He needs to change his fundamental worldview and submit to the revelation of God in order for any knowledge or experience to make sense. He at the same time needs to repent of his spiritual rebellion and sin against God. Because of the condition of his heart, he cannot see the truth or know God in a saving fashion.

Self-Deception

Until the sinner's heart is regenerated and his basic outlook changed, he will continue to resist the knowledge of God. As we just said, given his defective worldview and spiritual attitude, the unbeliever cannot justify any knowledge whatsoever and cannot come to know God in a saving fashion. This does not mean, however, that unbelievers do not have any knowledge, much less that they do not know God. What we said is that they cannot *justify* what they know (in terms of their unbelieving worldview), and they cannot know God in a *saving* way. The Bible indicates that unbelievers do, nevertheless know God—but it is a *knowledge in condemnation*, a knowledge which enables them to know things about themselves and the world around them, even though they suppress the truth of God which makes such knowledge possible.

According to Romans 1:18-21, unbelievers actually know God in their heart of hearts (v. 21). Indeed, that which is known of God is evident within them so that they are without excuse for their professed unbelief (vv. 19-20). Since He is not far from any of us, even pagan philosophers cannot escape knowing Him (cf. Acts 17:27-28). What unbelievers do is "suppress the truth in unrighteousness" (Rom. 1:18). They are guilty of self-deception. Although in one sense they very sincerely deny knowing God or being persuaded by His revelation, they nevertheless are mistaken in this denial. In fact they do know God, they are persuaded by His revelation of Himself, and they now are doing whatever they can to keep that truth from sight and to keep from dealing honestly with their Maker and Judge. Rationalization and any number of intellectual games will be enlisted to convince themselves and others that God's revelation of Himself is not to be believed. In this way unbelievers, who genuinely know God (in condemnation), work hard—even if habitually (and in that sense unconsciously)—to deceive themselves into believing that they do not believe in God or the revealed truths about Him.

It is the knowledge of God which all unbelievers inescapably have within themselves that makes it possible for them to know other things about themselves or about the world. Because they know God, they have a rationale for the laws of logic, the uniformity of nature, man's dignity and ethical absolutes. Accordingly they can pursue science and other aspects of life with some measure of success—even though they cannot *account for* that success (cannot provide the preconditions for the intelligibility of logic, science or ethics). For this reason, every bit of the unbeliever's knowledge is an evidence supporting the truth of God's revelation, and a further indictment against unbelief on the day of judgment.

The task of apologetics is to strip the unbeliever of his mask, to show him that he has really known God all along but suppressed the truth unrighteously, and that knowledge would be impossible otherwise. Apologetics in this way goes to the heart of the matter. It challenges the heart of the unbeliever's philosophical outlook, and it confronts the self-deception which grips the unbeliever's personal heart.

Notes:

[1] Whatever originates beyond man's temporal experience or exceeds that finite experience is said to "transcend" man.

[2] This view is also imprecise and naive regarding ordinary experience and the practice of science, but this is not the place to get into a long and detailed discussion of the theory-laden nature of all human knowing. Observing "there is a rose in the garden" itself necessarily presupposes a number of further beliefs which are theoretical and not observational in nature.

[3] "Empirical" is a term applied to that which is known by experience, observation, or sense perception. "Empiricism" as a school of thought boldly claims that all of man's knowledge is dependent upon empirical means.

[4] We would realize this if we paid attention to the history recorded in the Bible. The Israelites saw miracles first-hand in the wilderness, but still disbelieved and disobeyed God. The Jewish leaders saw Jesus raise Lazarus from the dead, and responded by plotting to kill Jesus! They paid the soldiers to lie about the Lord's own resurrection! The Lord has provided us with plenty of empirical evidence of His veracity, but the way evidence is treated is determined by more fundamental beliefs and commitments in a person's life. "If they hear not Moses and the prophets, neither will they be persuaded if one rises from the dead" (Luke 16:31).

[5] For instance, someone who rejects the reality of abstract entities (e.g., a nominalist like David Hume) will thereby not grant the legitimacy of intuition in his theory of knowledge (e.g., as Plato did by seeing knowledge as "recollection" of transcendent forms or ideas). Someone who thinks of the objects of knowledge as discrete and clearly categorizable as true or false (e.g. Hume again) will have a difficult time arguing meaningfully with someone who thinks of truth as the whole of reality and discrete propositions as nothing more than approximations (e.g. Hegel). A person's theory of knowledge and view of reality mutually affect each other.

[6] Of course there are a few cases where what the unbeliever needs is simply the evidence which is at our disposal in favor of certain claims in the Bible. For instance, a person may be so misled by the prejudiced and hostile voices about religion all around him (from the school classroom to the popular media) that he has the unstudied impression that absolutely "no thinking person" sees any credibility to creationism, the historical or textual accuracy of the Bible, etc. His mind needs to be cleared of such a misconception. He may be quite amazed to find that very competent scientists, historians and other scholars can present thoughtful evidence in favor of Christian claims in science or history. If that is all he needs in order to give a more open and honest reading to the message of Scripture, fine. However, in most cases, the resistance of unbelievers to the evidence is more principled and tenacious than this.

[7] We will see shortly that the unbeliever does not live consistently according to his professed principles. To a certain degree this is also true of the believer. Therefore the antithesis between them is not in actuality complete or absolute, although it would be in principle.

CHAPTER 27:

ANSWERING OBJECTIONS

Under Attack

Christians in the ancient world knew what it was to have accusations and ridicule directed at them for their religious convictions and practices. The report of Jesus' resurrection was taken as an idle tale (Luke 24:11), a lie (Matt. 28:13-15), an impossibility (Acts 26:8). For preaching it, believers were arrested by the Jews (Acts 4:2-3) and mocked by the Greek philosophers (Acts 17:32). On the day of Pentecost the disciples were accused of being drunk (Acts 2:13). Stephen was accused of opposing previous revelation (Acts 6:11-14). Paul was accused of introducing new gods (Acts 17:18-20). The church was accused of political insurrection (Acts 17:6-7). Experts openly contradicted what the Christians taught (Acts 13:45) and prejudicially vilified their persons (Acts 14:2). So, on the one hand, the Christian message was a stumblingblock to Jews and utter foolishness to Greeks (1 Cor. 1:23).

On the other hand, the early Christians had to guard against the wrong kind of positive acceptance of what they proclaimed. The apostles were confused for gods by advocates of pagan religion (Acts 14:11-13), given unwelcome commendation by soothsayers (Acts 16:16-18), and had their message absorbed by heretical legalists (Acts 15:1, 5). Twentieth-century believers can sympathize with their brothers in the ancient world. Our Christian faith continues to see the same variety of attempts to oppose and undermine it.

There is a large number of ways in which Christian truth-claims come under attack today. They are challenged as to their meaningfulness. The possibility of miracles, revelation, and incarnation are questioned. Doubt is cast upon the deity of Christ or the existence of God. The historical or scientific accuracy of the Bible is attacked. Scriptural teaching is rejected for not being logically coherent. Conscious life following physical death, everlasting damnation, and a future resurrection are not readily accepted. The way of salvation is found disgusting or unnecessary. The nature of God and the way of salvation are falsified by heretical schools of thought. Competing religious systems are set over against Christianity—or some try to assimilate it into their own thought forms. The ethics of Scripture is criticized. The psychological or political adequacy of Christianity is looked down upon.

These and many, many other lines of attack are directed against Biblical Christianity. It is the job of apologetics to refute them and demonstrate the truth of the Christian proclamation and worldview—to "cast down reasonings and every high thing that is exalted against the knowledge of God" (2 Cor. 10:5).

The Low Road

By studying the objections of unbelievers and preparing to reason with them, we take the high road of apologetics, the road of obedience to the direction of our Lord and Savior. His categorical claim was "I am the way, the truth, and the life; no one comes to the Father except through Me" (John 14:6). The apologist responds to the objections of unbelievers in a way which sets forth the objective truth of Christianity and the exclusive character of the system. He or she offers reasons for belief, vindicating the Christian worldview over against competing systems of thought and living.

Not all believers (or professing Christians) have chosen to take that high road. It has often happened that those speaking for the Christian faith settle for much less (especially but not exclusively in the current century). They have settled for much less than apologetics by reducing Christian commitment to subjectivism. It is certainly true that Christianity brings us a sense of personal peace and confidence before God, and this inner experience of the faith being right and our own coming to be right with God (cf. the witness of the Spirit, Rom. 8:16) cannot adequately be communicated in words. However appeals to this inner feeling do not constitute an argument which should persuade others of the truth of Christianity.

There is an important difference between confidence and certainty,[1] just as there is an important difference between subjective acceptability and objective truth. Confidence is a psychological property, a feeling assurance that some proposition is true. Many people feel quite confident of things, however, which prove to be notoriously false; yet the confidence of others turns out to be reliable. So the best we can say is that the presence of psychological assurance is not an adequate indicator of who possesses the truth and who does not. Certainty—as opposed to confidence—is technically the property of a proposition (or set of propositions), not of a person. The certainty of a proposition is the property that it cannot fail to be true. The truth of Christianity is not simply an autobiographical quality, telling us something about its acceptability to this or that individual person. The apologist defends the objective truth of the faith. That is, the apologist maintains that its truth has a public nature, open to inspection, and independent of what anybody thinks or feels about it (positively or negatively).

Another low road which some professing Christians take in response to unbelieving objections to the faith is the road of relativism. This is closely allied with subjectivism in many cases but constitutes a distinct error of its own. The subjectivist suppresses or denies the public nature of Christian truth, but still distinguishes truth from error; he believes Christianity to be true—and bases this on unargued feelings—and contrawise believes the non-Christian viewpoint to be false.

Relativism on the other hand believes that all beliefs and convictions (or all *religious* beliefs anyway) are conditioned by cultural factors and individual biases in such a way that there cannot be any absolute (unqualified) truth. If the Christian proclaims that God is a person, but Hindus teach that the supreme reality is impersonal, and if the Christian warns that all men will answer to God for their sins one day, but the master of some cult insists that God would never punish anyone for misdeeds—the relativist would say these disagreements cannot be resolved. What is "true for you" is not necessarily what is "true for me."[2] Relativism is either hypocritical or self-contradictory. Sometimes people play at relativism but do not really mean it. When the chips are down they want to insist that some things are absolutely true, even though other things are not—and of course they will be judge as to where to draw the line, as though truth could be a mere matter of personal convenience! Other times people contradict themselves by insisting quite absolutely that there is no absolute truth—thereby providing in what they say the very basis for rejecting what they say.

Christianity does not claim to be relatively true, but absolutely and universally so. Furthermore, as a religious system it claims to be exclusively true.[3] This is naturally quite offensive in a pluralistic, democratic age. "Everybody has a right to believe about God what they wish," we will be reminded. But that is not the point. The right to believe something does not translate it into something which is true. Some religious perspectives teach that there are a variety of ways of reaching God or serving Him (or It)—many paths to the top of the mountain. Christianity is not one of them, though. Eclectic and smorgasbord approaches to religion may wish to incorporate Christianity into their religious options (one more of many), but in the nature of the case Christianity cannot be assimilated to their outlook. Christianity claims that Christ alone is the divine Savior, claims that only through Him can anyone be right with God, and claims that what we believe about God is restricted to what He reveals about Himself (thus excluding human imagination).

The High Road of Sanctified Argumentation

As opposed to the low roads of subjectivism, relativism and eclecticism, the pages of the New Testament show us Christians who responded to the objections and challenges of unbelievers with apologetical arguments for the truth of the faith. The very term "apologetic" (found in 1 Peter 3:15) was used in the ancient world for the defense which an accused person offered in a court of law. Subjectivism and relativism and eclecticism would do a defendant absolutely no good in vindicating his innocence. The early Christians pressed the claims of truth and were able to defend them, clearly setting the truth of Christ in antithesis to the erroneous ideas which contradict it. And they did this whether they were formerly fishermen, tax-collectors, or academic students of the law.

Notice how the New Testament describes the proclamation and defense of Christian faith by its earliest adherents.

> Peter proclaimed, Let all the house of Israel therefore *know for certain* that God has made him [Jesus] both Lord and Messiah (Acts 2:36).

Saul increased the more in strength and confounded the Jews that dwelt at Damascus, *proving* that Jesus is the Messiah (Acts 9:22).

As his custom was, Paul went into the synagogue, and on three Sabbath days he *reasoned* with them from the Scriptures (Acts 17:2).

So he *reasoned* in the synagogue with the Jews and the God-fearing Greeks, as well as[4] in the marketplace day by day with those who happened to be there, [including] certain Epicurean and Stoic philosophers (Acts 17:17).

Every Sabbath he *reasoned* in the synagogue, trying to persuade Jews and Greeks (Acts 18:4).

Paul entered the synagogue and spoke boldly there for three months, *arguing* persuasively about the kingdom of God... [and later] *reasoning* daily in the school of Tyrannus (Acts 19:8-9).

When objections are raised to Christianity, it is our obligation to present reasoned answers in defense. We must *argue* with those who oppose the truth of God's word.

Offering arguments in favor of certain conclusions should not be confused with being "argumentative" or contentious in one's demeanor. The Bible exhorts us to the former, while prohibiting the latter. Presenting a reason for the hope that is within us does not demand that we do so in an offensive or arrogant way.[5] So well-meaning Christians who say "we shouldn't argue with people if we would be Christ-like" have something valuable to say, but are not saying it clearly and correctly. Arguing is not in itself wrong. The apostles quite obviously engaged in arguments with unbelievers. However the apostles also knew of a temperament and way of communication which dishonors the Lord. They could speak of "perverse disputing"—or as one translation puts it "constant friction between men of corrupt mind" (1 Tim. 6:5). The categorical moral injunction to those who would be Christian teachers is that they "must gently instruct, in hope that God will grant repentance [to the opponent] leading to a knowledge of the truth" (2 Tim. 2:25). Therefore "the Lord's servant must not quarrel" (v. 24). Arguing for the Christian faith can be and must be done in a way consistent with Christian piety.

The appropriate response to critics of the faith, then, is that of reasoning with them, refuting objections, proving conclusions, offering arguments. Let us understand more precisely what this involves. The Greek word used for "proving" in Acts 9:22 is used for "drawing things together," as one does with inferences or demonstrating conclusions from premises.

In an argument the truth of one proposition is asserted on the basis of the truth of other propositions (premises). The conclusion is said to be inferred from—to "follow upon"—the premises offered. This is not the same as what is called a conditional statement, one in the "if...then" format. "If Popeye is a sailor, then he is a drunkard" is a conditional statement, but not an argument—since no proposition is being *asserted* as following from the evidence provided in another proposition or set of propositions. But if someone claims that "Popeye is a drunkard because he is a sailor," then he is advancing an argument (a very poor one), basing a conclusion on other premises (in this case, one of those premises is suppressed or not mentioned).

It should be also noted here that an argument is not the same as an explanation. The presence of the word "because" in the preceding illustration can be misleading if we are not careful. The word "because" often asserts a causal connection between two things or events, rather than the giving of a reason (grounds for believing something). "The bread did not rise because Betty did not add the yeast" is a causal explanation, not an argument. The proposition following "because" does not aim to *establish the truth* of the proposition preceding it.

In apologetics our task is to analyze the arguments which are advanced by unbelievers against the truth of Christianity and to produce sound arguments in favor of it. This will call for an understanding of how the truth of a proposition can be based upon the truth of others—an understanding of empirical relations (evidence) and conceptual relations (logic). We take our best sanctified ability to reason and debate, using the empirical and logical tools of reasoning which God has granted us, and offer justification for believing Christianity to be true and rejecting the conflicting perspective of unbelievers.

Identifying the True Defendant

The last remark highlights the fact that apologetics is both defensive and offensive in nature; it not only responds to criticism, it also presents its own challenge to the thinking of unbelievers. Indeed, apologetics should bring out the irony of the fact that those who demand a defense from God are thereby the ones who in the end stand most in need of philosophical and personal defense.

Unbelievers take their intellectual autonomy so much for granted that they find it hard to believe that they are in no position, epistemologically or morally, to be questioning God and His revealed word. This is well described by C. S. Lewis:

> The trial may even end in God's acquittal. But the important thing is that Man is on the Bench and God in the Dock.[6]

God has, in His holy word, revealed the unholiness of this attitude. "You shall not make trial of Jehovah your God" (Deut. 6:16), as Moses decreed. When Satan tempted Jesus to do so--to push God into offering proof of the veracity of His word (as quoted by Satan)—Jesus rebuked Satan, "the accuser," with these very words from the Old Testament. He declared "It stands written that you shall not make trial of the Lord your God" (Matt. 4:7). It is not God whose integrity and veracity and knowledge is somehow suspect, really. It is that of those who would accuse Him and demand proof to satisfy their own way of thinking or living.

In answering the objections of unbelievers, the apologist must not lose sight of that profound truth. It is incumbent upon us to offer a reasoned defense to the unbeliever, dealing with the criticisms he has in an honest and detailed way. Christian apologetics is not served by obscurantism and generalities. Yet at the same time our apologetical arguments must serve to demonstrate that the unbeliever has no intellectual ground on which to stand in opposing God's revelation. Our argumentation should end up by showing that the unbeliever's presuppositions (worldview) would consistently lead to foolishness and the destruction of knowledge. In that case, and given the unbeliever's sinful lifestyle, it is really the unbeliever—and not God—who is after all "in the dock," both epistemologically and morally.

Notes:

[1] In popular English parlance this distinction is easily blurred, of course. We hear someone say that he "feels confident" that his team will win the World Series, and the same sentiment is expressed by him when he says he just "feels certain" they will win.

[2] The reader should not overlook the perversion of the English language which such an insidious idiom represents. Truth is not something which is person-relative. To say that some proposition is "true for me" is a misleading way of simply saying that I believe that proposition. Collapsing truth into belief has serious consequences for one's theory of knowledge.

[3] This should not be confused with saying that truth is restricted to the content of Christianity or the words of the Bible. There are many truths in addition to those found revealed in Scripture (e.g., the truth that water freezes at 32 degrees Fahrenheit). However there are no truths which conflict or compete with those found there.

[4] Notice that Paul's activity is the same whether his hearers already have a background in and respect for the word of God (Old Testament) or not. He "reasoned" with Jews in the synagogue and likewise with Greek philosophers on the street.

[5] This warning needs to be given since it seems that many believers who give themselves to apologetics are prone to a lack of gentleness in presenting their case. For the sake of their own sanctification and the honoring of the Lord whose word they defend, all apologists need to pray that their arguments not become contentious, that they not slip from defending their Lord into defending themselves. Humility is not incompatible with boldness.

[6] C. S. Lewis, *God in the Dock: Essays on Theology and Ethics*, ed. Walter Hooper (Grand Rapids: Eerdmans, 1970), p. 244.

CHAPTER 28:

TOOLS OF APOLOGETICS

An army cannot be expected to wage a successful battle if its soldiers are unfamiliar with the various weapons they have at their disposal for dealing with the enemy. Likewise a builder cannot construct or repair a house if he does not know what kinds of carpenter and plumbing tools are available to him and how to use them. In the same way, Christians who want to defend the faith should prepare for answering the criticisms of unbelievers by familiarizing themselves with the "tools" of reasoning and argumentation that can be enlisted in apologetics.

Being Rational, Broadly Speaking

> "God has not been so sparing to men to make them barely two-legged creatures, and left it to Aristotle to make them rational." So wrote John Locke (1632-1704).[1]

The quip refers to Aristotle's famous work on logic and syllogism, *Organon* ("The Instrument" or "tool" of knowledge), in which the ancient philosopher lays out rules of reasoning and distinguishes between correct and incorrect forms of argumentation. Locke was not sold on the epistemological benefit of the syllogistic form of reasoning (viz., major premise, minor premise, deduced conclusion) explored by Aristotle. Locke would have been far happier with Francis Bacon's *Novum Organum* ("New Instrument"), which was published in 1620 and explored the rules of inductive or scientific reasoning—which was later improved upon by John Stuart Mill's *System of Logic* (1843), whose own understanding of the tools of rationality in turn has been expanded and bettered by twentieth-century studies of logic, argument, and method.

Locke was, of course, the famous English socio-political philosopher who authored *Two Treatises of Government*, as well as a student of the human knowing process who became known as the father of "British empiricism." He was raised in a Puritan home and lived through the events which brought about the Westminster Assembly. He was a contemporary of Milton, Newton, and Boyle—and like these great men of letters, he openly professed Christian faith, having high regard for the Bible:

> The Holy Scripture is to me, and always will be, the constant guide of my assent; and I will always hearken to it, as containing the infallible truth relating to things of highest concernment.... Where I want the evidence of things, there yet is ground enough for me to believe, because God has said it; and I will presently condemn and quit any opinion of mine, as soon as I am shown that it is contrary to any revelation of the Holy Scripture."[2]

At age sixty-three, in the year 1695, Locke went to press with a treatise entitled *The Reasonableness of Christianity as Delivered in the Scriptures*.[3]

It was five years earlier (1690) that Locke had published his best-known work on the theory of knowledge, *An Essay Concerning Human Understanding*. In it he lamented the fact that the word "reason" is often used as though it were opposed to "faith." He wrote that, in his opinion, faith should not be afforded to anything "but upon good reason," thus dispensing with any tension between them. Locke insisted that to believe things arbitrarily, apart from reason, was to insult our Maker. This being so, Christians were called upon to understand, refine and train their faculty of reasoning. With that we must certainly agree— even if we cannot completely follow Locke's epistemology or theological conclusions. We should surely master the difference between reliable and unreliable ways of reasoning if we would honor Christ and become effective in His service.

God wishes for us to be rational: *to exercise and improve our reasoning ability* in understanding, propounding and defending the truths of

Scripture. And as Locke observed, this reasoning ability does not begin or end with the teaching of Aristotle. To be rational is a trait much broader than the use of syllogisms (although they certainly have their place). The kind of rationality or reasoning that we will employ in defending the Christian faith involves not only study of formal logic (patterns or abstract forms of inference), but also attention to informal fallacies in ordinary language, the use of inductive reasoning,[4] the handling of empirical evidence in history, science, linguistics, etc.,[5] and especially reflection upon the demands of an adequate worldview in terms of which all such thinking makes sense.[6]

Indeed, God has *not* been "sparing" in His provision of various tools which defenders of the faith can use to cross-examine opposing worldviews and rebut the argumentation of those who challenge the Scriptures. These tools are also beneficial in cogently formulating and advancing the Christian worldview, based on the teaching of the Bible. By exploring these tools of rationality (or the conspicuous ways in which they are violated) we can improve our ability to set forth an answer for the hope within us as believers, as well as get a grasp on the elementary errors in reasoning which are often committed by unbelievers.

Prejudicial Conjecture

One will often find that unbelievers, both educated and uneducated, take the offensive against Christianity before they have become familiar with what they are talking about. In the place of research and honest assessment of available evidence concerning some aspect of the Bible, many unbelievers have substituted personal conjecture about what "seems likely" to them.

For instance, since the Bible was supposed to be written so many hundreds of years ago, it just "seems likely" to many unbelievers that we cannot trust the text of the Bible which we have in our hands today. Surely scribes have altered and supplemented the original text so much that we cannot be sure what was actually written by Moses, Jeremiah, John or Paul (if these characters were in fact the authors in the first place); for all we know, what we read in our Bibles came from the pen of some monk in the "dark ages"! This kind of ignorant criticism seems intellectually sophisticated to some unbelievers. After all, in our natural human experience, messages which are passed from one speaker to another usually get garbled or distorted or augmented, don't they?

To unbelievers who reason this way (about this or many other subjects related to the Bible), we must not tire of pointing out that they are relying upon conjecture, not research. It may "seem likely" that the Biblical text would no longer be reliable or authentic after all these years, but that "likelihood" is an evaluation which rests upon prejudice. The *first* prejudice is the assumption that the Biblical text is no different from any other written document which we find in our natural human experience throughout history—which, of course, *begs the fundamental question* over which the believer and unbeliever are arguing! If the Bible is, as it claims, the inspired word of Almighty God, then the history of its textual transmission may very well be quite different than other human documents since God would have ordained that its text be preserved with greater integrity than that of ordinary books.

The *second* indication of prejudice is that the unbeliever does not offer any concrete evidence that (say) some medieval monk tampered with the text before us today. This kind of remark is simply and arbitrarily advanced as a hypothesis to be endorsed for its "likelihood," rather than its empirical credentials. If we want to play that way, of course, we could—with equal arbitrariness—conjecture that the words which came down to us as Paul's were actually written, not years later, but years before the time of Paul! Arbitrariness is a fickle friend to the scholar. Cut loose from any demand for evidence, we could believe any number of conflicting things.

The *third* indication of prejudice in the criticism of the unbeliever is that he or she has not taken account of the actual evidence which is publicly available regarding the text of Scripture. If the critic had taken time to look into this subject, he or she would not have offered the outlandish evaluation that the Biblical text is unreliable. This came home to me with great force after taking an advanced course on Plato in graduate school, a course which took account of the textual criticism of the literary corpus of Plato's works. Our earliest extant manuscript of a work by Plato dates from right before 900 A.D. ("Oxford B," found in a Patmos monastery by E. B. Clarke), and we must remember that Plato is thought to have written roughly 350 years before Christ—thus leaving us with a gap of over twelve centuries. By contrast, the earliest fragments of the New Testament date less than fifty years after the original writing; the bulk of our most important extant manuscripts dates from 200-300 years after original composition. The text of the New Testament is remarkably uniform and well established. The reliability of the Old Testament text has been demonstrated by the discovery of the Dead Sea scrolls.

The overall authenticity and accuracy of the Biblical text is well known to scholars. Frederick Kenyon concluded: "The Christian can take the whole Bible in his hand and say without fear or hesitation that he holds in it the true Word of God, handed down without essential loss from generation to generation, throughout the centuries."[7] Such assessments from competent scholars could be multiplied easily—which only goes to show the prejudice that operates in the thinking of unbelievers who offhand criticize the Bible for "very likely" having a dubious text.

When we defend our Christian faith, then, we must constantly be on the lookout for the way in which the reasoning of unbelievers rests upon prejudicial conjecture. It crops up repeatedly. I have even heard some people mouth the radical opinion that "we have no literary or historical basis for believing that Jesus of Nazareth actually ever lived"! Can you spot the obvious indications of *prejudice* here? Such a criticism simply takes it for granted that the Bible itself should not be taken in any way as a literary source of historical information—contrary to the general practice of even unbelieving historians of the ancient world. Moreover, such criticism does not show familiarity with the secular allusions to Jesus in ancient literature—such as the reference by the Roman historian Tacitus to "Christus" who suffered "the extreme penalty...at the hands of one of our procurators, Pontius Pilate" (*Annals* 15.44), or the reference by the Jewish historian Josephus to James "the brother of Jesus, who is called Christ" (*Antiquities* 20:9), etc. Criticism like this usually ends up telling us more about the critic (e.g., his prejudices, what he has not been reading) than about the object of his criticism.

There was a time when critics of the Old Testament ridiculed it for mentioning a tribe of people, the Hittites, which were (as yet) unknown outside the Bible; such presumed flaws in the Biblical record were taken as rendering it worthless as a historical document—until Hittite artifacts and monuments began to be uncovered around—Archemish by archaeologists, beginning in 1871. The Hittite civilization is today one of best known cultures of the ancient world!

Archaeology has over and over again proved to be the enemy of

Biblical critics, unearthing their negative prejudices and confirming the accuracy of the Scriptures in historical particulars. H. M. Orlinsky wrote:

> "More and more the older view that the biblical data were suspect and even likely to be false, unless corroborated by extra-biblical facts, is giving way to one which holds that, by and large, the biblical accounts are more likely to be true than false...."[8]

Even as unsympathetic an umpire as *Time* magazine, in a lead article entitled "How True Is the Bible?," had to admit:

> "After more than two centuries of facing the heaviest scientific guns that could be brought to bear, the Bible has survived—and is perhaps the better for the siege. Even on the critics' own terms—historical fact—the Scriptures seem more acceptable now than they did when the rationalists began the attack."[9]

The simple point which I want to make here is that apologists need to be prepared to expose the prejudicial conjectures of unbelievers when they appear. Many of the negative preconceptions held by those who criticize the Bible or Christianity prove to be arbitrary or embarrassing, when pressed; such pressure should be humbly but confidently applied. There are large numbers of those who reject the Scriptures on the basis of things, after all, about which they are really not familiar or well studied. We must point out how unreasonable it is to rest upon prejudice and conjecture in any area—but especially respecting matters of eternal consequence. The more people come to know "the facts" about the Bible's text and historical reports, the less likely they will be to dismiss the book out of hand.

Unargued Philosophical Bias

Another tool which the apologist may use in arguing with those who are critical of the Biblical message is to expose the philosophical precommitments of the critic which have been taken for granted, rather than openly argued and supported. Here is yet another broad indicator of how unbelievers fall short of being rational in their approach.

Consider this. Even if enough external, corroborating evidence were available from textual criticism, archaeology and related sciences to authenticate all of the ordinary data (linguistic, cultural, chronological, etc.) which we find in the literature of Scripture, there would still remain important features—indeed, the most important features—of the Biblical narrative over which conscientious unbelievers would intellectually stumble. We not only read of Hittites, high-places, houses, military battles, migrations and marriages in the Bible, we also come across healings, floating axheads, fiery chariots, water turned to wine, virgin birth and resurrections. When unbelievers read of miraculous events in the Bible, their first inclination is to say that such things cannot happen, thus disbelieving the written report of them. "We all know that people cannot walk on water; so this story must be fabricated."

Each of us is familiar with this line of reasoning. We engage in it ourselves at the checkout counter at the supermarket when we see the fantastic tabloid headlines ("Woman Gives Birth to Her Own Father!"). The implicit argument is that such things are impossible, therefore they could not have occurred. Unbelievers dismiss in advance the possibility of miraculous events, and in light of that unspoken premise they cast a doubtful eye upon the Biblical narrative. "Jesus did not rise from the dead because we all know that the dead do not rise." Unbelievers easily assume that people who live in the enlightened, scientific, twentieth century cannot accept the superstitions, myths and fairytales of the Bible. After all, we use refrigerators and computers today!

To conduct their thinking in a fully rational manner, however, unbelievers who doubt the Biblical narrative of miracles ought to pause to recognize and scrutinize their controlling premise. "We know that miracles are impossible." We *know* that? Unbelievers feel that they know that such events cannot take place because, having a scientific outlook, they are convinced that all of nature operates in a predictable, law-like fashion. "Miracles would run counter to the regularities of our ordinary experience, would not be predictable," they protest—to which the astute apologist ought to reply, "Isn't that just the point?" If miracles were not extraordinary, they would not be miracles.

The unbeliever's bias against extraordinary events needs to be challenged for its rational foundations. Does the unbeliever know that all of nature operates in a law-like fashion? that there can never be exceptions? That is a lot to know, involving as it does insight into the very nature of reality and the metaphysical limits of possibility. What justification does the unbeliever have for his or her views here? If instead the Christian worldview is true, miracles are not a philosophical problem in advance; an all-powerful Creator and Governor of the world could certainly do things which are out of the ordinary and contrary to the regularities of human experience—like raising the dead. To reject the Bible because of its account of miracles is, thus, philosophically to beg the question.

The fault here is *not* that critics of Christianity have philosophical presuppositions which they bring to the evidence and use in their reasoning. This is inevitable, for anyone—whether unbeliever or believer. The notion that we can be characterized by philosophical neutrality in scholarship and argumentation is naive and unrealistic; indeed, I would argue that it is impossible. The problem is not that unbelievers have their presuppositions, but rather that they frequently do not recognize those presuppositions for what they are and offer no warrant or defense for them—especially over against the conflicting presuppositions of others (like Christians).

Obviously believers and unbelievers approach the Biblical record of miracles with different controlling assumptions about what is possible, about God's existence and power, about God's intervention in the world, etc. It is part of the task of apologetics to disclose the character and function of these conflicting presuppositions in the argument between Christians and non-Christians. The debate must not, of course, end at that point, as though we are left with an irresolvable intellectual standoff between ultimate philosophical perspectives. The next step involves argumentation and comparison regarding the opposing presuppositions (or worldviews) of the believer and unbeliever, thus taking us closer to the heart of philosophical apologetics as discussed in previous studies. Only the Christian worldview makes sense out of the logic, science, morality, etc. to which both sides to the dispute appeal—not to mention, that this alone makes sense out of the very process of reasoning and arguing at all.

Key Intellectual Sins

The first tool of apologetical reasoning which we have considered is that of pointing to the *prejudicial conjecture* into which unbelievers easily fall when they look for a way to dispute the truth of Christianity. A second tool to be used in apologetics is to expose the *unargued philosophical bias* which is usually packed into the criticisms generated by unbelievers.

In utilizing such devices as these, the apologist seeks to uncover the "presuppositions" of the unbeliever which determine (unwittingly or sometimes self-consciously) the conclusions which he will reach. We are constantly on the lookout for unargued, crucial assumptions.

At other times the apologist needs to challenge not simply the nature of the unbeliever's presuppositions, but the fact that those presuppositions are either *arbitrary* or *inconsistent*. Indeed, these are precisely the two key sins for any scholar: arbitrariness in his thinking or incoherence between different aspects of his thinking (and living). Defenders of the faith must never tire of pointing this out.

If people are allowed to believe just anything they wish to believe out of convenience, tradition or prejudice, they have abandoned the course of rationality, which calls for having a good reason for the things we believe and do. On the other hand, if people are allowed to assert (or rely upon) certain premises, only later to abandon or contradict those very same premises, then they have violated the fundamental requirements for sound reasoning. In both cases a person's thinking and beliefs become unpredictable and unreliable.

Presuppositions Which Do Not Comport with Each Other

When we talk to unbelievers about their views—especially their worldviews—we should be especially sensitive to hear or discern what their controlling assumptions are about the nature of reality (metaphysics), about the nature of knowledge (epistemology), and about what is right or wrong in human behavior (ethics).

Although not everyone thinks clearly and specifically about such matters in the abstract (according to underlying principles), and although not everyone will be able openly and explicitly to state what his operating assumptions are, nevertheless *everybody* utilizes some basic perspective regarding reality, knowledge and conduct. As we say, everybody "does" philosophy, but not everybody does it well—not everybody reflects self-consciously about such matters and seeks a cogent and consistent outlook.

So Christians must learn to listen closely to what critics of the faith are saying and seek to identify what is being taken for granted by the critic. We must point out, then analyze and criticize, the presuppositions of our opponents. In the nature of the case, the conflict between the tenacious unbeliever and the faithful believer will come down to a matter of their differing presuppositions.

When we identify the presuppositions of the unbeliever, we will see in case after case (indeed, in every case ultimately) that the unbeliever has an unmanaged and irresolvable tension between his operating assumptions. His basic beliefs about reality, or about knowledge, or about ethics do not comport with each other—do not work harmoniously with each other or outright contradict each other. Let's look at a series of simple illustrations.

(1) Tension within one's ethical perspective: Imagine that your neighbor expresses an outlook which can be summarized in the words of a well-known beer commercial: "You only go around once in life, so go for all the gusto you can get!" That is, pleasure is the leading value in life, and there is no accountability for our conduct after this life. On the other hand, imagine that this same neighbor expresses indignation over a well-documented instance of police brutality, or over the oppression and invasion of a weaker nation by some tyrant, or over light sentences handed down to rapists, or over bribes accepted by government officials, or over racial hatred and discrimination, etc. (take your pick). These two views—that pleasure is the highest value, but brutality (etc.) is to be condemned—expose a conceptual tension within your neighbor's thinking. He is not being consistent. After all, if policemen or rapists or tyrants (etc.) get pleasure from what they are doing to others, then they should, on your neighbor's hypothesis ("go for all the gusto you can get"), pursue those very activities which your neighbor turns around and condemns.

(2) Tension within one's epistemological perspective: Imagine that you have a friend who is critical of your Christian faith, saying that you are superstitious and gullible. According to him, we should not believe anything that is not verified (or verifiable) by observation or more broadly by our sense perceptions: to put it simply, "seeing is believing." The problem with Christians, he thinks, is that they believe things simply on the alleged authority of God (speaking in the Bible). So you discuss this further with your friend. You ask how he came to hold the view that

knowledge is limited to observation. He explains that he has been taking a course at the local college (or reading some book from the library), and the teacher (writer) convinced him that we can only trust our senses in determining what to believe in this world. You spot the tension immediately! Your friend criticizes Christians for believing things, not by observational verification, but on the authority of another (God)—and yet he himself has come to believe what he does, not by observational verification, but on the authority of another (his teacher)!

Actually, the tension in his thinking is even worse. Regardless of how he came to his view that knowledge is limited to observation, that view itself is self-contradictory. Imagine some things which we know and can verify by the use of our senses. I know that there is a bird chirping outside my window. I know that fire is hot. I know that malaria is relieved by quinine. I know that my son mowed the lawn. And I know such things because I have perceived them (or could have perceived them) with my own senses. Now what about this? Your friend claims to know that knowledge is limited to observation. Did he have any sense perception of that alleged truth (as I do when I watch my son mow the lawn)? Of course he did not. He could not "observe" a conceptual limitation, much less a universal limitation. He did not "see" that all knowledge is limited to what we can see. Therefore, there is an irresolvable contradiction in your friend's thinking.

(3) Tension within one's metaphysical perspective: Imagine that your professor at school teaches a behavioristic view of man, claiming that all human behavior is determined by antecedent factors (particularly, stimulus-response conditioning) and is predictable, if we knew all those factors. Ultimately and in principle, the professor argues, human free will is an illusion. All of us think and do what we have been conditioned to think and do, given the variable factors of our environment. Imagine further that, when it comes time for you to take the final exam in his course, you cheat on the examination and are caught at it by the professor. He is indignant and insists upon imposing a strict penalty (say, flunking the course). If he does so, he exposes an open conflict within his views of human nature, does he not? By punishing you, he assumes that you were free to choose how to approach taking the test: you could study hard and prepare to answer the questions on your own, or you could more efficiently "ride" upon the effort put into the test by the student

from whose paper you copied. If you could not help doing what you did—given your previous conditioning and the variables of your environment—it would be senseless to punish you for doing what you predictably did. Yet this is precisely what the professor had taught you in class about human nature in the first place.

(4) Tension between one's epistemology and one's metaphysic: Imagine that you have a colleague at work who graduated from college and fancies himself somewhat intellectual about matters of religion. According to him, there is no God and no spiritual realm (or spiritual events, spiritual forces) whatsoever. This physical world is all there is to reality. Moreover, this colleague finds it intellectually impossible to accept the Christian outlook because it contains what he deems logical contradictions within itself (say, that God is one yet three, or that God is loving and all-powerful but there is evil in the world). According to him, we cannot know anything to be true which conflicts with the laws of logic. The veiled problem in the thinking of your colleague is that his view of reality (metaphysic) does not comport whatsoever with his view of knowledge (epistemology). He cannot simultaneously and consistently be committed to the laws of logic and the view that reality is solely physical in nature. And the reason is obvious: the "laws of logic" are not physical in nature. You cannot touch or taste a law of logic; nor could you identify one with a sophisticated instrument devised by a physicist. Laws of logic are not physical, and thus given your colleague's perspective, laws of logic are not real anyway.

Common Logical Fallacies

We have just mentioned the laws of logic (and how materialism would preclude them).[10] Because the laws of logic are so important to argumentation and reasoning—precisely what apologetics is all about, as we said before—we should pause to familiarize ourselves with some of the most common of those guidelines for reasoning. An effective defense of the faith will call for skillful use of logic in meeting the challenges of unbelievers and refuting their arguments, as well as in doing an internal critique of the unbeliever's own basic outlook.

Logic is the study of correct (reliable) and incorrect (unreliable) lines of reasoning or argumentation. The logician is concerned to learn what (a) kinds of premises or (b) patterns of inference can be relied upon to lead to truth in one's conclusions. When we consider the kinds of premises which are utilized in an argument formulated in ordinary conversation (in "natural languages" like English, German, Chinese, etc.), we are said to be dealing with *informal* logic—not because it is somehow casual, but because it does not concern itself with "formal" languages (systems of symbols, connectors, etc.). *Formal* logic, as the name would indicate, is concerned with forms of argumentation or patterns of reasoning (where the predicates or premises have been stripped of particular content and rendered abstract by assigning them a formal symbol or token, as one does in algebra).

Informal fallacies point out the unreliability of certain kinds of premises for insuring the truth of the conclusions inferred from them. Some of the most frequent informal fallacies in reasoning would be the following:

(1) Resting a conclusion upon an appeal to popular sentiment

(2) Resting a conclusion upon an appeal to emotion (pity, fear, etc.)

(3) Resting a conclusion upon an appeal against (or in favor of) the person, authority, circumstances or history of someone advancing a particular thesis

(4) Resting a conclusion upon an appeal to premises which prove (if anything) something else altogether

(5) Resting a conclusion upon an appeal to the absence (or ignorance) of premises proving the contrary

In each of the preceding kinds of fallacious reasoning (1-5), the truth of the premise (or premises) used in an argument is irrelevant to the truth of the proposed conclusion. Even granting the premise(s), the conclusion need not follow; consequently, such lines of thinking are unreliable. In other forms of fallacious reasoning (6-10), the truth of the conclusion does not reliably follow from the premise(s) because of ambiguous or confused thinking. Here are some common examples:

(6) Resting a conclusion upon appeal to a premise (or premises) where terms are not being used in the same sense, or where questions of grammar or emphasis render the sense (and thus truth) of the premise(s) uncertain

(7) Resting a conclusion upon appeal to a premise which is merely the restatement of the conclusion or takes the conclusion for granted

(8) Resting a conclusion upon appeal to a premise which is stated in an

overly general fashion (which does not recognize important qualifications, or which is known to be true only in a limited number
or atypical set of cases)

(9) Resting a conclusion upon appeal to a premise (or premises) in such
a way as to confuse the attributes of "parts" of something with the
attributes of the "whole"

(10) Resting a conclusion upon appeal to a premise (or premises) in
such a way as to confuse the causal and temporal connections between events, confuse different kinds of "causation," or overlook
the complexity of causes for something

Finally there are kinds of informal fallacies in reasoning (11-15) which
betray either an unfairness of mind and method in the person proposing
the argument in question or a distortion of the facts. Some examples of
this are:

(11) Resting a conclusion upon someone's inability to offer a single,
simple or clear answer to a complex question (raising more than
one issue), a trick question (emotionally loaded), or a (mis)leading
question (creating a false impression or diverting attention from
the specific issue)

(12) Resting a conclusion upon a forced choice between two alternatives
which are erroneously presented as the only options

(13) Resting a conclusion upon a line of reasoning which evidences the
use of a double-standard or special pleading

(14) Resting a conclusion upon an erroneous comparison between two
things (which do resemble each other, but in irrelevant or insignificant ways)

(15) Resting a conclusion upon the mistake of treating concrete attributes
or series of particular events as though they were an entity in themselves (metaphorical hypostatization or abstraction)

In addition to the above fifteen kinds of informal fallacies in reasoning,
Christians who wish to defend the faith effectively should be familiar with the common *formal* fallacies which are committed in
reasoning, as well as the most effective or frequent positive lines of
argumentation which are available. For instance:

(16) The fallacy of affirming the consequent is committed when someone asserts a conditional premise (If P, then Q), then affirms what
is implied (Q), and concludes that this proves what implied it (P).
Such a pattern of reasoning is not reliable, as we can see from ex-

amples: "If Milton wrote *Hamlet*, then Milton is a great author. But Milton is indeed a great author. Therefore he wrote *Hamlet*."

(17) The fallacy of denying the antecedent is committed when someone asserts a conditional premise (If P, then Q), then denies the premise from which the implication is drawn (P), and concludes that what was said to be implied (Q) must not be the case. Such a pattern of reasoning is just as unreliable as the one we just examined. Take an example: "If Castro shot Kennedy, then Castro is a scoundrel. But Castro did not shoot Kennedy. Therefore he is not a scoundrel."

(18) A very valuable form of argumentation, known as "disjunctive syllogism," progresses in the following way: you first establish the premise that (at least) one of two propositions is true: P or Q. You next prove that one of these propositions is not true (i.e., establish not-Q). From these two premises, one may validly infer that proposition P must be true. Example: "Samantha poisoned the tea, or her husband committed suicide. But Samantha did not poison the tea. Therefore her husband must have committed suicide."

(19) Another persuasive line of reasoning (when used cautiously) is known as arguing "*a fortiori*"—arguing from the lesser case to the greater case. If someone properly understands the nature of the greatness which is said to be increased, reasoning from the lesser case to the greater case can be very insightful. "If God holds those who have never heard the gospel accountable, how much more will He judge with severity those who have heard the gospel and openly repudiate it."

20) Perhaps the most powerful tool of rebuttal which apologists can use is the line of argument known as "*reductio ad absurdum*"—the project of reducing your opponent's particular premise or overall position to absurdity. In using this kind of argument your aim is to show that the opponent's premise entails a conclusion which is known to be false. Since it does so, the premise in question must itself also be false. (This is a rule in formal logic known as "*modus tollens*": from "If P, then Q" and the addition of "not-Q," the conclusion "not-P" necessarily follows.) Here is an example: "If there are no universal moral principles (as the relativist maintains), then it is invalid for one culture to condemn the activities of another culture. But surely it is morally appropriate for us to condemn in Germany the Nazi atrocities against the Jews (or in India the forced

incineration of a widow on her husband's funeral pyre, etc.). Therefore relativism is not true."

Behavior Which Betrays Professed Belief

Finally, in order to highlight a tool which is useful and necessary for Christian apologists, we should mention that it is not a mark of rationality for a person to assert one thing, but then live contrary to it. This can be considered a kind of moral hypocrisy, but it is equally a form of irrationality or inconsistency or tension within one's reasoning—since one belief is at work when he linguistically asserts a position, but a conflicting belief is evident when he behaves in a way contrary to that position.

The life of the unbeliever is riddled with such inconsistency. He will presuppose human dignity and attend a funeral to honor a dead friend or relative, even though he previously argued that man is, in principle, no different from any other product of evolution like a horse or dog. The unbeliever will insist that man is nothing more than a complex of bio-chemical factors controlled by the laws of physics—and then kiss his wife and children when he goes home, as though they share love with each other. He will argue that in sexual relations "anything goes" (there are no moral absolutes)—but then indignantly condemn child molesters or morally repudiate necrophilia. He will suggest that the things which happen in the universe happen randomly—by "chance"—but then turn around and look for regularities, law-like explanations of events, and uniformity or predictability in the things studied by natural science. The non-Christian does not have a workable worldview, and he exposes its weakness at every turn in his life.

Recap

God has not been "sparing" in His provision to us of a variety of effective tools for answering the criticisms of unbelievers and rebutting the claims of their conflicting worldviews. In dealing with the unbeliever, the Christian should be alert to point out the critic's

(1) prejudicial conjectures,
(2) unargued philosophical bias,
(3) presuppositions which do not comport with each other,
(4) logical fallacies, and
(5) behavior which betrays his professed beliefs.

In doing this we perform one of the key tasks of apologetics: refuting challenges and offering an internal critique of the position from which those criticisms arise.

Notes:

[1] *An Essay Concerning Human Understanding*, Book IV, Chapter XVII (New York: Dover Publications, 1959 [1690]), vol. 2, p. 391.

[2] Cited by the editor in the "Introduction" to John Locke, *The Reasonableness of Christianity as Delivered in the Scriptures*, ed. George W. Ewing (Chicago: Gateway Edition, Henry Regnery Co., 1964 [1695]), p. xi.

[3] Locke later explained that the book was chiefly designed as a rebuttal to the Deists; they nevertheless applauded Locke's emphasis upon the place of reason in religion, thus leading secondary scholars too hastily to class Locke as a deist. The English Calvinist, John Edwards (not to be confused with the American, Jonathan Edwards), distorted Locke's intentions even worse, maligning him with the epithets of atheism and Socinianism.

[4] For a helpful text on informal, formal, and inductive logic, see Irving M. Copi, *Introduction to Logic* (New York: Macmillan Publishing Co., 1978 [5th ed.]).

[5] Readers should consult here various beneficial texts on Christian "evidences," but they should also pursue discussions of the varying use of observational data in theory-formation and argumentation: for instance, W. V. Quine and J. S. Ullian, *The Web of Belief*, 2nd ed. (New York: Random House, 1978); Stephen Toulmin, *The Uses of Argument* (Cambridge: University Press, 1969); Thomas S. Kuhn, *The Structure of Scientific Revolutions*, 2nd ed. (Chicago: University Press, 1970).

[6] See the works of Cornelius Van Til here (available through Presbyterian and Reformed Publishing Co.): for instance, *The Intellectual Challenge of the Gospel* (1953), *The Defense of the Faith* (1955), *A Survey of Christian Epistemology* (1969).

[7] Cited in Greg L. Bahnsen, "The Inerrancy of the Autographa," *Inerrancy*, ed. Norman L. Geisler (Grand Rapids: Zondervan Publishing House, 1980), p. 187.

[8] *Ancient Israel* (Ithaca, New York: Cornell University Press, 1954), p. 6. Likewise, W. F. Albright has written that "archeological and inscriptional data have established the historicity of innumerable passages and statements of the Old Testament" ("Archeology Confronts Biblical Criticism," *The American Scholar*, vol. 7 [Spring, 1938], p. 181).

[9] Issue for December 30, 1974, p. 41.

[10] The immateriality of laws (of logic, of morality, etc.) indeed the immateriality of concepts, of justice, of love, etc. pose no automatic philosophical problem for the Christian worldview. Laws of logic are a human reflection of the mind of God and of God's thinking regarding the conceptual and/or evidential-proof relations between truths (or sets of truths). Logical laws are elaborations upon the fact that God does not contradict Himself (His word is not yes and no, 2 Cor. 1:18) and that it is impossible for Him to lie (Heb. 6:18).

CHAPTER 29:

APOLOGETICS IN PRACTICE

It is time to provide a concrete illustration or practical application of the principles and tools for defending the Christian faith which have been discussed in our previous studies. Training manuals on fire-fighting do not put out fires; the actual fighting of fires does. And when all is said and done, it is not the *theory* of apologetics which defends the faith and stops the mouths of critics. Only the *practice* of apologetics can do that.

Review

Let's summarize what has been said up to this point about how to approach the task of apologetics.

1. Engaging in apologetics is a moral necessity for every believer; we must be "always ready" to offer an answer for the hope within us (1 Peter 3:15)
2. To avoid misconceptions, we note that apologetics is *not*:
   (a) pugnacious,
   (b) a matter of persuasion, or
   (c) based on a different ultimate authority than theology.
3. For the Christian, "reason" should be used as a tool, not as the ultimate authority, in our thinking.
4. Our claim before the world is that believers "know" the Bible to be true—we have adequate justification for believing its claims.
5. The conflict between believers and unbelievers is ultimately over their differing worldviews—networks of presuppositions in terms of which all experience is interpreted and reasoning is guided.

6. Consequently we need to argue from "the impossibility of the contrary," showing that only Christianity provides the preconditions of intelligibility for man's experience and reasoning. If Christianity were not true, the unbeliever could not prove or understand anything.

7. Unbelievers are self-deceived: they know the truth about God, but suppress it (rationalizing the clear evidence within them and all around them).

8. The true defendant, intellectually and morally, is the unbeliever—not God.

9. There are a large variety of different kinds of attacks upon Christianity, and they cannot be dealt with adequately by defenses which rest upon:
    (a) subjectivism,
    (b) relativism, or
    (c) eclecticism.

10. Apologists must use argumentation. Sanctified argumentation need not be contentious; we find that sanctified arguing with unbelievers is warranted by Biblical example.

11. An argument asserts the truth of a proposition on the basis of others.

12. Rationality in argumentation is broader than simply using the rules of syllogistic deduction.

13. God wishes for us to master the tools of rationality in defending the faith. It is our task to refute the challenges of unbelievers and to offer an internal critique of the position from which those challenges arise.

14. The two key intellectual sins which are committed by people are
    (a) inconsistency and
    (b) arbitrariness.

15. In dealing with the unbeliever, the Christian should be alert to point out the critic's:
    (a) prejudicial conjectures,
    (b) unargued philosophical bias,
    (c) presuppositions which do not comport with each other,
    (d) logical fallacies, and behavior which betrays his professed beliefs.

Looking for a Fire to Fight (Bertrand Russell)

It would be instructive and helpful for readers if we could take the approach to apologetics which is advanced above and put it to use in a concrete case. We need a fire to put out, following the guidelines of our preceding fire-fighting manual.

An excellent opportunity to practice our defense of the Christian faith is provided by one of the most noteworthy British philosophers of the twentieth century: Bertrand Russell. Russell has offered us a clear and pointed example of an intellectual challenge to the truthfulness of the Christian faith by writing an article which specifically aimed to show that Christianity should not be believed. The title of his famous essay was "Why I Am Not a Christian."[1] Bertrand Russell (1872-1970) studied mathematics and philosophy at Cambridge University and began his teaching career there. He wrote respected works as a philosopher (about Leibniz, about the philosophy of mathematics and set theory, about the metaphysics of mind and matter, about epistemological problems) and was influential on twentieth-century developments in the philosophy of language. He also wrote extensively in a more popular vein on literature, education and politics. Controversy surrounded him. He was dismissed by Trinity College for pacifist activities in 1916; he was jailed in 1961 in connection with a campaign for nuclear disarmament. His views on sexual morality contributed to the annulment of his appointment to teach at the City University of New York in 1940. Yet Russell was highly regarded as a scholar. In 1944 he returned to teach at Cambridge, and in 1950 he became a recipient of the Nobel Prize for Literature.

For all his stature as a philosopher, Russell cannot be said to have been sure of himself and consistent in his views regarding reality or knowledge. In his early years he adopted the Hegelian idealism taught by F. H. Bradley. Influenced by G. E. Moore, he changed to a Platonic theory of ideas. Challenged by Ludwig Wittgenstein that mathematics consists merely of tautologies, he turned to metaphysical and linguistic atomism. He adopted the extreme realism of Alexius Meinong, only later to turn toward logical constructionism instead. Then following the lead of William James, Russell abandoned mind-matter dualism for the theory of neutral monism. Eventually Russell propounded materialism with fervor, even though his dissatisfaction with his earlier logical atomism left him without an alternative metaphysical account of the object of our empirical experiences. Struggling with philosophical problems not unlike those which stymied David Hume, Russell conceded in his later years that the quest for certainty is a failure.

This brief history of Russell's philosophical evolution is rehearsed so that the reader may correctly appraise the strength and authority of the intellectual platform from which Russell would presume to criticize the Christian faith. Russell's brilliance is not in doubt; he was a talented and intelligent man. But to what avail? In criticizing Christians for their views of ultimate reality, of how we know what we know, and of how we should live our lives, did Bertrand Russell have a defensible alternative from which to launch his attacks? Not at all. He could not give an account of reality and knowing which—on the grounds of, and according to the criteria of, his own autonomous reasoning—was cogent, reasonable and sure. He could not say with certainty what was true about reality and knowledge, but nevertheless he was firmly convinced that Christianity was false! Russell was firing an unloaded gun.

Bertrand Russell made no secret of the fact that he intellectually and personally disdained religion in general, and Christianity in particular. In the preface to the book of his critical essays on the subject of religion he wrote: "I am as firmly convinced that religions do harm as I am that they are untrue."[2] He repeatedly charges in one way or another that a free man who exercises his reasoning ability cannot submit to religious dogma. He argued that religion was a hindrance to the advance of civilization, that it cannot cure our troubles, and that we do not survive death.

We are treated to a defiant expression of metaphysical materialism—perhaps Russell's most notorious essay for a popular reading audience—in the article (first published in 1903) entitled "A Free Man's Worship." He there concluded: "Brief and powerless is man's life; on him and all his race the slow, sure doom falls pitiless and dark. Blind to good and evil, reckless of destruction, omnipotent matter rolls on its relentless way." In the face of this nihilism and ethical subjectivism, Russell nevertheless called men to the invigoration of the free man's worship: "to worship at the shrine that his own hands have built; undismayed by the empire of chance...."[3]

Hopefully the brazen contradiction in Russell's philosophy of life is already apparent to the reader. He asserts that our ideals and values are not objective and supported by the nature of reality, indeed that they are fleeting and doomed to destruction. On the other hand, quite contrary to this, Russell encourages us to assert our autonomous values in the face of a valueless universe—to act as though they really amounted to something worthwhile, were rational, and not merely the result of chance. But after all, what sense could Russell hope to make of an *immaterial value* (an ideal) in the face of an "omnipotent matter" which is blind to values? Russell only succeeded in shooting himself in the foot.

Why Russell Said He Could Not Be a Christian

The essay "Why I Am Not a Christian" is the text of a lecture which Russell delivered to the National Secular Society in London on March 6, 1927. It is only fair to recognize, as Russell commented, that constraints of time prevented him from going into great detail or saying as much as he might like about the matters which he raises in the lecture. Nevertheless, he says quite enough with which to find fault.

In broad terms, Russell argued that he could not be a Christian because:

(1) the Roman Catholic church is mistaken to say that the existence of God can be proved by unaided reason;

(2) serious defects in the character and teaching of Jesus show that he was not the best and wisest of men, but actually morally inferior to Buddha and Socrates;

(3) people accept religion on emotional grounds, particularly on the foundation of fear, which is "not worthy of self-respecting human beings"; and the Christian religion "has been and still is the principal enemy of moral progress in the world."

Internal Tensions

What is outstanding about this litany of complaints against Christianity is Russell's arbitrariness and inconsistency. The second reason offered above presupposes some absolute standard of moral wisdom by which somebody could grade Jesus as either inferior or superior to others. Likewise, the third reason presupposes a fixed criterion for what is, and what is not, "worthy" of self-respecting human beings. Then again, the complaint expressed in the fourth reason would not make any sense unless it is objectively wrong to be an enemy of "moral progress"; indeed, the very notion of moral "progress" itself assumes an established benchmark for morality by which to assess progress.

Now, if Russell had been reasoning and speaking in terms of the Christian worldview, his attempt to assess moral wisdom, human worthiness, and moral progress—as well as to adversely judge shortcomings in these matters—would be understandable and expected. Christians have a universal, objective and absolute standard of morality in the revealed word of God. But obviously Russell did not mean to be speaking as though he adopted Christian premises and perspectives! On what basis, then, could Russell issue his moral evaluations and judgments? In terms of what view of reality and knowledge did he assume that there was anything like an objective criterion of morality by which to find Christ, Christians, and the church lacking?

Russell was embarrassingly arbitrary in this regard. He just took it for granted, as an unargued philosophical bias, that there was a moral standard to apply, and that he could presume to be the spokesman and judge who applies it. One could easily counter Russell by simply saying that he had arbitrarily chosen the wrong standard of morality. To be fair, Russell's opponents must be granted just as much arbitrariness in choosing a moral standard, and they may then select one different from his own. And there goes his argument down in defeat.

By assuming the prerogative to pass moral judgment, Russell evidenced that his own presuppositions fail to comport with each other. In offering a condemning value-judgment against Christianity, Russell engaged in behavior which betrayed his professed beliefs elsewhere. In his lecture Russell professed that this was a chance world which shows no evidence of design, and where "laws" are nothing more than statistical averages describing what has happened. He professed that the physical world may have always existed, and that human life and intelligence came about in the way explained by Darwin (evolutionary natural selection). Our values and hopes are what "our intelligence can create." The fact remains that, according to "the ordinary laws of science, you have to suppose that human life... on this planet will die out in due course."

This is simply to say that human values are subjective, fleeting, and self-created. In short, they are relative. Holding to this kind of view of moral values, Russell was utterly inconsistent in acting as though he could assume an altogether different kind of view of values, declaring an absolute moral evaluation of Christ or Christians. One aspect of Russell's network of beliefs rendered another aspect of his set of beliefs unintelligible.

The same kind of inner tension within Russell's beliefs is evident above in what he had to say about the "laws" of science. On the one hand such laws are merely descriptions of what has happened in the past, says Russell. On the other hand, Russell spoke of the laws of science as providing a basis for projecting what will happen in the future, namely the decay of the solar system. This kind of dialectical dance between conflicting views of scientific law (to speak epistemologically) or between conflicting views of the nature of the physical cosmos (to speak metaphysically) is characteristic of unbelieving thought. Such thinking is not in harmony with itself and is thus irrational.

"Unaided Reason"

In the first reason given by Russell for why he was not a Christian, he alluded to the dogma of the Roman Catholic church that "the existence of God can be proved by the unaided reason."[4] He then turns to some of the more popular arguments advanced for the existence of God which are (supposedly) based upon this "unaided reason" and easily finds them wanting. It goes without saying, of course, that Russell thought that he was defeating these arguments of unaided reason by means of his own (superior) unaided reason. Russell did not disagree with Rome that man can prove things with his "natural reason" (apart from the supernatural work of grace). Indeed at the end of his lecture he called his hearers to "a fearless outlook and a free intelligence." Russell simply disagreed that unaided reason takes one to God. In different ways, and with different final conclusions, both the Roman church and Russell encouraged men to exercise their reasoning ability autonomously—apart from the foundation and restraints of divine revelation.

The Christian apologist should not fail to expose this commitment to "unaided reason" for the *unargued* philosophical bias that it is. Throughout his lecture Russell simply takes it for granted that autonomous reason enables man to know things. He speaks freely of his "knowledge of what atoms actually do," of what "science can teach us," and of "certain quite definite fallacies" committed in Christian arguments, etc. But this simply will not do. As the philosopher, Russell here gave himself a free ride; he hypocritically failed to be as self-critical in his reasoning as he beseeched others to be with themselves.

The nagging problem which Russell simply did not face is that, on the basis of autonomous reasoning, man cannot give an adequate and rational account of the knowledge we gain through science and logic. Scientific procedure assumes that the natural world operates in a uniform fashion, in which case our observational knowledge of past cases provides a basis for predicting what will happen in future cases. However, autonomous reason has no basis whatsoever for believing that the natural world will operate in a uniform fashion. Russell himself (at times) asserted that this is a chance universe. He could never reconcile this view of nature being random with his view that nature is uniform (so that "science" can teach us).

So it is with a knowledge and use of the laws of logic (in terms of which Russell definitely insisted that fallacies be avoided). The laws of logic are not physical objects in the natural world; they are not observed by man's senses. Moreover, the laws of logic are universal and unchanging—or else they reduce to relativistic preferences for thinking, rather than prescriptive requirements. However, Russell's autonomous reasoning could not explain or justify these characteristics of logical laws. An individual's unaided reason is limited in the scope of its use and experiences, in which case it cannot pronounce on what is universally true (descriptively). On the other hand, an individual's unaided reason is in no position to dictate (prescriptively) universal laws of thought or to assure us that these stipulations for the mind will somehow prove applicable to the world of thought or matter outside the individual's mind.[5]

Russell's worldview, even apart from its internal tensions, could not provide a foundation for the intelligibility of science or logic. His "unaided" reason could not account for the knowledge which men readily gain in God's universe, a universe sovereignly controlled (so that it is uniform) and interpreted in light of the Creator's revealed mind (so that there are immaterial laws of thought which are universal).

Prejudicial Conjecture and Logical Fallacies

We must note, finally, that Russell's case against being a Christian is subject to criticism for its reliance upon prejudicial conjecture and logical fallacies. That being the case, he cannot be thought to have established his conclusions or given good reason for his rejection of Christianity.

One stands in amazement, for instance, that the same Russell who could lavish ridicule upon past Christians for their ignorance and lack of scholarship, could come out and say something as uneducated and inaccurate as this: "Historically it is quite doubtful whether Christ ever existed at all, and if He did we do not know anything about Him." Even forgetting secular references to Christ in the ancient world, Russell's remark simply ignores the documents of the New Testament as early and authentic witnesses to the historical person of Jesus. Given the relatively early dates of these documents and the relatively large number of them, if Russell "doubted" the existence of Jesus Christ, he must have either applied a conspicuous double standard in his historical reasoning, or been an agnostic about virtually the whole of ancient history. Either way, we are given an insight into the prejudicial nature of Russell's thinking when it came to consideration of the Christian religion.

Perhaps the most obvious logical fallacy evident in Russell's lecture comes out in the way he readily shifts from an evaluation of Christian beliefs to a criticism of Christian believers. And he should have known better. At the very beginning of his lecture, Russell said, "I do not mean by a Christian any person who tries to live decently and according to his lights. I think that you must have a certain amount of definite belief before you have a right to call yourself a Christian." That is, the object of Russell's criticism should be, by his own testimony, not the lifestyle of individuals but the doctrinal claims which are essential to Christianity as a system of thought. The opening of his lecture focuses upon his dissatisfaction with those beliefs (God's existence, immortality, Christ as the best of men).

Nevertheless, toward the end of his lecture, Russell's discussion turns in the direction of fallaciously arguing against the personal defects of Christians (enforcing narrow rules contrary to human happiness) and the supposed psychological genesis of their beliefs (in emotion and fear). That is, he indulges in the fallacy of arguing *ad hominem*. Even if what Russell had to say in these matters was fair-minded and accurate (it is not), the fact would remain that Russell has descended to the level of arguing against a truth-claim on the basis of his personal dislike and psychologizing of those who personally profess that claim. In other settings, Russell the philosopher would have been the first to criticize a student for pulling such a thing. It is nothing less than a shameful logical fallacy.

Notice briefly <u>other defects</u> in Russell's line of thinking here. He <u>presumed to know the motivation of a person in becoming a Christian—</u> even though Russell's epistemology gave him no warrant for thinking he could discern such things (especially easily and at a distance). Moreover, he <u>presumed to know the motivation of a whole class of people</u> (including those who lived long ago), based on a very, very small sampling from his own present experience. These are little more than hasty and unfounded generalizations, telling us (if anything) only about the state of Russell's mind and feelings in his <u>obvious, emotional antipathy to Christians.</u>

But then this leaves us face to face with a <u>final, devastating fallacy</u> in Russell's case against Christianity—the use of <u>double standards</u> (and implicit special pleading) in his reasoning. Russell <u>wished to fault</u> Christians for <u>the emotional factor</u> in their faith-commitment, and yet Russell himself evidenced a similarly emotional factor in his own personal anti-Christian commitment. Indeed, Russell openly appealed to emotional feelings of courage, pride, freedom and self-worth as a basis for his audience to refrain from being Christians!

Similarly, Russell tried to take Christians to task for their "wickedness" (as though there could be any such thing within Russell's worldview)—for their cruelty, wars, inquisitions, etc. Russell did not pause for even a moment, however, to reflect on the far-surpassing cruelty and violence of non-Christians throughout history. Genghis Khan, Vlad the Impaler, Marquis de Sade and a whole cast of other butchers were not known in history for their Christian professions, after all! This is all conveniently swept under the carpet in Russell's hypocritical disdain for the moral errors of the Christian church.

Russell's essay "Why I Am Not a Christian" reveals to us that even the intellectually elite of this world are refuted by their own errors in opposing the truth of the Christian faith. There <u>is no credibility to a challenge to Christianity</u> which evidences <u>prejudicial conjecture, logical fallacies, unargued philosophical bias, behavior</u> which betrays professed beliefs, and <u>presuppositions which do not comport with each other.</u> Why wasn't Russell a Christian? Given his weak effort at criticism, one would have to conclude that it was not for intellectual reasons

Notes:

[1] The article is found in Bertrand Russell, *Why I Am Not a Christian, And Other Essays on Religion and Related Subjects*, ed. Paul Edwards (New York: Simon and Schuster, Clarion, 1957), pp. 3-23.

[2] *Ibid.*, p. vi.

[3] *Ibid*, pp. 115-16.

[4] In his lecture Russell displays a curious and capricious shifting around for the standard which defines the content of "Christian" beliefs. Here he arbitrarily assumes that what the Roman magisterium says is the standard of Christian faith. Yet in the paragraph immediately preceding, Russell claimed that the doctrine of hell was not essential to Christian belief because the Privy Council of the English Parliament had so decreed (over the dissent of the Archbishops of Canterbury and York). Elsewhere Russell departs from this criterion of Christianity and excoriates the teaching of Jesus, based upon the Bible, that the unrepentant face everlasting damnation. Russell had no interest in being consistent or fair in dealing with Christianity as his opponent. When convenient he defined the faith according to the Bible, but when it was more convenient for his polemical purposes he shifted to defining the faith according to the English Parliament or the Roman Catholic church.

[5] Those familiar with Russell's detailed (and noteworthy, seminal) work in philosophy would point out that, despite his brilliance, Russell's "unaided reason" could never resolve certain semantic and logical paradoxes which arise in his account of logic, mathematics and language. His most reverent followers concede that Russell's theories are subject to criticism.

CHAPTER 30:

THE PROBLEM OF EVIL

We want to turn now to examine some of the recurring and most basic kinds of objections which are raised against the Christian faith by those who disagree with the Biblical worldview—whether its intellectual antagonists, cultured despisers, or competing religions. Our aim will be to suggest how a presuppositional method of apologetics would answer these types of argument against Christianity (or alternatives to it) as a philosophy of life, knowledge and reality.

Perhaps the most intense, pained and persistent challenge which believers hear about the truth of the Christian message comes in the form of what is called "the problem of evil." The suffering and evil which we see all about us seems to cry out against the existence of God—at least a God who is both benevolent and almighty. This is thought by many to be the most difficult of all the problems which apologists face, not only because of the apparent logical difficulty within the Christian outlook, but because of the personal perplexity which any sensitive human being will feel when confronted with the terrible misery and wickedness that can be found in the world. Man's inhumanity to man is notorious in every age of history and in every nation of the world. There is a long story of oppression, indignity, unkindness, torture and tyranny. We find war and murder, greed and lust, dishonesty and lies. We encounter fear and hatred, infidelity and cruelty, poverty and racial hostility. Moreover, even in the natural world we come across so much apparently needless suffering and pain—birth defects, parasites, attacks of violent animals, radioactive mutations, debilitating diseases, deadly cancer, starvation, crippling injuries, typhoons, earthquakes, and other natural disasters.

When the unbeliever looks at this unhappy "vale of tears," he or she feels there is a strong reason to doubt the goodness of God. Why should there be so much misery? Why should it be distributed in such a seemingly unjust fashion? Is this what you would permit, if you were God and could prevent it?

Taking Evil Seriously

It is important for the Christian to recognize—indeed, to insist upon—the reality and serious nature of evil. The subject of evil is not simply an intellectual parlor game, a cavalier matter, a whimsical or relativistic choice of looking a things a certain way. Evil is real. Evil is ugly.

Only when we become emotionally charged and intellectually intense about the existence of evil can we appreciate the depth of the problem unbelievers have with the Christian worldview—but, likewise, realize why the problem of evil ends up confirming the Christian outlook, rather than infirming it. When we talk about evil with unbelievers, it is crucial that both sides "play for keeps." Evil must be taken seriously "*as evil.*"

A well known passage from the pen of the Russian novelist, Fyodor Dostoevski, readily stirs our emotions and makes us insistent about the wickedness of men, for instance men who are cruel to little children. It is found in his novel, *Brothers Karamazov.*[1] Ivan makes his complaint to Alyosha:

> "People talk sometimes of bestial cruelty, but that's a great injustice and insult to the beasts; a beast can never be so cruel as a man, so artistically cruel....
>
> I've collected a great, great deal about Russian children, Alyosha. There was a little girl of five who was hated by her father and mother.... You see, I must repeat again, it is a peculiar characteristic of many people, this love of torturing children, and children only.... It's just their defenselessness that tempts the tormentor, just the angelic confidence of the child who has no refuge and no appeal that sets his vile blood on fire....
>
> This poor child of five was subjected to every possible torture by those cultivated parents. They beat her, thrashed her,

kicked her for no reason till her body was one bruise. Then, they went to greater refinements of cruelty—shut her up all night in the cold and frost in a privy, and because she didn't ask to be taken up at night... they smeared her face and filled her mouth with excrement, and it was her mother, her mother did this. And that mother could sleep, hearing the poor child's groans! Can you understand why a little creature, who can't even understand what's done to her, should beat her little aching heart with her tiny fist in the dark and cold, and weep her meek unresentful tears to dear, kind God to protect her?... Do you understand why this infamy must be and is permitted?... Why, the whole world of knowledge is not worth that child's prayer to 'dear, kind God'!...

Imagine that you are creating a fabric of human destiny with the object of making men happy in the end, giving them peace and rest at last, but that it was essential and inevitable to torture to death only one tiny creature—that baby beating its breast with its fist, for instance—and to found that edifice on its unavenged tears, would you consent to be the architect on those conditions? Tell me, and tell the truth."

"No, I wouldn't consent," said Alyosha softly.

Incidents and soliloquies such as this could be multiplied over and over again. They elicit moral indignation within us. They also elicit moral indignation within the unbeliever—and that fact must not be disregarded by the apologist.

Once when I was doing a radio call-in show, a caller became very snide about my saying that we should worship and adore God. The caller wanted to know how anybody could adore a God who permitted sexual abuse and mutilation of a baby, such as the caller had witnessed in certain courtroom photographs at the trial of some horrible specimen of humanity. The description was sickening and surely evoked revulsion in everyone who heard it. I knew the caller meant to press his hostility to Christianity upon me hard, but I was actually glad that the caller was so irate. He was taking evil *seriously*. His condemnation of child abuse was not simply a matter of personal preference to him. For that reason, I realized it would not be difficult to show why the problem of evil is not really a problem for the believer—but rather for the unbeliever. More on this later.

Evil as a Logical Problem

The "problem" of evil has not always been properly understood by Christian apologists. They have sometimes reduced the difficulty of the unbeliever's challenge to Christianity by conceiving of the problem of evil as simply the angry presentation of evidence contrary to the alleged goodness of God. It is as though believers profess God's goodness, but then unbelievers have their counterexamples. Who makes the best case from the facts around us? The problem is presented (inaccurately) as a matter of who has weightier evidence on his side of the disagreement.

For instance, we read a popular apologist say this about the problem of evil: " But in the final analysis, the evidence for the existence of the good (God) is not vitiated by the anomaly of evil." And why not? "Evil remains a perplexing mystery, but the force of the mystery is not enough to demand that we throw out the positive evidence for God, for the reality of good.... *While we cannot explain the existence of evil, that is no reason for us to disregard the positive evidence for God.*"[2] This seriously underestimates the nature of the problem of evil. It is not simply a matter of weighing the positive evidence over against the negative evidence for goodness in God's world or in God's plan (say, for redemption, etc.). The problem of evil is a much more serious challenge to the Christian faith than that.

The problem of evil amounts to the charge that there is *logical incoherence* within the Christian outlook—regardless of how much evil there is in the universe, compared to how much goodness can be found. If Christianity is logically incoherent, *no amount* of positive, factual evidence can save its truth. The internal inconsistency would itself render Christian faith intellectually unacceptable, *even granting* there might be a great deal of indicators or evidence in our experience for the existence of goodness or for God, otherwise considered.

The 18th century Scottish philosopher, David Hume, expressed the problem of evil in a strong and challenging fashion: "Is [God] willing to prevent evil, but not able? then he is impotent. Is he able, but not willing? then he is malevolent. Is he both able and willing? whence then is evil?"[3] What Hume was arguing is that the Christian cannot logically accept these three premises: God is all-powerful, God is all-good, and nevertheless evil exists in the world. If God is all-powerful, then He must be able to prevent or remove evil, if He wishes. If God is all-good, then certainly He wishes to prevent or remove evil. Yet it is undeniable that evil exists.

George Smith states the problem this way in his book, *Atheism: The Case Against God*[4]: "Briefly, the problem of evil is this: ...If God knows there is evil but cannot prevent it, he is not omnipotent. If God knows there is evil and can prevent it but desires not to, he is not omnibenevolent." Smith thinks that Christians logically cannot have it both ways: God is completely good, as well as completely powerful.

Therefore, the charge which unbelievers make is that the Christian worldview is incoherent; it adopts premises which are inconsistent with each other, given the evil in this world. The unbeliever argues that, even if he were to accept the premises of Christian theology (regardless of evidence for or against them individually), those premises do not comport with *each other*. The problem with Christianity is an internal one—a logical defect which even the believer must acknowledge, as long as he realistically admits the presence of evil in the world. This evil, it is thought, is incompatible with either God's goodness or God's power.

For Whom is Evil Logically a Problem?

It should be obvious upon reflection that there can be no "problem of evil" to press upon Christian believers unless one can legitimately assert the existence of evil in this world. There is not even apparently a logical problem as long as we have only these two premises to deal with:

1. GOD IS COMPLETELY GOOD.
2. GOD IS COMPLETELY POWERFUL.

These two premises do not in themselves create any contradiction. The problem arises only when we add the premise:

3. EVIL EXISTS (HAPPENS).

Accordingly, it is crucial to the unbeliever's case against Christianity to be in a position to assert that there is evil in the world—to point to something and have the right to evaluate it *as* an instance of evil. If it should be the case that nothing evil exists or ever happens—that is, what people initially believe to be evil cannot reasonably be deemed "evil"—then there is nothing inconsistent with Christian theology which requires an answer.

What does the unbeliever mean by "good," or by what standard does the unbeliever determine what counts as "good" (so that "evil" is accordingly defined or identified)? What are the presuppositions in terms of which the unbeliever makes any moral judgments whatsoever?

Perhaps the unbeliever takes "good" to be whatever evokes public approval. However, on that basis the statement "The vast majority of the community heartily approved of and willingly joined in the evil deed" could never make sense. The fact that a large number of people feel a certain way does not (or should not rationally) convince anybody that this feeling (about the goodness or evil of something) is correct. Ethics does not reduce to statistics, after all. Ordinarily, people think of the goodness of something as evoking their approval—rather than their approval constituting its goodness! Even unbelievers talk and act as though there are personal traits, actions or things which possess the property of goodness (or evil) *irrespective* of the attitudes or beliefs or feelings people have about those traits, actions or things.[5]

There are even further problems with taking "good" to be whatever evokes the approval of the individual (rather than public at large). Not only does this too reduce to subjectivism, it absurdly implies that no two individuals can make identical ethical judgments. When Bill says "Helping orphans is good," he would not be saying the same thing as when Ted says "Helping orphans is good." Bill's utterance means "Helping orphans evokes Bill's approval," whereas Ted's would mean "Helping orphans evokes Ted's approval"—which are altogether different matters. Not only would this view make it impossible for two people to make identical ethical judgments, it would likewise (absurdly) imply that a person's own ethical judgments could never be mistaken, unless he happened to misunderstand his own feelings![6]

The unbeliever might turn, then, to an instrumental or consequential understanding of what constitutes objective goodness (or evil). For instance, an action or trait is good if it tends to achieve a certain end, like the greatest happiness of the greatest number. The irrelevance of such a notion for making ethical determinations is that one would need to be able to rate and compare happiness, as well as to be able to calculate all of the consequences of any given action or trait. This is simply impossible for finite minds (even with the help of computers). But more devastating is the observation that good may be taken to be whatever promotes general happiness *only* if it is antecedently the case that generalized happiness is itself "good." Any theory of ethics which focuses on the goodness of achieving a certain end (or consequence) will make sense only if it can establish that the chosen end (or consequence) is a good one to pursue and promote. Instrumental theories of goodness eventually must address the issue of intrinsic goodness, so that they can correctly determine what their goals *ought* to be.

Philosophically speaking, the problem of evil turns out to be, therefore, a problem for the unbeliever himself. In order to use the argument from evil against the Christian worldview, he must first be able to show that his judgments about the existence of evil are meaningful—which is precisely what his unbelieving worldview is unable to do.

Does the Unbeliever Take Evil Seriously, Then?

Unbelievers complain that certain plain facts about human experience are inconsistent with the Christian's theological beliefs about the goodness and power of God. Such a complaint requires the non-Christian to assert the existence of evil in this world. What, however, has been presupposed here?

Both the believer and the unbeliever will want to insist that certain things are evil, for instance cases of child abuse (like those already mentioned). And they will talk as though they take such moral judgments seriously, not simply as expressions of personal taste, preference or subjective opinion. They will insist that such things are truly—objectively, intrinsically—evil. Even unbelievers can be shaken from their easy and glib espousals of relativism in the face of moral atrocities like war, rape, and torture.

But the question, logically speaking, is how the unbeliever can make sense of taking evil seriously—not simply as something inconvenient, or unpleasant, or contrary to his or her desires. What philosophy of value or morality can the unbeliever offer which will render it meaningful to condemn some atrocity as objectively evil? The moral indignation which is expressed by unbelievers when they encounter the wicked things which transpire in this world does not comport with the theories of ethics which unbelievers espouse, theories which prove to be arbitrary or subjective or merely utilitarian or relativistic in character. On the unbeliever's worldview, there is no good reason for saying that anything is evil in nature, but only by personal choice or feeling.

That is why I am encouraged when I see unbelievers getting very indignant with some evil action as a matter of principle. Such indignation requires recourse to the absolute, unchanging, and good character of God in order to make philosophical sense. The expression of moral indignation is but personal evidence that unbelievers know this God in their heart of hearts. They refuse to let judgments about evil be reduced to subjectivism.

When the believer challenges the unbeliever on this point, the unbeliever will likely turn around and try to argue that evil is, in the final analysis, based on human reasoning or choices—thus being relative to the individual or culture. And at that point the believer must press home the *logical incoherence* within the unbeliever's set of beliefs. On the one hand, he believes and speaks as though some activity (e.g., child abuse) is wrong in itself, but on the other hand he believes and speaks as though that activity is wrong only if the individual (or culture) chooses some value which is inconsistent with it (e.g., pleasure, the greatest happiness of the greatest number, freedom). When the unbeliever professes that people determine ethical values for themselves, the unbeliever implicitly holds that those who commit evil are not really doing anything evil, given the values which they have chosen for themselves. In this way, the unbeliever who is indignant over wickedness supplies the very premises which philosophically condone and *permit* such behavior, even though at the same time the unbeliever wishes to insist that such behavior is *not* permitted—it is "evil."

What we find, then, is that the unbeliever must secretly *rely upon* the Christian worldview in order to make sense of his argument from the existence of evil which is *urged against* the Christian worldview! Antitheism presupposes theism to make its case.

The problem of evil is thus a logical problem for the unbeliever, rather than the believer. As a Christian, I can make perfectly good sense out of my moral revulsion and condemnation of child abuse. The non-Christian cannot. This does not mean that I can explain why God does whatever He does in planning misery and wickedness in this world. It simply means that moral outrage is consistent with the Christian's worldview, his basic presuppositions about reality, knowledge, and ethics. The non-Christian's worldview (of whatever variety) eventually cannot account for such moral outrage. It cannot explain the objective and unchanging nature of moral notions like good or evil. Thus the problem of evil is precisely a philosophical problem for unbelief. Unbelievers would be required to appeal to the very thing against which they argue (a divine, transcendent sense of ethics) in order for their argument to be warranted.

Resolving the Alleged Paradox

The unbeliever might at this point protest that, even if he as a non-Christian cannot meaningfully explain or make sense of the view that evil objectively exists, nevertheless there still remains a paradox within the set of beliefs which constitute the *Christian's own* worldview. Given his basic philosophy and commitments, the Christian certainly can and does claim that evil is real, and yet the Christian also believes things about the character of God which together seem incompatible with the existence of evil. The unbeliever might argue that, regardless of the ethical inadequacy of his own worldview, the Christian is still—on the Christian's own terms—locked into a logically incoherent position by maintaining the three following propositions:

1. GOD IS ALL-GOOD.
2. GOD IS ALL-POWERFUL.
3. EVIL EXISTS.

However the critic here overlooks a perfectly reasonable way to assent to all three of these propositions.

If the Christian *presupposes* that God is perfectly and completely good—as Scripture requires us to do—then he is committed to evaluating everything within his experience in the light of that presupposition. Accordingly, when the Christian observes evil events or things in the world, he can and should retain consistency with his presupposition about God's goodness by now *inferring* that God has a *morally good reason* for the evil that exists. God certainly must be all-powerful in order to be God; He is not to be thought of as overwhelmed or stymied by evil in the universe. And God is surely good, the Christian will profess—*so* any evil we find must be compatible with God's goodness. This is just to say that God has planned evil events for reasons which are morally commendable and good.

To put it another way, the apparent paradox created by the above three propositions is readily resolved by adding this fourth premise to them:

4. GOD HAS A MORALLY SUFFICIENT REASON FOR THE EVIL WHICH EXISTS.

When all four of these premises are maintained, there is no logical contradiction to be found, not even an apparent one. It is precisely part of the Christian's walk of faith and growth in sanctification to draw proposition 4 as the conclusion of propositions 1-3.

Think of Abraham when God ordered him to sacrifice his only son. Think of Job when he lost everything which gave his life happiness and pleasure. In each case God had a perfectly good reason for the human misery involved. It was a mark or achievement of faith for them not to waver in their conviction of God's goodness, despite not being able to see or understand why He was doing to them what He did. Indeed, even in the case of the greatest crime in all of history—the crucifixion of the Lord of glory—the Christian professes that God's goodness was not inconsistent with what the hands of lawless men performed. Was the killing of Christ evil? Surely. Did God have a morally sufficient reason for it? Just as surely. With Abraham we declare, "Shall not the Judge of all the earth do right?" (Gen. 18:25). And this goodness of God is beyond challenge: "Let God be true, though all men are liars" (Rom. 3:4).

The Problem is Not Logical, But Psychological

It turns out that the problem of evil is not a logical difficulty after all. If God has a morally sufficient reason for the evil which exists, as the Bible teaches, then His goodness and power are not challenged by the reality of evil events and things in human experience. The only logical problem which arises in connection with discussions of evil is the unbeliever's philosophical inability to account for the objectivity of his moral judgments.

The problem which men have with God when they come face to face with evil in the world is not a logical or philosophical one, but more a psychological one. We can find it emotionally very hard to have faith in God and trust His goodness and power *when we are not given the reason why bad things happen to us and others.* We instinctively think to ourselves, "why did such a terrible thing occur?" Unbelievers internally cry out for an answer to such a question also. But God does not always (indeed, rarely) provide an explanation to human beings for the evil which they experience or observe. "The secret things belong to the Lord our God" (Deut. 29:29). We might not be able to understand God's wise and mysterious ways, even if He told us (cf. Isa. 55:9). Nevertheless, the fact remains that He has not told us why misery and suffering and injustice are part of His plan for history and for our individual lives.

So then, the Bible calls upon us to trust that God has a morally sufficient reason for the evil which can be found in this world, but it does not tell us what that sufficient reason is. The believer often struggles with this situation, walking by faith rather than by sight. The unbeliever, however, finds the situation intolerable for his pride, feelings, or rationality. He refuses to trust God. He will not believe that God has a morally sufficient reason for the evil which exists, unless the unbeliever is given that reason for his own examination and assessment. To put it briefly, the unbeliever will not trust God unless God subordinates Himself to the intellectual authority and moral evaluation of the unbeliever— unless God consents to trade places with the sinner.

The problem of evil comes down to the question of whether a person should have faith in God and His word or rather place faith in his own human thinking and values. It finally becomes a question of ultimate authority within a person's life. And in that sense, the way in which unbelievers struggle with the problem of evil is but a continuing testimony to the way in which evil entered human history in the first place. The Bible indicates that sin and all of its accompanying miseries entered this world through the first transgression of Adam and Eve. And the question with which Adam and Eve were confronted way back then was precisely the question which unbelievers face today: should we have faith in God's word simply on His say-so, or should we evaluate God and

His word on the basis of our own ultimate intellectual and moral authority?

God commanded Adam and Eve not to eat of a certain tree, testing
them to see if they would attempt to define good and evil for themselves.
Satan came along and challenged the goodness and truthfulness of God,
suggesting He had base motives for keeping Adam and Eve from the delight of the tree. And at that point the whole course of human history
depended upon whether Adam and Eve would trust and presuppose the
goodness of God. Since they did not, the human race has been visited
with torments too many and too painful to inventory. When unbelievers
refuse to accept the goodness of God on the basis of His own self-revelation, they simply perpetuate the source of all of our human woes. Rather
than solving the problem of evil, they are part of the problem.

Therefore, it should not be thought that "the problem of evil" is
anything like an intellectual *basis* for a lack of faith in God. It is rather
simply the personal *expression* of such a lack of faith. What we find is
that unbelievers who challenge the Christian faith end up reasoning in
circles. Because they lack faith in God, they begin by arguing that evil is
incompatible with the goodness and power of God. When they are presented with a logically adequate and Biblically supported solution to the
problem of evil (viz., God has a morally sufficient but undisclosed reason
for the evil that exists), they refuse to accept it, *again* because of their lack
of faith in God. They would rather be left unable to give an account of
any moral judgment whatsoever (about things being good or evil) than to
submit to the ultimate and unchallengeable moral authority of God. That
is too high a price to pay, both philosophically and personally.

Notes:

[1] trans. C. Garnett (New York: Modern Library, Random House, 1950), from book V, chapter 4. The quotation here is taken from the selection found in *God and Evil: Readings on the Theological Problem of Evil*, ed. Nelson Pike (Englewood Cliffs, New Jersey: Prentice-Hall, 1964).

[2] R. C. Sproul, *Objections Answered* (Glendale, CA: Regal Books, G/L Publications, 1978), pp. 128, 129.

[3] *Dialogues Concerning Natural Religion*, ed. Nelson Pike (Indianapolis: Bobbs-Merrill Publications, 1981), p. 88.

[4] Buffalo, New York: Prometheus Books, 1979.

[5] Intuitionism would suggest that goodness is an indefinable (basic or simple) property which we do not come to know empirically or through nature, but "intuitively." What, however, is a "non-natural property" unless we are speaking of a "supernatural" property (the very thing in dispute for the unbeliever)? Further, intuitionism cannot provide a basis for *knowing* that our intuitions are correct: not only must we intuit the goodness of charity, we are also left to intuit that this intuition is true. It is a well known and embarrassing fact that not all people (or all cultures) have identical intuitions about good and evil. These conflicting intuitions cannot be rationally resolved within the unbeliever's worldview.

[6] Similar difficulties attend the notion that ethical terms do not function and are not used to describe anything at all, but simply to *give expression* to one's emotions. The related (performative) theory of ethical language known as "prescriptivism" holds that moral utterances do not function to describe things as good or evil, but simply to get one's hearer(s) to behave or feel in a certain way. On this theory, no attitude or action is good or evil in itself, and one is left without any explanation *why* people go around "directing" others with gratuitous and veiled imperatives like "Helping orphans is good."

CHAPTER 31:

THE PROBLEM OF
KNOWING THE "SUPER-NATURAL"

The Christian faith as defined by Biblical revelation teaches a number of things which are not restricted to the realm of man's temporal experience—things about an invisible God, His triune nature, the origin of the universe, the regularity of the created order, angels, miracles, the afterlife, etc. These are precisely the sort of claims which unbelievers most often find objectionable.

The objection is that such claims are about *transcendent* matters—things which go beyond day-to-day human experience. The triune Creator exists beyond the temporal order; the afterlife is not part of our ordinary observations in this world, etc. If the unbeliever is accustomed to thinking that people can only know things based upon, and pertaining to, the "here-and-now," then the Christian's claims about the transcendent are an intellectual reproach.

The Reproach of the Transcendent

Those who are not Christians will often assume that the natural world is all there is, in which case nobody can know things about the "super-natural" (whatever surpasses the limits of nature). In philosophical circles, discussions and debates about questions like these fall within the area of study known as "metaphysics." As you might expect, this division of philosophical investigation is usually a hotbed of controversy between conflicting schools of thought. More recently, the entire enterprise of metaphysics has in itself become a hotbed of controversy.

Over the last two centuries a mindset has developed which is hostile toward any philosophical claim which is metaphysical in character. It is clear to most students that antipathy to the Christian faith has been the primary and motivating factor in such attacks. Nevertheless, such criticism has been *generalized* into a pervasive antagonism toward any claims which are similarly "metaphysical." This anti-metaphysical attitude has been one of the crucial ingredients which have molded culture and history over the last two hundred years. It has altered common views regarding man and ethics, it has generated a radical reformulation of religious beliefs, and it has significantly affected perspectives ranging from politics to pedagogy. Consequently a very large number of the skeptical questions or challenges directed against the Christian faith are either rooted in, or colored by, this negative spirit with respect to metaphysics.

Defining the Metaphysical

Before we can elaborate on the anti-metaphysical arguments which are commonly heard today, it would help to understand better what is meant by "metaphysics." This is a technical word that is rarely used outside of academic circles; it will not even be part of the vocabulary of most Christians. Nevertheless, the conception of metaphysics and the reaction to it which can be found in academic circles will definitely touch and have an impact on the life of the believer—either in terms of the popular attacks on the faith which he or she must answer, or even in terms of the way in which the Christian religion is portrayed and presented in the pulpit.

It is often said that metaphysics is the study of "being." It might be more illuminating if we wrote that metaphysics studies "being"—that is, questions about existence ("to be, or not to be"). Metaphysics asks, *what is it* to exist? And, what *sorts* of things do exist? Thus the metaphysician is interested to know about fundamental *distinctions* (i.e., the basic classes of things that exist) and important *similarities* (i.e., the essential nature of the members of these classes). He seeks the *ultimate causes or explanations* for the existence and nature of things. He wants to understand the limits of possible reality, the modes of existing, and the interrelations of existing things.

It should be obvious, then, if only in an elementary way, that Christianity propounds a number of definite metaphysical claims.

Fundamental Distinctions

The Scripture teaches us that "there is one God, the Father, by whom are all things...and one Lord, Jesus Christ, through whom are all things" (1 Cor. 8:6). All things, of all sorts, were created by Him (John 1:3; Col. 1:16). But He is before all things, and by means of Him all things hold together or cohere (John 1:1; Col. 1:17). He carries along or upholds all things by the word of His power (Heb. 1:3). Therefore, to exist is to be divine or created. In God we live and move and have our being (Acts 17:28). He, however, has life in Himself (John 5:26; Ex. 3:14). The living and true God gives the distinguishable unity or common natures to things (Gen. 2:19), categorizing things by placing His interpretation on them (e.g., Gen. 1:5, 8, 10, 17; 2:9). It is He who also makes things to differ from each other (1 Cor. 4:7; Ex. 11:7; Rom. 9:21; 1 Cor. 12:4-6; 15:38-41). Similarity and distinction, then, result from His creative and providential work. Both the existence and nature of things find their explanation in Him—whether casual (Eph. 1:11) or teleological (Eph. 1:11). God is the source of all possibility (Isa. 43:10; 44:6; 65:11) and thus sets the limits of possible reality by His own will and decree.

A Comprehensive Metaphysic

"Metaphysics" can also be seen as an attempt to express the *entire scheme* of reality—of all existing things. The metaphysician must resolve conflicting accounts about the true nature of the world (over against mere appearances), and he does so in terms of an ultimate conceptual framework. Metaphysics tries to make sense of the world *as a whole* by articulating and applying a set of central, regulating, organizing, distinctive paradigms. These principles govern or guide the way in which a person interrelates and interprets the different parts of his life and experience. Everyone uses some such system of ultimate generalities about reality, evaluative criteria, and structuring relationships. We could not think or make sense of anything without some coherent view of the general nature and structure of reality.

Instead of dealing with simply one distinguishable department of study or one limited area of human experience (e.g., biology, history, astronomy), metaphysics is *comprehensive*—concerned with, and relevant to, the whole world. For this reason one's metaphysical views will affect every other inquiry in which he engages, illumine a wide range of subjects, and form the "first principles" for other intellectual disciplines.

The Christian Metaphysic

The Christian faith comprises a metaphysical system on this account also. Scripture teaches that all things are of God, through God, and unto God (Rom. 11:36). We must think His thoughts after Him (Prov. 22:17-21; John 8:31-32). In this way we can understand and interpret the world as a whole. The word of God gives us light (Ps. 119:130), and Christ Himself is the life-giving light of men (John 1:4), in whom are hid all the treasures of wisdom and knowledge (Col. 2:3). Hence we can discern the true nature of reality in terms of Christ's word: "in Thy light we see light" (Ps. 36:9).

The Bible sets forth a definite metaphysical scheme. It begins with God who is a personal, infinitely perfect, pure spirit (Ex. 15:11; Mal. 2:10; John 4:24). The triune God (2 Cor. 13:14) is unique in His nature and works (Ps. 86:9), self-existent (Ex. 3:14; John 5:26; Gal. 4:8-9), eternal (Ps. 90:2), immutable (Mal. 3:6), and omnipresent (Ps. 139:7-10). Everything else that exists has been created out of nothing (Col. 1:16-17; Heb. 11:3), whether the material world (Gen. 1:1; Ex. 20:11), the realm of spirits (Ps. 148:2, 5), or man. Man was created as the image of God (Gen. 1:27), a being who exhibits both a material and immaterial character (Matt. 10:28), surviving bodily death (Eccl. 12:7; Rom. 2:7) with personal awareness of God (2 Cor. 5:8), and awaiting bodily resurrection (1 Cor. 6:14; 15:42-44).

In creation God made all things according to His unsearchable wisdom (Ps. 104:24; Isa. 40:28), assigning all things their definite characters (Isa. 40:26; 46:9-10). God also determines all things by His wisdom (Eph. 1:11)—preserving (Neh. 9:6), governing (Ps. 103:19), and predetermining the nature and course of all things, thus being able to work miracles (Ps. 72:18). The decree by which God providentially ordains historical events is eternal, effectual, unconditional, unchangeable, and comprehensive (e.g., Isa. 46:10; Acts 2:23; Eph. 3:9-11).

These truths are paradigmatic for the believer; they are ultimate principles of objective reality, to be distinguished from the delusions set forth in contrary views of the world. What the unbelieving world sees as wisdom is actually foolish (1 Cor. 1:18-25). Since the minds of the unbelieving are blinded (2 Cor. 4:4), they err according to the faith described above, thus having only a "knowledge falsely so-called" (1 Tim. 6:20-21). For instance, resting in the appearance of total regularity, an unbelieving metaphysic does not teach that Christ will come again to intervene in the cosmic process to judge men and determine their eternal destinies (cf. 2 Peter 3:3-7).

Distinguishing Appearance from Reality

Therefore, the Bible distinguishes appearance from reality, and it provides an ultimate conceptual framework that makes sense of the world as whole. The Biblical metaphysic affects our outlook and conclusions regarding every field of study or endeavor, and it serves as the only foundation for all disciplines from science to ethics (Prov. 1:7; Matt. 7:24-27).

Ultimate Questions

So then, "metaphysics" studies such questions or issues as the nature of existence, the sorts of things that exist, the classes of existent things, limits of possibility, the ultimate scheme of things, reality versus appearance, and the comprehensive conceptual framework used to make sense of the world as a whole. It is not hard to understand, then, how the term "metaphysics" has come to connote the study of that which is "beyond the physical realm." Simple eyeball inspection of isolated and particular situations in the physical world cannot answer metaphysical questions like those just enumerated. An individual's limited personal experience cannot warrant a comprehensive framework encompassing every sort of existent there may be. Empirical experience merely gives us an appearance of things; empirical experience cannot *in itself* correct illusions or get us beyond appearance to any world or realm of reality lying beyond. Nor can it determine the limits of the possible. A particular experience of the physical world does not deal with the world as whole. Nor does the nature of existence manifest itself in simple sense perception of any physical object or set of them.

Suprasensible Reality

Consequently, metaphysics eventually studies non-sensuous or *suprasensible* reality. In the nature of the case the metaphysician examines issues transcending physical nature or matters removed from particular sense experiences. And yet the results of metaphysics are alleged to give us intelligible and informative statements about reality. That is, metaphysics makes claims which have substantive content, but which are not fully dependent on or restricted to empirical experience (observation, sensation).

For that reason the means by which metaphysical claims are intellectually supported is not limited to natural observation and scientific experimentation. Herein lies the offense of metaphysics to the modern mind.[1] Metaphysics presumes to tell us something about the objective world which we do not directly perceive in ordinary experience and which cannot be verified through the methods of natural science.

Of course, antipathy to metaphysics is even more pronounced in the case of Christianity because its claims about the entire scheme of things include declarations about the existence and character of God, the origin and nature of the world, as well as the nature and destiny of man. Such teachings do not stem from direct, eyeball experience of the physical world, but transcend particular sensations and derive from divine revelation. They are not verified empirically in a point by point fashion. Scripture makes absolute pronouncements about the nature of the real world as a whole. Biblical doctrine presents truths which are not circumscribed or limited by personal experience and which are not qualified or relativized by an individual's own way of looking at things. Such authoritarian claims about such difficult and wide-ranging matters are offensive to the skeptical mood and religious prejudices of the present day. The modern age has a contrary spirit regarding philosophical (especially religious) claims which speak of anything super-natural, anything "beyond the physical," anything metaphysical.

Pure Motives?

It would be profitable to pause and reflect upon an insightful comment by a recent writer in the area of philosophical metaphysics. W. H. Walsh has written, "It must be allowed that the reaction against [metaphysics] has been ... so violent indeed as to suggest that the issues involved in the controversy must be something more than academic."[2] Precisely. The issues are indeed more than academic. They are a matter of life and death—eternal life and death. Christ said, "And this is life eternal, that they should know thee the only true God, and him whom thou didst send" (John 17:3). However, if the unbeliever can stand on the claim that such a God *cannot be known* because nothing transcending the physical (nothing "metaphysical") can be known, then the issue of eternal destiny is not raised. Accordingly, men may think and do as they please, without distracting questions about their nature and destiny.

Men will, as it were, build a roof over their heads in hopes of keeping out any distressing revelation from a transcendent God. The anti-metaphysical perspective of the modern age functions as just such a protective ideological roof for the unbeliever.

The fact is that one cannot avoid metaphysical commitments. The very denial of the possibility of knowledge transcending experience is *in itself* a metaphysical judgment. Thus the question is not *whether* one should have metaphysical beliefs, but it comes down to the question of *which kind* of metaphysic one should affirm. In considering that question remember the candid observation of Friedrich Nietzsche:

> What provokes one to look at all philosophers half suspiciously, half mockingly, is ... [that] they all pose as if they had discovered and reached their real opinions through self-development of a cold, pure, divinely unconcerned dialectic...; while at bottom it is an assumption, a hunch, indeed a kind of "inspiration"—most often a desire of the heart that has been filtered and made abstract—that they defend with reasons they have sought after the fact. They are all advocates [paid lawyers] who resent that name, and for the most part even wily spokesmen for their prejudices which they baptize "truths".... Gradually it has become clear to me what every great philosophy so far has been: namely, the personal confession of its author and a kind of involuntary and unconscious memoir; also that the moral (or immoral) intentions in every philosophy constituted the real germ of life from which the whole plant had grown.[3]

The apostle Paul teaches us that all unbelievers (including Nietzsche) "suppress the truth in unrighteousness" (Rom. 1:18); they attempt to hide the truth about God from themselves due to their immoral lives. "The carnal mind is enmity against God" (Rom. 8:7) and "minds earthly things" (Phil. 3:18-19). Those who are enemies in their minds due to evil works

(Col. 1:21), and are foolish in their reasoning (Rom. 1:21-22; 1 Cor. 1:20), are led in particular to an anti-biblical metaphysic (e.g., "The fool has said in his heart there is no God," Ps. 10:4)—disguised as an anti-metaphysical posture in general.

The Case Against Metaphysics

The most common philosophical reason advanced by unbelievers, from Kant to the Logical Positivists of our century, for antagonism to metaphysical claims is quite simply the allegation that "pure reason" apart from sense experience cannot itself provide us with factual knowledge. Metaphysical statements speak of a suprasensible reality which is not directly experienced or verified by natural science; it might be said quite baldly, then, that metaphysics is a kind of "news from nowhere." Those antagonistic to metaphysics argue that all informative or factual statements about the objective world must be derived empirically (based on experience, observation, sensation), and therefore human knowledge cannot transcend particular, physical experience or the appearance of the senses.

According to Kant, metaphysical discussions trade in purely verbal definitions and their logical implications; hence they are arbitrary, suspended in the sky, and result in irresolvable disagreements. Metaphysical statements have no real significance. By nature, human knowledge is dependent on the senses, and thus reasoning can never take one to conclusions that apply *outside* the empirical realm.

Logical Positivism

The Logical Positivists intensified Kant's criticism. For them metaphysical claims were not simply empty definitions without significance (without existential referents), they were quite literally *meaningless*. Because metaphysical claims could not be brought to the critical test of sense experience, they were concluded to be senseless.

So then, opponents of metaphysics (and thereby of the theology of the Bible) view metaphysical reasoning as conflicting with empirical science as the one and only way to acquire knowledge. Whereas the scientist arrives at contingent truths about the way things appear to our senses, the metaphysician aims at absolute or necessary truths about the reality which somehow lies behind those appearances. A gulf is posited between the truths of empirical fact (arrived at on the basis of information from the senses) and truths of speculative reason (which could only be arbitrary verbal conventions or organizing concepts that are inapplicable outside the sphere of experience). In that case, according to modern dogma, all meaningful and informative statements about the world were judged to be empirical in nature.

The case against metaphysical claims, then, can be summarized in this fashion:

(1) THERE CANNOT BE A NON-EMPIRICAL SOURCE OF KNOWLEDGE OR INFORMATION ABOUT REALITY, AND

(2) IT IS ILLEGITIMATE TO DRAW INFERENCES FROM WHAT IS EXPERIENCED BY THE SENSES TO WHAT MUST LIE OUTSIDE OF EXPERIENCE.

In short, we can only know as factually significant what we can experience directly with our senses—which nullifies the meaningfulness of metaphysical claims and the possibility of metaphysical knowledge.

Double Standards and Begging the Question

We can begin our response by considering (2) above. We should first ask why it is that metaphysicians (and theologians) should not reason from what is known in sense experience to something lying beyond sensation. After all, isn't this precisely what empirical scientists do from day to day? They continually reason from the seen to the unseen (e.g., talking of subatomic particles, computing gravitational forces, warning against radiation simply on the basis of its effects, prescribing medicine for an unseen infection on the basis of an observed fever, etc.) It certainly appears capricious for those with anti-metaphysical leanings to prohibit the theologian from doing what is allowed to the scientist! Such an inconsistency betrays a mind that has been made up in advance against certain kinds of conclusions about reality. Everybody should be expected to play by the same rules.

Moreover, it is important to notice that (2) above is not really relevant to making a case against biblical metaphysics. Christianity does not view its metaphysical (theological, supernatural) claims as unguided or arbitrary attempts to reason from the seen world to the unseen world—unwarranted projections from nature to what lies beyond it. In the first place, the Christian claims that God created this world to reflect His glory and to be a constant testimony to Him and His character. God also created man as His own image, determined the way in which man would think and learn about the world, and coordinated man's mind and the objective world so that man would unavoidably know the supernatural Creator through the conduit of the created realm. God Himself intended and made it unavoidable that man would learn about the Creator from the world around him. This amounts to God coming to man through the temporal and empirical order, not man groping toward God. This amounts to saying that the natural world is not in itself random and without a clue as to its ultimate meaning, leaving man to arbitrary speculation and metaphysical projections.

Moreover, given the intellectually corrupting effects of man's fall into sin and rebellion against God, man's mind has not been left to know God on the basis of man's own unaided experience and interpretation of the world. God has undertaken to make Himself known to man by means of verbal revelation—using words (chosen by God) which are exactly appropriate for the mind of man (created by God) to come to correct conclusions about His Creator, Judge and Redeemer.

Christian theology is not the result of a self-sufficient exploration of, and argument from man's unaided and brute empirical experience, to a god lying beyond and behind experience. Rather the Christian affirms, on the basis of Scripture's declaration, that our theological tenets rest on the *self-revelation* of the transcendent Creator. Theology does not work from man to God, but from God to man (via infallible, verbal revelation; cf. 2 Peter 1:21).

Therefore, the anti-metaphysical polemic—already seen to be arbitrary and inconsistent—begs the main question. If God as portrayed in the Bible does indeed exist, then there is no reason to preclude the possibility that man who lives in the realm of "nature" can gain a knowledge of the "supernatural." God created and controls all things, according to the Biblical account. Given that perspective, God could certainly bring it about that man learns the truth about Him through both the created order and a set of divinely inspired messages. When the unbeliever contends that nothing in man's temporal, limited, natural experience can provide knowledge of the metaphysical or supernatural, he is simply taking a roundabout way of saying that the Biblical account of a God who makes Himself clearly known in the created order and Scripture is mistaken.

This begging of the question is sometimes veiled from the unbeliever by his tendency to recast the nature of theological truth as man-centered and rooted initially in human, empirical experience. However, the very point in contention between the believer and unbeliever comes down to the claim that Christian teaching is rooted in God's self-disclosure of the truth as found in the world around us and in the written word. There is no reason to think that theology would be intellectually required to be built upon the foundation of human sense experience, unless someone were presupposing in advance that all knowledge must ultimately derive from empirical procedures. But that is the very question at hand. The anti-metaphysical polemic is not a supporting reason for rejecting Christianity; it is simply a rewording of that rejection itself.

Philosophical Self-deception

We are brought, then, to number (1) above, the first and foundational step in the case against metaphysics. What are we to make of the assertion that "all significant knowledge about the objective world is empirical in nature"? The most obvious and philosophically significant reply would be that if the preceding statement were true, then—on the basis of its claim—we could *never know* that it were true. Why? Simply because the statement in question is *not itself* known as the result of empirical testing and experience. Therefore, according to its own strict standards, the statement could not amount to significant knowledge about the objective world. It simply reflects the subjective (perhaps meaningless!) bias of the one who pronounces it. Hence the anti-metaphysician not only has his own preconceived conclusions (presuppositions), but it turns out that he cannot live according to them (cf. Rom. 2:1). On the basis of his own assumptions he *refutes himself* (cf. 2 Tim. 2:25). As Paul put it about those who suppress the truth of God in unrighteousness: "They became futile in their speculations" (Rom. 1:21)!

Further Difficulties

There are other difficulties with the position expressed by (1) as well. We can easily see that it amounts to a presupposition for the unbeliever. What rational basis or evidence is there for the position that all knowledge must be empirical in nature? That is not a conclusion supported by other reasoning, and the premise does not admit of empirical verification since it deals with what is universally or necessarily the case (not a historical or contingent truth). Moreover, the statement itself precludes any other type of verification or support other than empirical warrants or evidence. Thus the anti-metaphysical opponent of the Christian faith holds to this dogma in a presuppositional fashion—as something which controls inquiry, rather than being the result of inquiry.

That anti-metaphysical presupposition, however, has certain devastating results. Notice that if all knowledge must be empirical in nature, then the uniformity of nature cannot be known to be true. And without the knowledge and assurance that the future will be like the past (e.g., if salt dissolved in water on Wednesday, it will do likewise and not explode in water on Friday) we could not draw empirical generalizations and projections—in which case the whole enterprise of natural science would immediately be undermined.

NoPredictability

Scientists could not arrive at even one dependable, rationally warranted conclusion about future chemical interactions, the rotation of the earth, the stability of a bridge, the medicinal effects of a drug, or anything else. Each and every premise that entered into their reasoning about a particular situation at a particular time and in a particular place would need to be individually confirmed in an empirical fashion.

Nothing experienced in the past could become a basis for expectations about how things might happen at present or in the future. Without certain beliefs about the nature of reality and history—beliefs which are supra-empirical in character—the process of empirical learning and reasoning would become impossible.

At this point we can press even harder, arguing that if one presupposes that all knowledge must be empirical in nature, then not only has he undermined science and refuted himself, but he has actually scuttled all argumentation and reasoning. To engage in the evaluation of arguments is to recognize and utilize propositions, criteria, logical relations and rules, etc. However, such things as these (propositions, relations, rules) are not empirical entities which can be discovered by one of the five senses.

According to the dogma of empiricism, it would not make sense to speak of such things—not make sense, for instance, to speak of validity and invalidity in an argument, nor even to talk about premises and conclusions. All you would have would be one contingent electro-chemical event in the physical brain of a scholar followed contingently by another.

If these events are thought to follow a pattern, we must (again) note that on empirical grounds, one does not have a warrant for speaking of such a "pattern"; only particular events are experienced or observed. Moreover, even if there were a pattern within the electro-chemical events of one's brain, it would be accidental and not a matter of attending to the rules of logic. Indeed, the "rules of logic" would at best be personal imperatives expressed as the subjective preference of one person to another. In such a case there is no point to argument and reasoning at all. An electro-chemical event in the brain cannot meaningfully be said to be "valid" or "invalid."

Naturalism versus Supernaturalism as Worldviews

Enough has now been said to make it clear what kind of situation we have when an unbeliever argues against the Christian's claim to knowledge about the "super-natural"—when the unbeliever takes an anti-metaphysical stand against the faith. The believer holds, on the basis of infallible revelation from the transcendent Creator, certain things about unseen reality (e.g., the existence of God, providence, life after death, etc.). Knowledge of such matters is not problematic within the worldview of the Christian: God knows all things, having created everything according to His own wise counsel and determining the individual natures of each thing; further He created man as His own image, capable of thinking His thoughts after Him on the basis of revelation, both general (in nature) and special (in Scripture). Thus man has the rational and spiritual capability to learn and understand truths about reality which transcend his temporal, empirical experience—truths which are disclosed by his Creator. It is evident that the Christian defends the *possibility* of metaphysical knowledge, therefore, by appealing to certain metaphysical truths about God, man, and the world. He reasons presuppositionally, arguing on the basis of *the very metaphysical premises* which the unbeliever claims are *impossible* to know in virtue of their metaphysical nature.

However, the anti-metaphysical unbeliever has his own metaphysical commitments to which he is presuppositionally committed and to which he appeals in his arguments (e.g., only sensible individuals or particulars exist). His materialistic, naturalistic, atheism is taken as a final truth about reality, universally characterizing the nature of existence, directing us how to distinguish appearance from reality, and resting on intellectual considerations which take us beyond simple observation or sense experience. The this-worldly outlook of the unbeliever is *just as much* a metaphysical opinion as the "other-worldly" viewpoint he attributes to the Christian.

What is glaringly obvious, then, is that the unbeliever rests upon and appeals to a metaphysical position in order to prove that there can be no metaphysical position known to be true! He ironically and inconsistently holds that nobody can know metaphysical truths, and yet he himself has enough metaphysical knowledge to declare that Christianity is wrong!

It turns out that two full-fledged presuppositional philosophies stand over against one another when the anti-metaphysician argues with the Christian. The metaphysical claims of Christianity are based on God's self-revelation. Moreover, they are consistent with the assumptions of science, logical reasoning, and the intelligibility of human experience. On the other hand, the unbeliever who claims metaphysical knowledge is impossible reasons on the basis of presuppositions which are arbitrarily applied, self-refuting, unable to pass their own strict requirements, and which undermine science and argumentation—indeed undermine the usefulness of those very empirical procedures which are made the foundation of all knowledge!

This is simply to say that the anti-metaphysical position has as its outcome the total abrogation, not simply of metaphysical knowledge, but of all knowledge whatsoever. In order to argue against the faith, the unbeliever must commit intellectual suicide—destroying the very reasoning which he would feign to use against the truth of God! This is too high a personal and philosophical price to pay for prejudices and presuppositions which one hopes can form a roof to protect him from the revelation of God.

Notes:

[1] Antony Flew writes: "Not surprisingly, many critics have argued that the achievement of some at least of these [metaphysical] aims is in principle impossible. Thus, it has been held that the human mind has no means of discovering facts outside the realm of sense experience.... Another criticism is that since no conceivable experience could enable us to decide between, for example, the statements that reality consists of only one substance (monism) or of infinitely many (monadology), neither serves any purpose in the economy of our thought about the world, and they are alike neither true nor false but meaningless" ("metaphysics" in *A Dictionary of Philosophy*, rev. 2nd ed. New York: St. Martin's Press, 1984, pp. 229-230).

[2] *Metaphysics* (New York: Harcourt, Brace, & World, 1963), p. 12.

[3] *Beyond Good and Evil*, "On the Prejudice of Philosophers," trans. Walter Kaufmann (New York: Vintage Books, 1966), pp. 12, 13.

CHAPTER 32:

THE PROBLEM OF FAITH

Does Christian Commitment Sacrifice Reason?

According to an old, humorous quip: "Faith is believing what you know ain't true." It is not hard to see why this would be said. The tendency for people—whether they believe fantastic claims about UFO visitors or pathetic claims about the honor of a discredited politician—who have meager evidence or reasoning to support their personal convictions is to fall back easily on the claim that they "simply have faith" that what they believe is true,[1] even though there appear to others many good reasons for disbelieving it. People *should* know that what they are saying is not true, and yet they persist in believing it anyway—in the name of "faith."

This conception of faith as blind personal commitment is one of the chief obstacles that stands in the way of unbelievers giving Christianity an honest hearing. They have a fierce and fundamental difficulty in becoming Christians, they imagine, because religious faith would require them to sacrifice reason altogether and blindly trust some purported revelation in an arbitrary, undiscerning fashion.

In his *Dictionary of Philosophy*, Peter Angeles offers as two definitions of "faith" among others: "belief in something despite the evidence against it" and "belief in something even though there is an absence of evidence for it."[2] Given either of these popular understandings of the term—whereby the Christian call to "faith" is conceived of as either contrary to reason or at least without reasons—Christianity does indeed look quite irrational. "Faith" becomes a buzz-word for putting your intellect out of gear, suspending a cautious and critical attitude toward things, and making a personal commitment without sound evidence.

Varieties of Irrationalism

Christianity is charged with irrationality by lots of people, but not all critics mean the same thing. Some distinctions should be drawn for clarity.

Some people pit Christian faith against reason because they feel that the teachings of the Bible are themselves irrational. For instance, some people look upon the idea of God becoming man (the incarnation) as a contradictory notion; for them, the concept of the God-man is incoherent, a violation (allegedly) of some elementary logical laws which all men recognize. When they charge Christianity with being irrational, they mean that its dogmas are illogical in this sense.

Other people believe that there is utterly no empirical (observational) substantiation for certain magnificent historical claims found in the Bible: for instance, that the sun stood still, that Jesus multiplied the loaves, or that men have risen from the dead. If Christian faith calls for affirming these kinds of unfactual matters (as they see them), people will deem it contrary to reason.

The previous two types of critics have wanted to charge Christianity with irrationality because of specific intellectual imperfections within the set of propositions which believers affirm—either logical imperfection or empirical imperfection. These kinds of attacks upon Biblical particulars call for apologists to offer focused answers which deal with the details of each different challenge—at least to do so at the *outset* of responding to such charges by the unbeliever. (Ultimately, presuppositional matters will need to be engaged and discussed, of course.) But our present concern is really with a more devastating version of the claim that Christianity is irrational.

Affirming the Absurd

Much more intellectually vicious is the class of critics who judge the Christian faith to be irrational because they conceive of Christians as dedicated to believing the absurd (for its absurdity). As they see it, religious believers glory in the fact that the object of their faith is without rational support, is apparently untrue, and must be endorsed in the face of good sense and contrary reasons. Some unbelievers have been given the impression—not without the damnable "help" of many modern theologians—that Christianity is indifferent to logic, science, evidence or (even) truth.

Some people have been so misled as to feel that Christians actually elevate the value of one's personal faith in direct proportion to the degree that it must be dubious, blind or mystical.[3] Likewise, it is thought that believers degrade the worth of faith to the extent that it accords well with good reason. In *The Antichrist: Attempt at a Critique of Christianity* (1895), Friederich Nietzsche expressed his derision toward this attitude by saying: "'Faith' means not *wanting* to know what is true."

However, all criticism in this vein flows from a fundamental mistake as to the *nature* of Christian faith. As J. Gresham Machen boldly put the matter in his book, *What is Faith?*, "we believe that Christianity flourishes not in the darkness, but in the light." Machen wrote that "one of the means which the Spirit will use" to bring a revival of the Christian religion "is an awakening of the intellect." He fervently resisted "the false and disastrous opposition which has been set up between knowledge and faith," arguing that "at no point is faith independent of the knowledge upon which it is logically based." Reflecting upon the famous Biblical remark about faith in Hebrews 11:1 ("the evidence of things not seen"), Machen declared: "Faith need not be too humble or too apologetic before the bar of reason; Christian faith is a thoroughly reasonable thing."[4]

Regardless of what certain misguided spokesmen may say—whether enthusiasts, mystics, emotionalists, voluntarists, or fideists—the Bible itself (the sourcebook and standard of Christianity) is not indifferent to logical blunders or factual mistakes. The Christian religion does not pit "faith" against reason, evidence or (above all) truth.

It was just in order to vindicate the truth of his religious claims and conceptions that Moses challenged the magicians of Pharaoh's court, and that Elijah competed with and taunted the priests of Baal on Mount Carmel. The Old Testament prophets knew that their words would be demonstrated to be true when their forecasts or predictions were fulfilled in history for all to see.

When Christ appeared, he himself claimed to be "the Truth"! His resurrection was a mighty sign and wonder, providing evidence for the veracity of His claims and for the apostolic message. Despite what the Jews and Greeks might think to themselves, wrote Paul, the gospel is in fact the very wisdom of God which destroys the arrogance of worldly philosophy (1 Cor. 1:18-25). He said that those who oppose the gospel are the ones who have only a "knowledge falsely so-called" (1 Tim. 6:20).

Because of this attitude Paul was eager to "reason" (dispute, debate) daily in the marketplace with the philosophers at Athens (Acts 17:17-18). He did not hesitate to argue his case before the Athenian tribunal which judged new and controversial teachers, declaring "what you worship displaying your ignorance, I authoritatively declare unto you" (v. 23). He was clearly not promoting the value of absurdities! Indeed, if the cardinal claims of the faith were demonstrably false, Paul would have been compelled to admit that our religious faith is wrong-headed and futile (e.g., 1 Cor. 15:14).

Peter's own attitude, even as an uneducated fisherman, was made unmistakably clear when he asserted with confidence, "we have not followed cunningly devised fables" (2 Peter 1:16)—as well as when he required every believer to be ready to present a *reasoned defense* for the hope that was within him (1 Peter 3:15). Jesus categorically taught of God's word in Scripture: "Thy word is truth" (John 17:17). The Bible's bold perspective maintains that on the great and final day of judgment, the reason men will be condemned by God is that they preferred to believe "a lie" (Rom. 1:25), rather than to trust the claims of God's own Son.

Consequently, when unbelievers repudiate Christianity for its alleged *goal* of religious irrationality, the apologist must decisively correct that mistaken conception. Christian faith does not aim to affirm what is absurd, reveling in irrationality. Such a thought misconstrues the nature of faith as it is presented by the Bible. The Christian notion of faith—unlike most other religions—is not an arbitrary leap of emotion, a blind stab of commitment, a placing of the intellect on hold. For the Christian, faith (or belief) is well-grounded.

Indeed, as Christians we claim that the content of our faith is what any reasonable man should endorse, not only because it completely accords with logic and fact (when they are properly viewed), but also because without the Christian worldview "reason" itself becomes arbitrary or meaningless—becomes unintelligible.

Faith versus Proof

Other opponents of Christian faith, as a further class of critics in addition to those considered in our last study, protest the presence of any attitude of faith (or trust) at all in a person's system of thought. They maintain, arrogantly if not naively, that they will not believe anything which has not first been fully proven to them. They are led by proof, not by faith!

They like to think that theirs is the spirit of Rene Descartes (1596-1650), the French scholar and theoretician of knowledge who became the primary philosopher of "the Age of Reason." Descartes was concerned that men should strive to realize and follow a reliable and proper method for arriving at their beliefs.[5] According to Descartes' way of thinking, this method would be that of doubting and criticizing everything he could, accepting nothing as true which was not clearly recognized as such (things which are self-evident) or which was not completely supported by other clear and distinct, foundational truths.

Descartes sought to doubt every thought that came into his head (e.g., is he really eating an apple or only dreaming that it is so?) until he would come upon something which was indubitable. Systematic doubt would open the door to final certainty for him.[6] Yet Descartes recognized that he could not ultimately doubt everything. The indubitable would turn out to be the stopping-point of his method—and the theoretical starting-point for all other reasoning.

The modern-day apes of Descartes who claim they will doubt absolutely everything and accept nothing except upon proof act or talk like arrogant fools. Nobody can doubt everything. Nobody. If a person were truly to doubt everything—his memory of past experiences, his present sensations, the "connections" between experiences, the meanings of his words, the principles by which he reasons—he would not be "thinking" at all (much less doubting), and there would be no "he" to think or not to think. A fundamental (logically basic) set of beliefs—a faith—is inescapable for anyone.

Men only succeed in deluding themselves when they say that they will not accept anything without proof or demonstration—that they allow no place for "faith" in their outlook or in the living of their lives. Accordingly, such unbelievers who criticize Christians for appealing to "faith" are intellectual hypocrites—men who cannot and do not live by their own declared standards for reasoning.

"No Assumptions" Makes No Sense

The attitude which feigns that there ought to be no element within Christian commitment which has not been independently proven is illustrated by the statement of C. Gore: "It seems to me that the right course for anyone who cannot accept the mere voice of authority, but feels the imperative obligation to 'face the arguments' and to think freely, is to begin at the beginning and to see how far he can reconstruct his religious beliefs stage by stage on a secure foundation, as far as possible without any preliminary assumptions...."[7] Here we are told to examine the religious hypothesis from the beginning without preliminary assumptions—without presuppositions.

Of course, this is quite literally impossible. A complete demonstration of each of our beliefs by means of other independent beliefs cannot be given. When I demonstrate the truth that ice melts at room temperature, I press into service certain standards and procedures of demonstration. But the question can be asked whether I have chosen the correct criteria to use for demonstrating my conclusion. Further, can I be sure that I have properly used the chosen procedures and standards? In order to proceed "without assumptions," I would need to demonstrate that my methods of demonstration are the correct ones and that my execution of these methods was faultless. *But* that will call for *further* argumentation or proof *about* the *proof* used for the veracity and validity of my original demonstration. And on and on we would go.

If there can be no assumed starting point for a demonstration, then no demonstration can get started—or finished, depending upon how you look at it.

If an unbeliever considers Christianity to be irrational simply on the basis that it allows for something to be accepted without independent demonstration, then the unbeliever in question is unrealistic and must be pressed to see that he ends up refuting *himself* (not simply Christians) in terms of such values and demands. Thus *his* unbelieving attitude turns out to be the truly *irrational* attitude, for it inconsistently requires something of its opponents which it does not live up to itself. Such an attitude would make knowledge of anything whatsoever impossible for finite and faulty creatures—and thus shows itself to be supremely unreasonable.

The Kind of Evidence on Which Faith Rests

The problem with Christian faith, then, cannot be that it involves presuppositional commitments. So we move on to consider one last category of unbelievers who criticize Christian "faith" as irrational. These critics acknowledge that believers have evidence and reasoning which they enlist in support of their beliefs, and they admit that nobody—not even religious skeptics—can proceed intellectually without assumptions nor prove *everything* they believe by independent considerations. What they object to, however, is the *kind* of evidence to which Christians appeal and the *kind* of presuppositions in terms of which they reason. To put it briefly: they object to the idea of believing something *on the basis of God's personal authority*, rather than on the basis of impersonal and universally accepted norms of observation, logic, utility, etc.

Christians may have evidence, then, for their faith, but it is completely the wrong kind of evidence, says the unbeliever. For instance, in his candidly titled book *Religion without Revelation*, Julian Huxley says: "I believe firmly that the scientific method, although slow and never claiming to lead to complete truth, is the only method which in the long run will give satisfactory foundations for beliefs," and "we quite assuredly at present *know* nothing beyond this world and natural experience."[8] For Huxley, Christian faith should not be grounded in revealed authority (since all metaphysical knowledge is precluded by decree), but in the authority of natural science.

What Huxley openly displays here is his own faith-commitment with its prejudice against Christianity. Having said on the one hand that the scientific method cannot give the *complete* truth, he turned around on the other hand and, based on the authority of the alleged scientific method, *completely* ruled out knowing anything beyond the natural world! Why does Huxley count out the *kind* of evidence offered by Christians for their faith (revelation from God)? Because of his *own faith* and devotion to natural science.

In *God and Philosophy*, Antony Flew likewise expresses the unbeliever's criticism of Christian faith for resting upon authority. "An appeal to authority here cannot be allowed to be final and overriding. For what is in question precisely is the status and authority of all religious authorities.... [It is] inherently impossible for either faith or authority to serve as themselves the ultimate credentials of revelation."[9] The teaching of Scripture cannot be accepted on the authority of God speaking therein, says Flew, because it is precisely that authority which is under question by the unbeliever.

This can only mean, then, that Flew has determined in advance that God cannot be the *ultimate* authority. For him, there must always be something independent of God which is more authoritative and in terms of which the authority of God can be accepted. Nor can God's authority be inescapable and *self-validating*, according to Flew: "the philosopher examining a concept is not at that time himself employing it; however much he may at other times wish and need to do so."[10]

Does Flew really pretend that he himself as a philosopher strictly and purely adheres to this general prerequisite—that we may not examine something while simultaneously employing it? This is simply not so, and Flew should know better. Those who *examine* and argue about logic simultaneously *employ* that same logic in their examinations. Those who *examine* and evaluate the powers and reliability of the eyeball simultaneously *employ* their eyeballs. To wave off and automatically preclude the possibility that Christians could examine and argue about the authority of God's revelation while simultaneously employing (assuming, applying) the authority of God's revelation is little more than arbitrary prejudice on Flew's part.

Flew simply will not permit the thought that God's authority is *self-*validating. What is remarkable about his or any other unbeliever's refusal to submit in faith to God's authority *on the basis of that very authority* is that he thereby only discloses that he is committed *in advance against* Christian teaching. That is, it reveals an obvious and personal faith commitment to the proposition that there cannot be a God who speaks with a voice of inescapable, ultimate, self-validating authority over man and his thinking.[11]

God cannot have this kind of final authority for Flew, but only such an authority which will first be *authorized* by the reasoning of man. In the long run Flew and other unbelievers insist that man must not be reduced to bowing in abject dependence upon his Creator as the final authority. There can be *other* self-validating authorities acknowledged or entertained as a possibility, but *not God*. They will tolerate the Creator in their thinking only on the terms dictated by the *creature*—notably that He never confront men with the rational inescapability and ultimate authority of their *Creator*!

As Van Til observes: "The natural man then assumes that he has the final criterion of truth *within himself*. Every form of authority that comes to him must justify itself by standards inherent in man and operative *apart from* the authority that speaks."[12] Elsewhere he had noted that "If we must determine the foundations of the authority, we no longer accept authority on authority."[13] This is just to say that God cannot be permitted by the unbeliever to be and to speak *as God*—to be the ultimate and self-authenticating authority. Such a position and privilege will be assigned by the unbeliever to something else, something which is part of the creation (such as man's reasoning, experience)[14] and thus is implicitly treated as an idol. "They worshipped and served the creature rather than the Creator" (Rom. 1:25).

The bottom line, then, is that to criticize the Christian's irrational "faith" is itself nothing more than to express a different religious faith—a faith which in one way or another adopts the ultimate authority and self-sufficiency of the human mind and reasoning. *That* is irrational "faith" indeed, given the sad experience and history of mankind—as well as the unresolved, rational tensions within autonomous science and philosophy.

Notes:

[1] People who speak this way seem oblivious to the trivial or tautological character of such a claim. To "have faith" that something is true (e.g., that Elvis is alive and residing in Idaho) is the same as "believing" that the claim in question is true; these are different semantic ways of expressing the same thing. Accordingly, when a person says he "believes" something "simply on faith" (without specifying further), he has merely told us that "he believes because he believes."

I am not unaware that many religious people, including philosophers who reflect upon religious issues, think of "faith" as being in another category from "believing." The former is supposed to be a personal matter of trust or commitment, while the latter is a matter of intellect. For instance, in an essay entitled "Faith and Belief," the Oxford philosopher, H. H. Price, asserted: "Faith, then, is something very unlike belief 'that' and certainly not reducible to it nor definable in terms of it.... Surely when a person is actually in the faith attitude, he would never say he believed that God loves him. It is rather that he *feels* God's love for him.... It does not seem to be a matter of believing at all" (*Faith and the Philosophers*, ed. John Hick [New York: St. Martin's Press, 1964], p. 11). Such verbal stipulations may be made and often are, I realize, but it would require a heroic effort to bring such a conceptual distinction into verbal conformity with the New Testament use of the Greek verb "*pisteuo*" and noun "*pistis*."

[2] Peter A. Angeles, *Dictionary of Philosophy* (New York: Barnes & Noble, 1981), p. 94.

[3] Cf. "Doubt, as the dark side of the cognitive aspect of faith, is an essential ingredient for faith.... A lively mind stands in *Angst* at the crossroads daily, and daily makes a choice, making it, as Kierkegaard would say, 'in fear and trembling.'" Geddes MacGregor, *Philosophical Issues in Religious Thought* (Boston: Houghton Mifflin, 1973), p. 239.

[4] J. Gresham Machen, *What is Faith?* (Grand Rapids: Wm. B. Eerdmans Publishing, 1925), pp. 18, 26, 94, 243.

[5] What about their beliefs *about proper method*, then? Are *these* beliefs also arrived at by means of that proper method? If so, they have no independent (non-question-begging) authority or foundation! If not, then what has been deemed the proper method for arriving at beliefs is not foundational, after all.

[6] Descartes felt that his method brought him finally to the indubitable and foundational truth that he himself existed. Even if everything else he believed was an illusion, he at least needed to exist in order to do the doubting in the first place. Thus the famous dictum: "I think, therefore I am." But Descartes was here not scrupulous enough as a philosopher. By taking as his premise "I think," he had already begged the question of his existence (asserting the "I"). This was no more helpful, really, than arguing: "I stink, therefore I exist." Descartes should have more stringently premised only that "Thinking is occurring"—from which it does *not* logically follow that "I exist."

[7] C. Gore, *Belief in God* (New York: Penguin, 1939), p. 12.

[8] Julian Huxley, *Religion without Revelation* (New York: Mentor, 1957), pp. 15, 17.

[9] Antony Flew, *God and Philosophy* (New York: Harcourt, Brace and World, 1966), pp. 159, 161.

[10] Ibid, p. 26.

[11] Part of the self-validating (self-authenticating) character of that authoritative revelation is that without it, reasoning and science and ethics become unintelligible, philosophically speaking. God's authority is necessary to the (subordinate) intellectual authority and usefulness of those very principles which unbelievers propose to use in testing God's authority. Nobody can utilize reasoning without simultaneously, even if implicitly and without acknowledging it, employing the outlook of God's revelation. Thus Christian claims about the self-validating character of God's revelation are not merely subjective testimony or beyond rational discussion or demonstration.

[12] Cornelius Van Til, *The Defense of the Faith* (Philadelphia: Presbyterian and Reformed, 1955), pp. 145.

[13] Ibid, p. 49.

[14] Note well that "reason" is here criticized as an authority or standard (which stands above God in judgment), but *not* at all as a tool or instrument (which is used under God for His glory). Of course the unbeliever must use his reasoning ability in hearing, weighing and (hopefully) adopting the claims of God's word. This does not mean that the controlling norm by which he uses his reasoning must be reason itself. (In such discussions, it would be good to ask just exactly what is meant by "reason.")

CHAPTER 33:

THE PROBLEM OF
RELIGIOUS LANGUAGE

Is God-talk Even Meaningful?

In philosophical circles during much of the twentieth century, two issues which have dominated discussions in philosophy of religion—and thus two of the most popular polemics against the intellectual credibility of Christian commitment—have centered on the meaningfulness of religious discourse.

Religious discourse involves *talk* about God, immortality, miracles, salvation, prayer, values, ethics, etc. To speak of the existence or attributes of God, for example, is to make religious *utterances*. All religions which are promulgated publicly must in some measure use religious discourse. And Christians in particular engage extensively in utterances concerning God and their faith; after all, Christianity is preeminently a religion of verbal revelation from God and personal profession of faith. Thus Christians are always talking "religiously"—in sermons, prayers, confessions, didactic lessons, catechisms, personal testimonies, songs, exclamations, counsel and encouragement, etc.

The challenge made by many modern philosophers has been that talk of this kind is not really meaningful (in any cognitive sense), even if it has the deceptive appearance of being so. For years and years and years it may have seemed that when Christians used language about God and salvation, it was possible to make pretty good sense out of what they were saying. Not everybody believed that what Christians would utter was *true*, of course, but the God-talk of believers was at least thought to make (or entail) assertions which carried rationally intelligible, if not also spiritually intoxicating, meaning. But not so, according to many philosophers of recent vintage.

Worse Than False

The magnitude of the charge which has been made against the intelligibility of Christianity must be appreciated by believers. When philosophers claim that God-talk is *meaningless*, they are saying something far stronger and far more devastating than that talk about God is *false*. Their criticism is that religious utterances do not even qualify to be false (or true) because they do not amount to talk that makes cognitive sense—that aims to convey information—in the first place. (Think about it this way: it is one thing to criticize the Chicago Cubs for not *winning* the 1991 pennant, and altogether another thing to charge that the Cubs were not even a *baseball team* to begin with.)

Thus religious language, many would charge, is simply meaningless. "It snowed in Dallas last summer" is a sentence which is meaningful, but false. It makes a cognitively meaningful claim which happens to be in error. However, "Sum last dallies snow" makes no intelligible claim at all, but is simply meaningless (on any ordinary reading), conveying nothing which could be true *or* false.

Many critics of Christianity claim that its utterances, similarly, are not subject to being either true or false. They make no significant claims about the world (or about the world of human experience anyway). Thus they are cognitively meaningless, in one of the following ways.

The utterance of an exclamation like "Ouch!" is neither true nor false (it does not claim that anything is the case), but merely *expressive* in linguistic function. Many have maintained that religious language should be interpreted in the same way, as emotive talk rather than informative.

Others have gone further. For them, talk about God makes absolutely *no practical difference* to a person's observations of, or operations upon, the physical world. That is, the claims made by religious believers and the counterclaims made by their opponents have no distinct, conflicting cash-value in the public domain. Believers and unbelievers perceive and do the very same things. Accordingly, their respective interpretations or explanations of what they perceive and do are taken as quite meaningless—a difference which "makes no difference." Empty talk.

Others have gone even further than that. Religious discourse is for them simply unintelligible, like *superstitious gibberish* which cannot be rationally translated. When people talk about God, the after-life, miracles or salvation, they are engaging in a kind of linguistic ritual which is learned by imitation and passed along without cognitive understanding. That explains why the uninitiated—unbelievers—cannot have religious utterances "put in their own language," do not "catch on," do not feel intellectually compelled to affirm what believers say, and indeed care very little about it anyway. It is just meaningless babble.

(1) Verificationism

As indicated above, the meaningfulness of religious language has come under attack in philosophical circles in *two ways* during this century. We need to look at each one of them. The first can be designated the "verificationist" challenge to religious discourse, and the second designated the "falsificationist" challenge. Neither has proven successful.

In the earlier part of this century a school of thought known as logical positivism zealously promoted empirical science and disparaged any kind of metaphysics. According to the positivists, any proposition could be tested for meaningfulness by applying to it the "verification principle."

Logical positivism acknowledged two different kinds of meaningful sentences. Certain sentences in a language will be known to be true simply by means of analyzing them logically and linguistically (for instance: "all bachelors are unmarried" can be verified by reference to laws of logic and semantic definitions). However, such truths (called "analytical") are devoid of significant information about the world of experience or observation, and thus are trivial. For a sentence to tell us something interesting or have a factual component to it, its truth must be verifiable by looking beyond logic and meaning to one's observations or experiences in the world. Thus a significant (non-trivial) sentence is meaningful, according to the verificationist, only if it can be empirically confirmed; its truth or falsity would make a difference in our experience of the world. Meaningful sentences should be translatable either into observation terms alone (descriptions of immediate experience) or into a procedure used to confirm the sentence empirically.

The effect of applying the verification principle, the positivists concluded, would be the dismissal of all metaphysical claims (including theology) and all ethical claims as non-sense from a scientific standpoint. Since the religious language of Christians is filled with terms which are not taken from observation (e.g., God, omnipotence, sin, atonement) and claims for which there is no empirical means of confirmation (e.g., God is triune, Jesus intercedes for the saints), logical positivism's verification principle seemed to rule out the meaningfulness of what Christians said.

What's Sauce for the Goose is Sauce for the Gander

As it turns out, though, the effect of applying the verification principle of meaningfulness was much different than what the logical positivists had envisioned and intended. The result of applying the verification criterion across the board was, in fact, more than embarrassing to the critics of religious language.

You see, the logical positivist—just like the Christian—holds a particular view of the world, man, and reality as a whole. And this outlook leads the logical positivist—just like the Christian—to endorse and follow certain standards or rules for human behavior and reasoning. For the logical positivist, there is no supernatural reality, and man is simply one more random component of the physical world (though amazingly—almost miraculously!—complex). Given this outlook, men are obliged to live and speak in a certain way. Talk about persons, things or events which transcend the physical world must be forbidden; such talk must not even be countenanced as meaningful.

On the other hand, the Christian—as we have indicated—also has convictions about the nature of reality (e.g., God is a spirit who created the world) in terms of which men are obliged to live and speak in a certain way (e.g., offering praise to their Maker for all things, not talking as though there is anything more certain or authoritative as Him, etc.).

The logical positivist and the Christian both have worldviews, to put it briefly. Now, is it possible that the verification principle could disqualify the meaningfulness of the Christian's worldview as a worldview and *not do equal damage* to *the positivist's* worldview *as a worldview* as well? Not at all. As strictly empirical as the logical positivist may wish to be (sticking close to observational particulars), even he cannot escape using philosophical notions or abstract principles in his reasoning and theorizing.

The key component in the verificationist challenge to religious language was naturally the verification principle itself. This standard or rule was crucial to the worldview of the logical positivist. Accordingly, the Christian apologist must ask whether the verification principle itself is either (1) a trivial truth of logic and semantics, or (2) a sentence which can be empirically confirmed. Clearly, the answer is no to both options—in which case, the verificationist challenge to Christianity undermines *itself* (if it undermines anything).

This reply to the verification principle, used as a weapon against religious language and the intelligibility of Christianity in particular, reveals that verificationism was nothing but a rationalization of religious prejudice. And this prejudice against God-talk was so openly foolish that it self-destructed; it ruled out *its own* meaningfulness along the way.

The Dedicated Faith of the Positivist

For all his intellectual hostility to religion and Christianity, the verificationist was clearly just as "religious" in his devotion to his underlying presuppositions as was any devotee of Christianity.

For logical positivism, the practice of natural science, with its impressive results, was perfectly acceptable just the way it is; its authority and supremacy were taken for granted—in the same way that the Christian takes the Bible's ultimate authority for granted. Natural science did not call for critical appraisal and possible correction or reform, any more than the Christian thinks the Bible has errors to be rectified. Instead, according to logical positivism, the only thing natural science required was to have its empirical basis elucidated—which the verification principle attempted to do. Likewise, the Christian simply feels that the Bible needs to be elucidated and explained, for its value and truth should be obvious to any honest hearer.

Logical positivism was, ironically, very much like a religious faith— a faith in natural science (which might be called "scientism"). This became very apparent when the positivist attempt to elucidate the strictly empirical foundation of natural science came to grief over the self-refuting character of the verification principle. When the elucidation failed, the logical positivist did not relinquish his original faith in natural science at all. He acted like a "true believer." He held on to that commitment to science, regardless of its philosophical problems.

Of course, this dedicated faith of the logical positivist in natural science had not been acquired through the rigorous application of anything like the scientific method. Commitment to the foremost authority of natural science was not scientifically founded. It was a personal leap of faith.

Too Restrictive While Too Inclusive

The other embarrassing thing about using the verification principle to challenge the meaningfulness of any language about metaphysics, theology or ethics was that the principle was simultaneously too narrow *and yet* too broad!

First, it was too narrow or restrictive because it ruled out sentences which any reasonable man, even positivists, would be willing to assert as meaningful (such as "There is a past," "Every person has a mother").

Moreover, the verification principle would have resulted in judging the intended result of natural science—the darling of the logical positivists!—to be meaningless. It is characteristic of natural science to aim to make universally quantified statements (such as "All whales are mammals") or to generalize laws which are likewise universal in character (such as "In all cases, water expands upon freezing"). Because of their universal character, however, no such statement can be fully verified by any finite person or finite group of researchers. In that case, scientific generalizations would fall into the limbo of meaninglessness.

It also proved impossible for dedicated logical positivists to successfully reduce even the simplest observation sentences completely to reports of sense-data. "An apple is on the table" became something akin to "A set of qualities [a, b, c...] is at x;y;z [three-dimension specifications] at t [temporal specification]." Even Rudolf Carnap's famous efforts to perform this kind of reductionistic translation were left encumbered with the language of logic and math (e.g., "sets") and language about location (e.g., "is at") which were undefined and alien expressions which did not express sense-data.

Thus the verification principle did not in the end prove friendly to those advocating it since it ruled out expressions and generalizations they would have wanted to retain as meaningful. Logical positivists have a dedicated faith in natural science, and yet their own verification principle would have rendered the program, procedures, and results of natural science meaningless. In a conspicuous way, the verification principle became unreasonably restrictive for the positivist.

On the other hand, though, there was a sense in which the verification principle proved embarrassingly open-ended, allowing *too many* expressions the privileged status of qualifying as meaningful. This rendered it unreasonably inclusive.

A. J. Ayer was perhaps the best known logical positivist in the English world. In the first edition of his famous book, *Language, Truth and Logic,* Ayer maintained that a sentence is meaningful when, in conjunction with other premises, an observation statement can be deduced which could not have been derived from the other premises alone.[1] This was entirely unhelpful. With a little imagination, a logician could use this criterion and show that *any* statement whatsoever can pass the test[2]—in which case Ayer's criterion of verifiability allows *all* statements to count as meaningful!

Keeping the Faith

It will not surprise the reader that Ayer attempted to remedy this situation by *revising* the verifiability criterion in the second edition of his famous book. This maneuvering reveals that Ayer was not a disinterested scholar, seeking in some neutral fashion to follow the evidence wherever it happened to lead. He had a particular conclusion in mind from the outset, thus desiring to shape and revise his espoused principles until they would (hopefully) prove what he originally wanted. Unbelievers are not very subtle about letting their own religious prejudices or presuppositions show. *They too* "keep the faith"!

Ayer now allowed for statements to be verified *either* directly or indirectly. But more importantly, he further prescribed that *the premises* which are conjoined with any test statement to deduce a further observation statement must include only observation statements, analytical truths, or independently verifiable statements.[3] This did not help. On Ayer's revised approach, a clever logician can still show any test statement whatsoever or its negation to be verifiable (directly or indirectly)[4]—thus rendering *all* statements once again meaningful.

What we find, then is that "verificationism" simply could not state its own position cogently. The verification principle of cognitive meaning was self-defeating; further, it was simultaneously too restrictive and yet too inclusive. Accordingly, verificationism was never in a position to successfully challenge the meaningfulness of religious discourse.

(2) Falsificationism

The second way in which unbelieving philosophers have attempted to criticize the meaningfulness of religious language in the twentieth century can be called "falsificationism." The falsificationists were dedicated to the authority of natural science, just like the logical positivists. However, the falsificationists were painfully aware of the failure of the logical positivists to formulate cogently, or save themselves from the fatal application of, the verification principle of meaning.

Still, they wanted to guard the honorific position of natural science and distinguish it clearly from disreputable ways of thinking, such as superstition, magic, metaphysics and religion. The language of religion (etc.), according to the falsificationist, does not belong to the domain of "genuine science." Science is tied to an empirical basis or procedural commitment which does not characterize religion. Upon analysis, the falsificationist said, the religious talk of believers was ultimately meaningless.

For the falsificationist, what makes genuine science "scientific" is that the theories which it will affirm are in principle *falsifiable* by means of empirical methods. This is a necessary condition for a truly scientific approach to what rational men will believe. Accordingly, if some theory or claim is not empirically falsifiable, this defect alone is sufficient to dismiss it as being cognitively meaningless. A meaningful claim in science must be, according to the falsificationist, subject to refutation (in theory). This does not mean that scientific claims must be refuted in order to be "scientific" (which would make all scientific claims false by definition!)—but that they must be empirically *refutable* in some conceivable circumstance.

The great advantage of taking this approach, if you advocate the supremacy of natural science and its procedures, is that the generalizations after which the scientist aspires (e.g., "all planets rotate around an axis") are not ruled out as meaningless by virtue of their not being fully verifiable. The generalizations of natural science, even those which are true, will always be open to refutation or falsification (e.g., just in case we ever find a planet that does not rotate around an axis). No longer is the incompleteness of induction a strike against the meaningfulness or scientific character of an empirical generalization concerning the natural world.

Flew's Famous Challenge

Perhaps the best known critique of religious language in the second half of the twentieth century came from the witty pen of the English philosopher, Antony Flew, and attacked the meaningfulness of religious discourse from the perspective of falsificationism. Flew made his point by rehearsing a parable once told by John Wisdom, then commenting upon the defect of theological utterances which the parable illustrated:

> Once upon a time two explorers came upon a clearing in the jungle. In the clearing were growing many flowers and many weeds. One explorer says, 'Some gardener must tend this plot'. The other disagrees, "There is no gardener'. So they pitch their tents and set a watch. No gardener is ever seen. 'But perhaps he is an invisible gardener.' So they set up a barbed-wire fence. They electrify it. They patrol with bloodhounds.... But no shrieks ever suggest that some intruder has received a shock. No movements of the wire ever betray an invisible climber. The bloodhounds never give cry. Yet still the Believer is not convinced. 'But there is a gardener, invisible, intangible, insensible to electric shocks, a gardener who has no scent and makes no sound, a gardener who comes secretly to look after the garden which he loves.' At last the Sceptic despairs, 'But what remains of your original assertion? Just how does what you call an invisible, intangible, eternally elusive gardener differ from an imaginary gardener or even from no gardener at all?'[5]

Having told the story, Flew continued with his commentary in sharp criticism of religious language: Someone may dissipate his assertion completely without noticing that he has done so. A fine brash hypothesis may thus be killed by inches, the death by a thousand qualifications.

> And in this, it seems to me, lies the peculiar danger, the endemic evil, of theological utterance....
> For if the utterance is indeed an assertion, it will necessarily

be equivalent to a denial of the negation of that assertion. And
anything which would count against the assertion, or which
would induce the speaker to withdraw it and to admit that it
had been mistaken, must be part of (or the whole of) the meaning of the negation of that assertion.... And if there is nothing
which a putative assertion denies then there is nothing which
it asserts either: and so it is not really an assertion.[6]

Flew was suspicious of religious discourse because he noticed that
believers tend to hold on securely to their convictions, even when they
are aware of apparent counter-evidence to those beliefs. They qualify
and defend, then qualify and defend some more. It begins to look as
though they would guard their theological claims against any and all objections or rebuttals. But if so, that would make religious convictions
impervious to falsification—would render the religious language compatible with every conceivable state of affairs in the world. Since God-talk
would not amount to denying anything, there would be nothing intellectually at stake in theological utterances. And thus, being unfalsifiable,
they would not amount to genuine or meaningful assertions in the first
place, suggested Flew. This is the problem with religious language.

Are Strong Convictions As Such Non-cognitive?
Many subsequent writers who have reflected upon Flew's criticism
of the meaningfulness of religious discourse have observed in one way or
another that he failed to distinguish adequately between a *proposition*
logically resisting falsification and the *person* who believes that proposition psychologically resisting its falsification.
A proposition or linguistic claim which is *logically* compatible with
any and all states of affairs could, indeed, be said to resist falsification; as
Flew properly observed, in theory nothing could then conceivably contradict the proposition. It should be judged to be vacuous. But a person
can resist being *persuaded* that his belief has been falsified by
counter-evidence, *even when* the proposition he believes logically contra-
dicts (rules out) certain states of affairs. He should be simply judged to be
tenacious.
Flew confused a characteristic of human behavior (diligently defending one's beliefs) with a conceptual characteristic of some linguistic utter-

Polemic— art of disputation

ances (logically never needing a defense). And in so doing, he apparently did not notice that his polemic against "religious" discourse was in fact a polemic against all "committed" discourse—the utterances and linguistic responses of people who maintain certain beliefs dogmatically.

If we think about it for a moment, it is obvious that people can and do hold strong convictions about a number of things, not simply religious topics (narrowly understood). Sometimes beliefs about historical events are fervently propounded and defended (for instance, that Lee Harvey Oswald did not act alone in assassinating President Kennedy). Sometimes beliefs about scientific matters are zealously championed (for instance, that silicone breast implants do not cause cancer, etc.). Just about any kind of belief can be held tenaciously and defended at great lengths—from auto mechanics to family honor. Part of what it means to say that people hold their convictions "strongly" is precisely that they *resist* having those convictions refuted. Does that imply the conviction must be non-cognitive?

Now then, scientists often display intellectual stubbornness with respect to their theories about the natural world. They can be quite committed to the conclusions they have reached and published. When evidence or reasoning is urged contrary to their views, they defend or qualify those views, and many times "dig in their heels" against refutation.[7] This is *not* usually taken as a mark that their scientific theories must be vacuous of any significant claim about the world—thus, being cognitively meaningless. It is usually just taken as a mark of a deep-seated belief about which they are strongly persuaded (or at least personally motivated). The logical status of the belief in question is not affected by the personal demeanor of the individual propounding or defending it (that is, the degree of his readiness to abandon the belief).

Since natural scientists—and anybody who has strong convictions about anything at all—behave the very same way that religious believers do, then Flew's criticism of the cognitive meaningfulness of religious language would, in fairness, need to be applied to the language of natural science as well. Scientific discourse which resists refutation, as it often does, would be consigned to the status of cognitive meaninglessness. That is not what Flew intended to accomplish! Indeed, in terms of any subject matter at all, the *only* "meaningful" discourse, according to Flew's line of thought, would be the discourse of those who are tentative, doubtful, or unsure of themselves—which is surely an unreasonable assessment.

The One-By-One Myth

Antony Flew's commentary upon the parable of the invisible gardener gains its persuasiveness from the myth that the beliefs held by people are accepted or rejected against the empirical evidence in a one-by-one fashion. That is, it is thought (erroneously) that we observationally test and rationally evaluate only one individual belief at a time. Supposedly the scientifically directed scholar takes a single proposition as *isolated* from every other proposition he would assert to be true, and then compares it to the empirical evidence which is available (as though the relevance and strength of such evidence are independently and indisputably established in advance).

This is, however, not at all an accurate description of the way in which people actually come to beliefs or test them against the empirical evidence. Moreover, from a conceptual standpoint, the picture of one-by-one scrutinizing of beliefs for empirical falsification is entirely artificial and impossible.

The beliefs which people hold are always connected to *other* beliefs by relations pertaining to linguistic meaning, logical order, evidential dependence, causal explanation, indexical and self conceptions, etc. To assert "I see a ladybug on the rose" is to affirm and assume a *number* of things simultaneously—some rather obvious (e.g., about the usage of English words, one's personal identity, a perceptual event, categories of bugs and flowers, physical relations), others more subtle (e.g., about one's linguistic, entomological, and botanical competence, the normalcy of one's eyes and brain-stem, theories of light refraction, shared grammar and semantics, the reality of the external world, laws of logic, etc.).

The network of *all* these beliefs together encounters the tribunal of any empirical experience.[8] When a conflict is detected between this network of beliefs and empirical experience, all we know is that *some kind* of adjustment in one's beliefs will need to be made to restore order or consistency. But there is no way to determine in advance *what specific change* a person will choose to make in order to eliminate the conflict within his thinking.

If Sam says that he saw a ladybug on the rose, but his friends all say that they saw no ladybug, which of his beliefs will he surrender? There are any *number* of possibilities. Maybe his friends do not know the difference between aphids and ladybugs. Maybe there was a spot on his glasses. Maybe the lighting was not right. Maybe he does not understand the use of the English word "rose." Maybe his friends are on drugs. Maybe they were looking at a different rose. Maybe the ladybug quickly flew away. Maybe he is dreaming. Maybe our senses deceive us. Maybe only the "pure of heart" can see gentle ladybugs, and his friends are perverse.... There are so many possibilities for correcting previous assumptions, ranging from what will seem reasonable to what seems to be fanatic or extreme. The point is simply that it is ambiguous or unclear just what the counter-evidence to Sam's remark will turn out to falsify.

Remember the story of the psychiatrist who was treating a man who believed that he was dead. Counseling the poor man about his neurosis seemed to get nowhere. Finally one day the psychiatrist decided to use an empirical test to convince the patient of his error. He asked the man whether dead men bleed, to which the man said no. At that point the psychiatrist pricked the man's finger with a pin and told the man to look and see: he was bleeding, so he could not be dead. To this the patient responded that he must, then, have been wrong: dead men *do* bleed after all! The psychiatrist in this joke mistakenly thought that the bleeding finger would be counter-evidence that would falsify one particular belief of the patient (viz., that he was dead), when in fact it was equally possible that it falsified a related belief instead (viz., that dead men do not bleed).

Since empirical experience or evidence never decisively falsifies any particular belief within a person's network of convictions, it turns out that it is possible (even if it seems unreasonable to others) that a person can choose to treat *any* of his beliefs—about anything whatsoever—as central convictions relative to which any other belief should first be surrendered when counter-evidence is offered. That is, given the fact that a whole network of beliefs, rather than isolated individual beliefs, meet the test of observational evidence, then any belief *may* be treated as unfalsifiable. This is a characteristic of all beliefs. Falsifiability is not inherently a feature of any specific belief or a belief on any specific subject. It is as true of "religious" beliefs (narrowly understood) as it is of beliefs about the natural world.

The falsificationist does not successfully relegate religious language to the disgrace of meaninglessness, unless it is at the cost of consigning *all* discourse to the same disgrace. While there may be something wrong or fanatical about the particular *way* in which a believer guards his convictions from refutation, that fact still does not impugn the meaningfulness of his religious *language*. It is simply the language of strong conviction and firmly entrenched belief—the language of presupposition.

Flew Too Has His Presuppositions

Every thinker grants preferred status to *some* of his beliefs and the linguistic assertions which express them. These privileged convictions are "central" to his "web of beliefs," being treated as immune from revision—until the network of convictions itself is altered.[9] These central beliefs have cognitive significance (i.e., are not simply stipulated truths in virtue of definitions and logic), and yet they resist empirical falsification to one degree or another (depending on how fixed and central they are in the system).[10] The reality of human nature and behavior should be recognized: our thoughts, reasoning and conduct are governed by presuppositional convictions which are matters of deep personal concern, which are far from vacuous or trivial, and to which we intend to intellectually cling and defend "to the end."

As irreligious as Antony Flew is as a person, he too has fundamental commitments to which he "religiously" adheres. He attempts to bring his thinking and living into line with these personal presuppositions—which means that, when faced with what appears to be counter-evidence, he will qualify and defend the language by which he expresses those presuppositions. He treats utterances about them as unfalsifiable! As pointed out by John Frame, "both Flew and the Christian are in the same boat." Each have their presuppositions for which they believe there is extensive evidence, and each would make extensive changes within their respective systems of thought to guard those presuppositions—those heart commitments and life-governing convictions—from refutation.

Frame illustrates this by means of a clever parody which reverses the point of Flew's famous parable:

> Once upon a time two explorers came upon a clearing in the jungle. A man was there, pulling weeds, applying fertilizer, trimming branches. The man turned to the explorers and introduced himself as the royal gardener. One explorer shook

his hand and exchanged pleasantries. The other ignored the gardener and turned away: "There can be no gardener in this part of the jungle," he said; "this must be some trick." They pitch camp. Every day the gardener arrives, tends the plot. Soon the plot is bursting with perfectly arranged blooms. "He's only doing it because we're here—to fool us into thinking this is a royal garden." The gardener takes them to a royal palace, introduces the explorers to a score of officials who verify the gardener's status. Then the sceptic tries a last resort: "Our senses are deceiving us. There is no gardener, no blooms, no palace, no officials. It's still a hoax!" Finally the believer despairs: "But what remains of your original assertion? Just how does this mirage, as you call it, differ from a real gardener?"[11]

Like the challenge of the logical positivists, Flew's falsificationist challenge to the cognitive meaningfulness of religious language was a failure. In attempting to discredit the worldview of Christian faith, he (like the positivists) ended up discrediting the meaningfulness of all language, including the language of science and discourse about *his own* most cherished convictions. Self-refutation is the most painful refutation of all.

So we may conclude our response. The allegation of "problems" with the meaningfulness of religious language which have been advanced by both verificationists and falsificationists in this century have disclosed, rather, the religious prejudices and inconsistencies of Christianity's critics.

Notes:

[1] A. J. Ayer, *Language, Truth and Logic* (New York: Dover Press, 2nd. ed. 1952), p. 39.

[2] Any test statement whatever (T) can be conjoined with the premise "If T, then O" (where O stands for an observation statement). Notice that the premise just stated does not by itself logically imply the observation statement (O); nor does the observation statement follow directly from the test statement (T). Yet when T is taken with the premise suggested here, the observation statement (O) can indeed be deduced.

[3] *Language, Truth and Logic* (2nd ed.), p. 13.

[4] Alonzo Church briefly but devastatingly demonstrated this in his review of the second edition of Ayer's book (*Journal of Symbolic Logic* v. 14 [1949], p. 53). Where O^n stands for an observation statement, any test statement whatever (T) can be conjoined with any observation statement (O^1) and the following complex premise: [(not-O^1 and O^2) OR (O^3 and not-T). When we do so, not-T passes the test of being *directly* verifiable (by disjunctive syllogism), whereas T can be joined with the complex premise given here to pass Ayer's test of being *indirectly* verifiable.

[5] See Karl Popper, *The Logic of Scientific Discovery* (London: Hutchinson, University Library, 1959 [German original, 1935]).

[6] Antony Flew, "Theology and Falsification," *New Essays in Philosophical Theology*, eds. Antony Flew & Alasdair MacIntyre (New York: Macmillan Co., 1964 [1955]), pp. 96, 97, 98.

[7] Cf. Thomas Kuhn, *The Structure of Scientific Revolutions*, 2nd rev. ed. (Chicago: University of Chicago Press, 1970 [1962]).

[8] "Our statements about the external world face the tribunal of sense experience not individually but only as a corporate body." This was observed and discussed by Willard Van Orman Quine in "Two Dogmas of Empiricism," *From a Logical Point of View*, 2nd ed. (New York: Harper Torchbooks, 1961), p. 41.

[9] This does not imply that theory of knowledge is ultimately relativistic or voluntaristic. It does point to the necessity of transcendental argumentation in apologetics—showing how the Christian's presuppositions provide the preconditions of intelligibility (in science, logic, ethics, etc.) and doing an internal critique of competing philosophies of life to demonstrate that they do not.

[10] Presuppositions are not the only factor in the development of one's system of beliefs. Because of different secondary commitments, social influences, personal experiences, criteria of rationality, intellectual abilities (etc.), two people with shared presuppositions may nevertheless generate differing "networks" of belief.

[11] John M. Frame, "God and Biblical Language," *God's Inerrant Word*, ed. J. W. Montgomery (Minneapolis: Bethany Fellowship, 1974), p. 171.

CHAPTER 34:

THE PROBLEM OF MIRACLES

More often than not the modern mind finds abhorrent the occurrence—or even the possibility—of miracles. Miracles would disrupt our simplistic (and impersonalistic) views of the predictability and uniformity of the world around us. Miracles would indicate that there is a realm of inscrutable mystery for the (pretended) autonomy of man's mind. Miracles would testify to a transcendent and self-conscious Power in the universe which unbelievers find unnerving. So rather than examine whether miracles have in fact occurred or take seriously their reports and significance, it is better, thinks the unbeliever, to dismiss their possibility in advance.

So we will hear critics of Christianity say things like: "How can anybody with even a smattering of high school science believe that a virgin can conceive a child, a man can walk on water, a storm can be calmed upon command, the blind or lame can be instantly healed, or a dead corpse can resuscitate? The modern world knows better! The miracle-claims of Christianity are evidence of its irrationality and superstitious character." In the face of such ridicule and challenge, Christians sometimes cower in silence, when in fact it should be the critic who is intellectually ashamed—put to shame by his historical ignorance, as well as the logical defects in his thinking.

Slandering the Past

You will notice in the hypothetical challenge to Christianity's credibility which is expressed above (meant to be representative of the actual negative mindset and comments of unbelievers which we encounter), there is an unquestioned and arrogant assumption that a critical mindset about miracles is the exclusive property of "the modern world." The philosopher David Hume snidely remarked that it forms a strong presumption against all supernatural and miraculous relations that they are observed chiefly to abound among ignorant and barbarous nations; or if a civilized people has ever given admission to any of them, that people will be found to have received them from ignorant and barbarous ancestors....[1]

Over and over again you will find non-Christians who simply take it for granted that people in the ancient world believed miracles took place, to be blunt, because: (a) they were too scientifically stupid to know better, (b) they were gullible and naive, and/or (c) they were fascinated and eager to find anywhere they could traces of magic in their experience.

Of course, on those three scores we should wonder if the enlightened modern world has any reason for pride, really. It is not the least bit difficult *today* to locate scientifically stupid people, even college graduates. Watch them try to "fix" things with a hammer, deal with an unwanted cockroach or rationalize their smoking; listen to their home-cures for a hangover. And as for gullibility and magic! In our oh-so-smart "modern" world have you ever heard about get-rich-quick investment schemes, diet fads, lottery fever, or the wonder of crystals (or pyramids, etc.)?

Or listen to all those respected entertainers on TV talk-shows telling large, attentive audiences about their "former lives," or about the healing power of meditation, or about "social Karma" and "mother earth," or about the "human face" of communist tyranny in our century, etc. These are hardly evidences of a critical mind or superior rationality.

Believe It or Not, Skepticism Has Been Around

Clear-thinking people should beware of sloppy and self-serving generalizations about, or comparisons between, one age (or culture) and another.

Even more, they should refrain from manifesting the kind of historical ignorance which imagines that people who lived before our entlightened, modern age were, in general, never critically minded or were readily fooled (or more easily than we would be) into accepting tales of miracles. After all, what is the source of the expression occasionally still used in our day "he's just a doubting Thomas"? Remember Thomas, called Didymus (the "Twin"), from the gospel of John's account of Christ's resurrection (John 20:24-29)? Down through subsequent history he has come to be called "Doubting Thomas" *just because* of his skeptical mindset regarding one of the greatest miracles in the Bible. Thomas would not readily accept the testimony of the other apostles that they had seen the resurrected Savior.

And he was not alone in that spirit of disbelief. Even those who personally encountered Christ after He rose from the dead were not excitedly awaiting or jumping with eagerness at the opportunity to believe that a wonder had taken place. Two disciples on the Road to Emmaus (Luke 24:13-31) as well as Mary Magdalene (John 20:1, 11-16) were so *disinclined* to believe such a miracle that they did not even recognize Jesus when they saw him. (Gestalt psychology helps us understand that kind of experience, which all of us have had when "seeing" somebody we know, but not recognizing him "out of normal context" or in an *unexpected* setting.) Matthew relates that even in the presence of the resurrected Lord and knowing who He was supposed to be, "some doubted" (Matt. 28:17).

When the gospel of the resurrected Savior was taken out into the ancient world, there was then—even as now—a general antagonism to the credibility of such claims. Paul proclaimed the resurrection of Christ before the Council of Areopagus in Athens, but the Greek poet Aeschylus many years before had related, in the story of the very founding of the Areopagus, that it was there declared that once a man has died "there is no resurrection." The ancient world knew its share of skepticism and denunciation of miracles. Luke writes that when Paul's address to the Areopagus brought him to the claim about Christ's resurrection, his audience could hardly be characterized by general gullibility and a predisposed willingness to affirm the miracle! Instead: "now when they heard of the resurrection of the dead, some *mocked*," and others more politely put Paul off to another time (Acts 17:32). Ridicule of miracles did not begin in the modern world of enlightened science.

Just like our own culture today, the ancient world was an intellectually mixed-bag. Like us, it had its share of superstitious and mystically minded people; as we do, it had people whose thinking was ignorant, misinformed, lazy, stupid, illogical and silly. But also like our own age, the ancient world had *plenty* of people who were skeptical and cynical. (Indeed, those were even the names for two prominent schools of ancient Greek philosophy in the period of the New Testament!) Plenty of people in the ancient world were critically minded about reports of natural wonders and magical powers. Many not only doubted claims to miracles and found them incredible, but even precluded the very possibility that such things could occur.

The Truth Claims of Christianity

This was so much the case that you will notice the apostle Peter felt it necessary to make this declaration in his second general epistle: "For we did not follow cunningly devised fables when we made known unto you the power and coming of our Lord Jesus Christ, but we were eyewitnesses of His majesty" (2 Peter 1:16). Peter knew that it would be easy for people to "write off" the claims of Christians as just so much more idle chatter and story-telling; he knew that people in his own generation had dismissed the church's proclamation about Jesus because they would not believe such claims regarding miracles. Far from being stupid and gullible, Peter's contemporaries had to be assured that apostolic accounts of Jesus were not cunningly devised fables, but the eyewitness truth.

It was important for the Christian testimony in the midst of an unbelieving culture that followers of Jesus have a reputation for not "giving heed to fables" (1 Tim. 1:4) or entertaining "old wives' tales" (1 Tim. 4:7)—that is, fictitious accounts which are the very opposite of "the truth" of Christianity (2 Tim. 4:4). The hostile world of unregenerate men would only too gladly dismiss the claims of the gospel narrative as being of the same mythical nature—fabulous, unreliable, exaggerated.

The point here, very simply, is that contemporary critics of the Christian faith who automatically dismiss and ridicule the miracle-claims of the Bible because of the alleged widespread ignorance and gullibility of the ancient world only bring shame to themselves for their own ignorant prejudices and unwarranted generalizations. Like today, defenders of the faith in the ancient world encountered significant opposition and negativity about the alleged occurrence of miracles—hostility ranging from sophisticated philosophical repudiations to gut-level mockery. If people living in those days came to believe that Jesus was born of a virgin, walked on water, healed the sick and was raised from the dead, it was *not* because they categorically were weak-minded and ignorant fools, ready to believe any and every fable that came their way.

Begging the Question

The unbeliever who dismisses in advance the Biblical account of miracles should not only be ashamed of his arrogant slander against the ancient world's alleged ingorance and gullibility, he should also be embarrassed by the logically fallacious character of his "reasoning." Consider again our earlier statement from a hypothetical unbeliever, summarizing the actual comments which we hear from non-Christians: "How can anybody with even a smattering of high school science believe that a virgin can conceive a child, a man can walk on water, a storm can be calmed upon command, the blind or lame can be instantly healed, or a dead corpse can resuscitate? The modern world knows better! The miracle-claims of Christianity are evidence of its irrationality and superstitious character."

Unbelievers who speak this way are usually quite unaware of the fatuous and fallacious character of what they are saying and suggesting. They often think that they are treating the miracle-claims of the Bible as independent evidence that the Christian worldview is rationally unacceptable. Their reasoning is something like this: we already *know* miracles do not occur ("How could anybody believe..."), and since Christianity claims that such impossible things did occur (e.g., virgin birth, resurrection), we can draw the conclusion that Christianity must be false. But that conclusion is not so much "drawn" as it is taken for granted from the very outset. The denial of the very possibility of miracles is not a piece of evidence *for* rejecting the Christian worldview, but simply a specific manifestation *of* that very rejection.

Only if the Christian worldview happens to be false could the possibility of miracles be cogently precluded. According to Scripture's account, God is the transcendent and almighty Creator of heaven and earth. Everything owes its very existence and character to His creative power and definition (Gen. 1; Neh. 9:6; Col. 1:16-17). He makes things the way they are and determines that they function as they do. "His understanding is infinite" (Ps. 147:5). Moreover, God sovereignly governs every event that transpires, determining what, when, where, and how anything takes place—from the movement of the planets to the decrees of kings to the very hairs of our heads (Eph. 1:11). According to the Bible, He is omnipotent and in total control of the universe. Isaiah 40 celebrates in famous phraseology the creation, delineating, direction, providence, and power of Jehovah (vv. 12, 22-28). He has the freedom and control over the created order that the potter has over the clay (Rom. 9:21). As the Psalmist affirms, "Our God is in the heavens; He has done whatsoever He pleased" (Ps. 115:3).

Faith vs. Faith

Very simply, according to the Biblical witness: "The Lord God omnipotent reigneth" (Rev. 19:6). Therefore, in terms of the Christian worldview, there is nothing "too hard" for God to do according to His own holy will (Gen. 18:14). Because of who He is, "with God all things are possible" (Matt. 19:26; cf. Mark 14:36). Nothing can stay His hand or prevent Him from accomplishing what He wishes.

Now then, if this God depicted in the pages of the Bible actually exists, then it would be preposterous to try and rule out the *possibility* of miracles. God could accomplish anything—from parting the Red Sea to raising the dead. It is important to keep this in mind when we encounter unbelievers who confidently reject Christianity and ridicule its credibility on the basis of its fantastic claims about miracles which have taken place in history. To declare in advance that the miracles narrated in the Bible *did not* occur because such miracles *could not* occur, and that "therefore" Christianity is false, is simply to "beg the question" that separates believers from unbelievers. It is to take for granted what the unbeliever needs to prove—that the Christian worldview is not true.

So you see, given the common ridicule of unbelievers about the incredibility of miracles, the alleged problem with such events comes down to nothing more than the unbeliever's personal prejudices masquerading as "modern rationality." The unbeliever who brashly and rhetorically asks "show how anybody with a modern education could believe in miracles," thereby repudiating the intellectual respectability of Christianity, has *upon analysis* asserted no more than this: "Unless the Christian worldview is true, the presence of miracle-claims in the Bible is evidence that the Christian worldview is not true." How trivial.

What we usually find, then, is that unbelievers who reject the miracle accounts in the Bible are simply giving expression to their own philosophical prejudices—their presuppositional commitment to a solely natu-ralistic understanding of the world in which we live. This hostile philo-sophical precommitment has not been demonstrated to be true, but sim-ply taken for granted in an uncritical fashion.

The presuppositional nature of the dispute over miracles becomes very clear once we stop and analyze what we mean in speaking of a "miracle."

The concept of the "miraculous"

The word "miracle" does not appear in the text of Scripture. The events recorded in the Bible which we would be inclined to label "miracles" are rather called in the Old and New Testaments "signs," "wonders," "works/acts [of God]," "what is wondrous, astonishing," "omens," or "powers." The Biblical words thus lay emphasis upon one or more of these features:

1. THE AMAZING AND EXTRAORDINARY CHARACTER OF THE EVENTS BEING DESCRIBED (FULL OF WONDER, EVOKING ASTONISHMENT),
2. THE DIFFICULTY OF THESE EVENTS EXCEEDING NORMAL HUMAN ABILITY (FULL OF POWER, AN ACT OF DIVINE STRENGTH), AND/OR
3. THE PURPOSE OF SUCH EVENTS POINTING BEYOND THEMSELVES TO SOME SPECIAL THEOLOGICAL LESSON OR TRUTH (SIGNS, OMENS).

What is interesting for our purposes is that, while hinting at it, these characteristics do not in themselves amount to the full concept of a miracle as discussed in religious and philosophical circles. The connotative stress of the Biblical words is somewhat different from (though not contrary to) what is accentuated in the modern English word "miracle".

There are events which clearly go beyond ordinary human strength or ability (cf. 2); yet they too would not (apart from rhetorical flourish, again) seriously be called "miracles." A hurricane is much stronger than a man, and no mere man has the ability to generate or thwart a hurricane. But hurricanes are not miraculous events in themselves. Indeed, there are some meteorologists who can explain in extensive detail the natural fac-tors which bring about hurricanes, can account for how they operate and dissipate, and can even do a reasonably accurate job of predicting when they will occur and what course they will take. But no meteorologist can give a causal account of Jesus stilling the raging storm at sea with a simple verbal command.

We should observe, as well, that human beings are exposed to natural things and events —like the beauty of the sea or grandeur of the stars— which point beyond themselves to the theological wonder and glory of God the Creator, according to Psalm 19 and Romans 1. Nevertheless, in our ordinary discourse we do not speak of the surging sea or orbiting planets as "miracles." They are signs, even signs which leave us with a sense of wonder. Yet they are also quite "natural." Not at all like turning water into wine or raising the dead.

What we call "miracles" are more than amazing events, more than powerful occurrences, more than parabolic theological lessons. What distinguishes the "miraculous" event from all these other grand things which happen is its specifically supernatural character. The miracle is an extraordinary and awe-inspiring event which in its character (or sometimes in its timing) cannot be explicated by known natural principles or controlled by mere human beings. That is its *super*-natural quality.

Some Conceptual Misdirections

The supernaturalness of an event which is to be classified as a "miracle" has often been misconstrued, even by well-meaning apologists for the faith. Before we look more pointedly at the supernatural quality of miracles, we should be warned away from certain misleading theological or philosophical paths.

Miracles As a Personal Directive

It is sometimes thought that miracles are *super*-natural because they amount to divine intrusions into the ordinary and predictable operations of an otherwise "closed" and self-perpetuating domain of "nature." Mechanical metaphors are often used to give a picture of this natural order, for instance the metaphor of a well-designed clock which God devised, wound up, stood back from, and now runs on its own—except for those rare occasions when the clock-maker steps in to interfere with the way He intended the clock to operate.

The more philosophically sophisticated way to describe this situation is to speak of "natural law." The events which transpire in the universe, whether monumental or minuscule, are viewed as inevitable and predictable according to causal factors which can, in theory, be described in systematic, law-like principles. Many ancient Greek philosophers (e.g., Heraclitus, the Stoics) conceived of an eternal and impersonal "logos" or "reason" governing or flowing through the realm of matter, thus organizing all motion or activity into a rational order.

The religious version of this notion that there are "laws of nature" postulates a personal God as the origin of the material world and of the causal principles by which it operates, but this God (and the free or arbitrary exercise of His almighty will) is nevertheless "separated" from the ordinary and ongoing workings of the world He made. God has chosen not to directly govern every detail in the created world on a moment by moment basis, and thus "nature" has laws inherent in it which determine what things are like and how things happen. Variations on this conception of God's world as governed by impersonal natural laws are found in a wide range of Christian professions, from Deism to Thomism (Roman Catholicism) to evangelical Arminianism.

Given the above conception, the *super*-naturalness of a "miracle" consists in its "violation" of the laws of nature. God interferes with the machinery of the world in its law-directed actions and procedures. This is a flawed and terribly misleading way of thinking about the cosmos and about God, however. God's self-revelation in the Scriptures offers no support for the idea that there are impersonal laws of nature which make the world operate mechanically and with an inevitability which is free (ordinarily) from the choices of God's will. In fact, the Bible offers us a view of the world which is quite contrary to this, one where God and His agents are seen as intimately, continuously, and directly involved in all of the detailed events which transpire in the created order.

God personally created and now *personally directs* all the affairs of the world. Thus sustaining of all animal life and renewing of the plants in this world is the work of God's Spirit (Isa. 63:14; Ps. 104:29-30); Jehovah's Spirit is intimately involved with the processes of the created world, from the withering of the flowers to driving the rushing streams (Isa. 40:7; 59:19). God's decretive will governs all things which happen, from the changing of the seasons (Gen. 8:22) to the hairs on our head (Matt. 10:30). Even the apparently fortuitous events in this life are planned and carried out by His sovereign will (Prov. 16:33; 1 Kings 22:28, 34). Paul declares that God "works *all things* according to the counsel of His will" (Eph.

1:11). That is, He causes everything to happen which happens. There is no semi-autonomous, self-operating realm of "nature" whose impersonal laws are occasionally "violated" by the God who reveals Himself in the pages of the Bible. Nothing is independent of Him and His sovereign, immanent, personal will.

Miracles As Super-Ordinary Providence

Another misconception of the *super*-natural quality of miraculous events holds that, while God plans and causes every thing that happens in the world, sometimes He carries out His choices by more "direct" or "immediate" power, rather than through the ordinary means of His providence personally at work in the natural world. As an example of the difference, we might think of the way in which God usually exercises His providence to bring loaves of bread into the world—planting and harvesting the wheat over time, working in the kitchen with a recipe, baking the dough, taking it from the oven, etc. By contrast, it is thought, God can "miraculously" bring about the same effect, but do so without using the normal means within the created world. He can "immediately" bring loaves of bread into existence, as Jesus did with the multiplying of five loaves to feed five thousand people (Matt. 14:19-21). A miracle comes, then, to be viewed as an "extraordinary providence," an unusual event produced by the "immediate" power of God.

This generalization is unclear. Why is not the baking of bread said to be accomplished by God's "immediate" power? Because it utilizes the means of heat produced by burning wood. Well then, why is not the burning of wood (or the chemical interactions involved, etc.) said to be accomplished by God's "immediate" power? It seems like the mediate and immediate exercises of God's will are only relatively (or subjectively) distinguished by how we choose to look at the process involved. The generalization we are considering is also hasty and fallacious. Not all Biblical "miracles" can be readily classified as "immediate" acts of God's power. The parting of the Red Sea for the escape of the Hebrews from Egypt was one of the greatest and well-remembered wonders of the Old Testament. Yet Exodus tells us that God accomplished it *by means of* the natural phenomenon of a strong east wind. One day Jesus healed a blind man through the natural means of applying mud (spittle and dirt) to his eyes. When Jesus stilled the storm on the lake, He utilized the natural means of His human voice to rebuke the waves. The notion of a miracle being *super*-natural because it is a "direct" act of God intervening in the ordinary operation of the world creates more conceptual headaches than it resolves.

Miracles of Darkness

A further misunderstanding of the supernaturalness of miraculous events is detected in the common conviction that "miracles" can be genuinely performed only by the living and true God—in which case any duly authenticated case of a miraculous occurrence functions as a marker or evidence that God is at work, usually verifying the divine approval of the message or the person of the miracle-worker. But this premise is simply out of step with the Biblical witness itself.

On the day of judgment there will be people who had worked mighty works, even casting out demons, who will not have the approval or acceptance of God (Matt. 7:22-23). When Moses worked miracles by the power of God before the Pharoah, Scripture tells us that the court magicians were able to replicate some of them, obviously by the evil power of Satan (e.g., Ex. 7:11-12). False prophets (Deut. 13:1-2) and false messiahs (Matt. 24:24) are recognized in God's word as having the power to perform miracles. A beastly leader in Revelation 13:13-15 has attributed to him the working of great miracles, like calling fire down from heaven and causing a statue to speak. Why do evil men perform such miraculous deeds? To deceive men and lead them into theological error, to lure them into lies (cf. Deut. 13:2; Rev. 13:14). Accordingly, the Bible can describe these evil miracles as "lying wonders" (2 Thess. 2:9) because they are amazing events which lie about God and mislead His people—*not* (as some interpreters illegitimately foist upon the text) because they are "pseudo" miracles (fake, pretend, illusory). They are real wonders which mislead people from the truth.

And thus the "supernatural power" behind the working of a miracle may be the living and true God whom people should worship and obey, but it might also be the Prince of Darkness, the Devil, who wishes to deceive men and lead them into soul-damning error. (Of course, as the book of Job teaches us, even the workings of Satan take place subject to the sovereign direction of God. Satan is not a genuinely autonomous power in the universe.)

Notes:

[1] David Hume, "Of Miracles" in *An Inquiry Concerning Human Understanding,* ed. Charles W. Hendel (Indianapolis: Boobs-Merrill Co., [1748] 1955), p. 126.

APPENDIX:

BIBLICAL EXPOSITION OF ACTS 17

APPENDIX:

THE ENCOUNTER OF
JERUSALEM WITH ATHENS

What indeed has Athens to do with Jerusalem? What concord
is there between the Academy and the Church?... Our instructions come from "the porch of Solomon".... Away with all
attempts to produce a mottled Christianity of Stoic, Platonic,
and dialectic composition! We want no curious disputation
after possessing Christ Jesus...!

So said Tertullian in his *Prescription against Heretics* (VII). Tertullian's
question, what does Athens have to do with Jerusalem?, dramatically
expresses one of the perennial issues in Christian thought—a problem
which cannot be escaped by any Biblical interpreter, theologian, or apologist. We all operate on the basis of *some* answer to that question, whether
we give it explicit and thoughtful attention or not. It is not a matter of
whether we will answer the question, but only of *how well* we will do so.

What does Tertullian's question ask? It inquires into the proper
relation between Athens, the prime example of secular learning, and Jerusalem, the symbol of Christian commitment and thought. How does the
proclamation of the Church relate to the teaching of the philosophical
Academy? In one way or another, this question has constantly been
before the mind of the church. How should faith and philosophy inter-
act? Which has controlling authority over the other? How should the

---

This chapter was first published in the *Ashland Theological Bulletin* XIII:1 (spring,
1980).

believer respond to alleged conflicts between revealed truth and extrabiblical instruction (in history, science, or what have you)? What is the proper relation between reason and revelation, between secular opinion and faith, between what is taught outside the church and what is preached inside?

This issue is particularly acute for the Christian apologist. When a believer offers a reasoned defense of the Christian hope that is within him (in obedience to 1 Peter 3:15), it is more often than not set forth in the face of some conflicting perspective. As we evangelize unbelievers in our culture, they rarely hold to the authority of the Bible and submit to it from the outset. The very reason most of our friends and neighbors *need* an evangelistic witness is that they hold a different outlook on life, a different philosophy, a different authority for their thinking. How, then, does the apologist respond to the *conflicting* viewpoints and sources of truth given adherence by those to whom he witnesses? What should he think "Athens" has to do with "Jerusalem" just here?

Christians have long disagreed over the proper strategy to be assumed by a believer in the face of unbelieving opinions or scholarship. Some renounce extrabiblical learning altogether ("Jerusalem versus Athens"). Others reject Biblical teaching when it conflicts with secular thought ("Athens versus Jerusalem"). Some try to appease both sides, saying that the Bible and reason have their own separate domains ("Jerusalem segregated from Athens"). Others attempt a mingling of the two, holding that we can find isolated elements of supportive truth in extrabiblical learning ("Jerusalem integrated with Athens"). Still others maintain that extrabiblical reasoning can properly proceed only upon the foundation of Biblical truth ("Jerusalem the capital of Athens").

The Biblical Exemplar

Now it turns out that the Bible has not left us in the dark in answering Tertullian's important question. Luke's account of the early church, The Acts of the Apostles, offers a classic encounter between Biblical commitment and secular thought. And appropriately enough, this encounter takes place between a superb representative of "Jerusalem"—the apostle Paul—and the intellectuals of Athens. The exemplary meeting between the two is presented in Acts 17.

Throughout the book of Acts Luke shows us how the ascended Christ established His church through the apostles. We are given a selective recounting of main events and sermons which exhibit the powerful and model work of Christ's servants. They have left us a *pattern* to follow with respect to both our message *and* method today. Thus, it is highly instructive for contemporary apologists to study the way the apostles, like Paul, reasoned and supported their message of hope (cf. 1 Peter 3:15). Paul was an expert at suiting his approach to each unique challenge, and so the manner in which he confronted the Athenian unbelievers who did not profess submission to the Old Testament Scriptures—like most unbelievers in our own culture—will be noteworthy for us.

We know that Paul's approach to such pagans—for instance, those at Thessalonica, where he had been shortly before coming to Athens—was to call them to turn from idols to serve the living and true God and to wait for His resurrected Son who would judge the world at the consummation (cf. 1 Thess. 1:1-10). In preaching to those who were dedicated to *idols* Paul naturally had to engage in *apologetical* reasoning. Proclamation was inseparable from defense, as F. F. Bruce observes:

> The apostolic preaching was obliged to include an apologetic element if the stumbling-block of the cross was to be overcome; the *kerygma*... must in some degree be *apologia*. And the *apologia* was not the invention of the apostles; they had all "received" it—received it from the Lord.[1]

The currently popular tendency of distinguishing witness from defense, or theology from apologetics, would have been preposterous to the apostles. The two require each other and have a common principle and source: Christ's authority. Paul's Christ-directed and apologetical preaching to pagans, especially those who were philosophically inclined (as in Acts 17), then, is paradigmatic for apologists, theologians, and preachers alike today.

Although the report in Acts 17 is condensed, Luke has summarized the main points of Paul's message and method.

But is this Paul at His Best?

Some biblical interpreters have not granted that Acts 17 is an exemplar for the proper encounter of Jerusalem with Athens. Among them there are some who doubt that Paul was genuinely the author of the speech recorded in this chapter, while others think that Paul actually delivered this speech but repudiated its approach when he went on to minister at Corinth. Both groups, it turns out, rest their opinions on insufficient grounds.

A non-evangelical attitude toward the Scripture allows some scholars a supposed liberty to criticize the authenticity or accuracy of its contents, despite the Bible's own claim to flawless perfection as to the truth. In Acts 17:22 Luke identifies the speaker of the Areopagus address as the apostle Paul, and Luke's customary historical accuracy is by now well known among scholars of the New Testament. (Interestingly, classicists have been more generally satisfied with the Pauline authenticity of this speech than have modernist theologians.) Nevertheless, some writers claim to discern a radical difference between the Paul of Areopagus and the Paul of the New Testament epistles. According to the critical view, the Areopagus focuses on world-history rather than the salvation history of Paul's letters, and the speaker at Areopagus teaches that all men are in God by nature, in contrast to the Pauline emphasis on men being in Christ by grace.[2]

These judgments rest upon an excessively narrow perception of the writings and theology of Paul. The Apostle understood his audience at Athens: they would have needed to learn of God as the Creator and of His divine retribution against sin (even as the Jews knew these things from the Old Testament) before the message of grace could have meaning. Thus the scope of Paul's theological discussion would necessarily be broader than that normally found in his epistles to Christian churches. Moreover, as we will see as this study progresses, there are conspicuous similarities between the themes of the Areopagus address and what Paul wrote elsewhere in his letters (especially the opening chapters of Romans). Johannes Munch said of the sermon: "its doctrine is a reworking of thoughts in Romans transformed into missionary impulse."[3] Finally, even given the broader perspective on history found in the address of Acts 17, we cannot overlook the fact that it, in perfect harmony with Paul's more restricted salvation-history elsewhere, is bracketed by creation and final judgment, and that it finds its climax in the resurrected Christ. The speech before the Areopagus was a "plea for the Jewish doctrine of God, and for the specifically Christian emphasis on a 'Son of Man' doctrine of judgment"[4] (*not* an "idealized scene" printing a message about man's [alleged] "dialectical relation to God").[5] The Paul on Areopagus is clearly the same Paul who writes in the New Testament epistles.

Did Paul suddenly shift his apologetical strategy after leaving Athens though? It has sometimes been thought that when Paul went on from Athens to Corinth and there determined to know nothing among the people except Christ crucified, repudiating the excellency of wisdom (1 Cor. 2:1-2), he confessed that his philosophical tactics in Athens had been unwise. Disillusioned with his small results in Athens, Paul prematurely departed the city, we are told, and then came to Corinth and became engrossed in the word of God (Acts 18:5), never to use philosophical style again.[6] This outlook, while intriguing, consists of more speculation and jumping to conclusions than hard evidence.

In the first place, Paul is herein portrayed as a novice in Gentile evangelism at Athens, experimenting with this and that tactic in order to find an effective method. This does not square with the facts. For several years Paul had already been a successful evangelist in the world of pagan thought; moreover, he was not of an experimental mindset, and elsewhere he made plain that favorable results were not the barometer of faithful preaching. Besides, in Athens his results were *not* completely discouraging (17:34). And of a *premature* departure from Athens the text says nothing. After leaving Athens, Paul can hardly be said to have abandoned the disputing or "dialogue" for which he became known at Athens (cf 17:17); it continued in Corinth (18:4), Ephesus (18:19), and Troas (20:6-7)—being a daily exercise for two years in the school of Tyrannus (19:8-9). It is further inaccurate to project a *contrast* between post-Athens Paul, engrossed in the word, and Athenian Paul, absorbed in extrabiblical thought. Some Greek texts of Acts 17:24-29 (e.g., Nestle's) list up to 22 Old Testament allusions in the margin, thus showing *anything but* a neglect of the Scriptural word in Paul's Athenian preaching!

Mention can again be made of the enlightening harmony that exists between Paul's writings, say in Romans 1 and 1 Corinthians 1, and his speech in Acts 17. The passages in the epistles help us understand the apologetical thrust of the Areopagus address, rather than clashing with it—as the subsequent study will indicate. Finally, it is quite difficult to imagine that Paul, who had previously declared "Far be it from me to glory save in the cross of our Lord Jesus Christ" (Gal. 6:14), and who incisively taught the inter-significance of the death and resurrection of Christ (e.g., Rom. 4:25), would proclaim Christ as the resurrected one at Athens *without* explaining that He was also the crucified one—only later (in Corinth) to determine not to neglect the crucifixion again. We must conclude that solid evidence of a dramatic shift in Paul's apologetic mentality simply does not exist.

What Luke portrays for us by way of summary in Acts 17:16-34 can confidently be taken as a speech of the Apostle Paul, a speech which reflected his inspired approach to Gentiles without the Bible, a speech consistent with his earlier and later teachings in the epistles. His approach is indeed an exemplar to us. It was specially selected by Luke for inclusion in his summary history of the early apostolic church. "Apart from the brief summary of the discourse at Lystra..., the address at Athens provides our only evidence of the apostle's direct approach to a pagan audience."[7] With respect to the author's composition of Acts, Martin Dibelius argues: "In giving only one sermon addressed to Gentiles by the great apostle to the Gentiles, namely the Areopagus speech in Athens, his primary purpose is to give an example of how the Christian missionary should approach cultured Gentiles."[8] And in his lengthy study, *The Areopagus Speech and Natural Revelation*, Gartner correctly asks this rhetorical question: "How are we to explain the many similarities between the Areopagus speech and the Epistles if the speech did not exemplify Paul's customary sermons to the Gentiles?"[9] In the encounter of Jerusalem with Athens as found in Paul's Areopagus address, we thus find that it was genuinely Paul who was speaking, and that Paul was at his best. Scripture would have us, then, strive to emulate his method.

Intellectual Backgrounds

Before looking at Acts 17 itself, a short historical and philosophical background for the speaker of and listeners to, the Areopagus address would be helpful.

Paul was a citizen of Tarsus, which was not an obscure or insignificant city (Acts 21:39). It was the leading city of Cilicia and famed as a city of learning. In addition to general education, Tarsus was noted for its schools devoted to rhetoric and philosophy. Some of its philosophers gained significant reputations, especially the Stoic leaders Zeno of Tarsus (who cast doubt on the idea of a universal conflagration), Antipater of

Tarsus (who addressed a famous argument against Carneade's skepticism), Heraclides of Tarsus (who abandoned the view that "all mistakes are equal"), and Athenodorus the Stoic (who was a teacher of Augustus); Nestor the Academic followed Athenodorus, evidencing thereby the *variety* of philosophic perspectives in Tarsus. The city surely exercised an academic influence on Paul, an influence which would have been broadened later in Paul's life when he came into contact with its culture again for some eight years or so, three years following his conversion. In his early years Paul was also educated by Gamaliel in Jerusalem (Acts 22:3), where he excelled as a student (Gal. 1:14). His course of study would have included critical courses in Greek culture and philosophy (as evidence from the Talmud indicates). When we add to this the extensive knowledge of Greek literature and culture which is reflected in his letters, it is manifest that Paul was neither naive nor obscurantist when it came to a knowledge of philosophy and Gentile thought. Given his background, training, and expertise in Scriptural theology, Paul was the ideal representative for the classic confrontation of Jerusalem with Athens.

Athens, the philosophical center of the ancient world, was renowned for its four major schools: The Academy (founded ca. 287 B.C.) of Plato, the Lyceum (335 B.C.) of Aristotle, the Garden (306 B.C.) of Epicurus, and the Painted Porch (300 B.C.) of Zeno.

The outlook of the Academy was radically altered by Arcesilaus and Carneades in the third and second centuries before Christ; respectively, they moved the school into utter skepticism and then probabilism. Carneades relegated the notion of god to impenetrable mystery. When Antiochus of Ascalon claimed to restore the "old Academy" in the first century B.C., in actuality he introduced a syncretistic dogmatism which viewed Stoicism as the true successor to Plato. The Platonic tradition is remembered for the view that man's soul is imprisoned in the body; at death man is healed, as his soul is released from its tomb.

This anti-materialist emphasis was somewhat challenged by Aristotle's Peripatetic school, which denied the possibility of immortality and invested much time in specialized empirical study and classification of the departments of knowledge. The influence of this school had greatly weakened by the time of the New Testament. However, its materialistic proclivity was paralleled in the atomism of Epicureanism.

Democritus had earlier taught that the universe consisted of eternal atoms of matter, ever falling through space; the changing of combinations and configurations of these falling atoms was explained by reference to chance (an irrational "swerve" in the fall of certain atoms). This metaphysic, in combination with an epistemology which maintained that all knowledge stemmed from sense perception, led the Epicurean followers of atomism to believe that a naturalistic explanation of all events could and should be given. By their doctrine of self-explanatory naturalism the Epicureans denied immortality thereby declaring that there was no need to fear death. Moreover, whatever gods there may be would make no difference to men and their affairs. Epicurus taught that long-lasting pleasure was the goal of human behavior and life. Since no after-life was expected (at death a person's atoms disperse into infinite space), human desires should focus on this life alone. And in this life the only genuine long-term pleasure was that of tranquility—being freed from disturbing passions, pains, or fears. To gain such tranquility one must become insulated from disturbances in his life (e.g., interpersonal strife, disease), concentrating on simple pleasures (e.g., a modicum of cheese and wine, conversations with friends) and achieving serenity through the belief that gods never intervene in the world to punish disobedient behavior. Indeed, whatever celestial beings there are, they were taken merely as dream-like images who—in deistic fashion—care nothing about the lives of men. Thus Philodemus wrote: "There is nothing to fear in god. There is nothing to be alarmed at in death." The Epicureans were, as is evident here, antagonistic to theology. Epicurus had taught them to appeal to right reason against superstition. Accordingly Lucretius denied any need for recourse to "unknown gods" in order to explain the plague at Athens or its alleviation.

Zeno, the founder of the Stoic school, agreed that sensation was the sole origin of knowledge, and that the mind of man was a *tabula rasa* at birth. However, against Epicurean materialism, he taught that reason governs matter in both man and the world, thus making man a microcosm of the universal macrocosm. Man was viewed as integrated with nature—man's reason seen as being of a piece with the ever-living fire which permeates the world order. This was the "Logos" for the Stoics. As a kind of refined matter that actively permeates all things and determines what will happen, the Logos was the unchanging rational plan of historical change. Nature's highest expression, then, was reason or the world-soul, being personified eventually as god. In addition to this pantheistic thrust, Zeno expounded a cyclic view of history (moving through conflagration-regeneration sequences) which precluded individual immortality. Being subordinated to immanent forces (the divine world-soul and historical determinism) the individual was exhorted to "live in harmony with nature," not concerning himself with matters which were beyond his control. If life was to be conducted "conformably to nature," and reason was nature's basic expression, then virtue for man was to live in harmony with reason. The rational element in man was to be superior to the emotional. Epictetus wrote that men cannot control events, but they can control their attitude toward events. So everything outside reason, whether it be pleasure, pain, or even death, was to be viewed as indifferent. Stoicism gave rise to a serious attitude, resignation in suffering, stern individualism, and social self-sufficiency. In turn, these achievements produced pride. Aratus and Cleanthes, two pantheistic Stoics of the mid-third century B.C., viewed Zeus as a personification of the unavoidable fate which governs man's life. Later Stoics either abandoned or modified much of Zeno's teaching. For instance, a century after Cleanthes, Panaetius essentially became a humanist who saw theology as idle chatter; and a century after Panaetius another Stoic leader, Posidonius (Cicero's instructor), opted for a Platonic view of the soul, the eternality of the world (contrary to the idea of conflagration), and the dynamic continuity of nature under fate. The famous Roman Stoic, Seneca, was a contemporary of Paul.

A final line of thinking which was influential in Athens in Paul's day (mid-first century A.D.) was that of the neopythagoreans. In the late sixth century B.C. Pythagoras had taught a mathematical basis for the cosmos, the transmigration of souls, and a regime of purity. Mixed with the thought of Plato, the Peripatetics, and Stoicism, his thought reappeared in the first century B.C. with the *neo*pythagoreans, who emphasized an exoteric and mystical theology which took a keen interest in numbers and the stars. The neophythagoreans influenced the Essene community as well as Philo—Paul's other philosophical contemporary[10]

In Paul's day Athenian intellectual life had come to be characterized by turmoil and uncertainty. Skepticism had made heavy inroads, which in turn fostered various reactions—notably: interaction between the major schools of thought, widespread eclecticism, nostalgic interest in the

past founders of the schools, religious mysticism, and resignation to he-
donism. Men were turning every which way in search for the truth and
for security. On the other hand, over four hundred years of philosophical dispute with its conflicts, repetitions, and inadequacies had left many
Athenians bored and thirsty for novel schemes of thought. Thus one can
understand Luke's accurate and insightful aside to the reader in Acts 17:21,
"Now all the Athenians and the strangers sojourning there spent time in
nothing else, but either to tell or to hear some new thing." The curiosity
of the Athenians was indeed proverbial. Earlier, Demosthenes had re-
proached the Athenians for being consumed with a craving for "fresh
news". The Greek historian, Thucydides, tells us that Cleon once declared, "You are the best people for being deceived by something new
which is said." With this background let us now examine Paul's apologetic to secular intellectuals.

Paul's Encounter with the Philosophers

Acts 17:16-21 (American Standard Version)

(16) NOW WHILE PAUL WAITED FOR THEM AT ATHENS, HIS SPIRIT WAS PRO-
VOKED WITHIN HIM AS HE BEHELD THE CITY FULL OF IDOLS.

(17) SO HE REASONED IN THE SYNAGOGUE WITH THE JEWS AND THE DEVOUT
PERSONS, AND IN THE MARKETPLACE EVERY DAY WITH THEM THAT MET
HIM.

(18) AND CERTAIN ALSO OF THE EPICUREAN AND STOIC PHILOSOPHERS EN-
COUNTERED HIM. AND SOME SAID, WHAT WOULD THIS BABBLER SAY?
OTHERS, HE SEEMETH TO BE A SETTER FORTH OF STRANGE GODS: BE-
CAUSE HE PREACHED JESUS AND THE RESURRECTION.

(19) AND THEY TOOK HOLD OF HIM, AND BROUGHT HIM UNTO THE AR-
EOPAGUS, SAYING, MAY WE KNOW WHAT THIS NEW TEACHING IS, WHICH
IS SPOKEN BY THEE?

(20) FOR THOU BRINGEST CERTAIN STRANGE THINGS TO OUR EARS: WE WOULD
KNOW THEREFORE WHAT THESE THINGS MEAN.

(21) (NOW ALL THE ATHENIANS AND THE STRANGERS SOJOURNING THERE
SPENT THEIR TIME IN NOTHING ELSE, BUT EITHER TO TELL OR TO HEAR
SOME NEW THING.)

In the early 50's of the first century Paul was on something of a
"missionary furlough," waiting in Athens for Silas and Timothy. (Luke's

rehearsal of this situation, Acts 17:14-16, is confirmed by Paul's own account in 1 Thess. 3: 1-2). However, his brief relief was broken when he became internally provoked at the idolatry of the city, being reminded anew of the perversity of the unbeliever who suppresses God's clear truth and worships the creature rather than the Creator (Acts 17:16; cf. Rom. 1:25). Paul's love for God and His standards meant he had a corresponding hatred for that which was offensive to the Lord. The idolatry of Athens produced a strong and sharp emotional disturbance within him, one of exasperated indignation. The Greek word for "provoked" is the same as that used in the Greek Old Testament for God's anger at Israel's idolatry (e.g., at Sinai). The Mosaic law's prohibition against idolatry was obviously *binding* outside of Old Testament Israel, judging from Paul's attitude toward the idolatrous society of Athens. Paul was thinking God's thoughts after Him, and strong emotion was generated by the fact that this "city full of idols" was "without excuse" for its rebellion (Rom. 1:20)—as also had been Israel of old.

The profligate Roman satirist, Petronius, once said that it was easier to find a god in Athens than a man; the city simply teemed with idols. Visitors to Athens and writers (e.g., Sophocles, Livy, Pausanius, Strabo, Josephus) frequently remarked upon the abundance of religious statues in Athens. According to one, Athens had more idols than all of the remainder of Greece combined. There was the altar of Eumenides (dark goddesses who avenge murder) and the hermes (statues with phallic attributes, standing at every entrance to the city as protective talismans). There was the altar of the Twelve Gods, the Temple of Ares (or "Mars," god of war), the Temple of Apollo Patroos. Paul saw the image of Neptune on horseback, the sanctuary of Bacchus, the forty foot high statue of Athena, the mother goddess of the city. Sculptured forms of the Muses and the gods of Greek mythology presented themselves everywhere around Paul.[11] What is today taken by tourists as a fertile field of aesthetic appreciation—the artifacts left from the ancient Athenian worship of pagan deities—represented to Paul not art but despicable and crude religion. Religious loyalty and moral considerations precluded artistic compliments. These idols were not "merely an academic question" to Paul. They provoked him. As Paul gazed upon the Doric Temple of the patron goddess Athena, the Parthenon, standing atop the Acropolis, and as he scrutinized the Temple of Mars on the Areopagus, he was not only struck with the inalienable religious nature of man (v.22), but also outraged at how fallen man exchanges the glory of the incorruptible God for idols (Rom. 1:23).

Thus Paul could not keep silent. He began daily to reason with the Jews in the synagogue, and with anybody who would hear him in the agora, at the bottom of the Acropolis, the center of Athenian life and business (where years before, Socrates had met men with whom to discuss philosophical questions) (v.17). Paul's evangelistic method was always suited to the local conditions—and portrayed with historical accuracy by Luke. In Ephesus Paul taught in the "school of Tyrannus," but in Athens his direct approach to the heathen was made in the marketplace. Paul had already approached the unbelieving Jews and God-fearing Gentiles at the synagogue in Athens. Now he entered the marketplace of ideas to "reason with" those who met him there. The Greek word for Paul's activity recalls the "dialogues" of Plato wherein Socrates discusses issues of philosophical importance; it is the same word used by Plutarch for the teaching methods of a peripatetic philosopher. Paul did not simply announce his viewpoint; he discussed it openly and gave it a reasonable defense. He aimed to educate his audience, not to make common religious cause with their sinful ignorance.

Paul was well aware of the philosophical climate of his day. Accordingly he did *not* attempt to use premises agreed upon with the philosophers, and then pursue a "neutral" method of argumentation to move them from the circle of their beliefs into the circle of his own convictions. When he disputed with the philosophers *they* did not find any grounds for agreement with Paul at any level of their conversations. Rather, they utterly disdained him as a "seed-picker," a slang term (originally applied to gutter-sparrows) for a peddler of second-hand bits of pseudo-philosophy—an intellectual scavenger (v. 18). The word of the cross was to them foolish (1 Cor. 1:18), and in their pseudo-wisdom they knew not God (1 Cor. 1:20-21). Hence Paul would not consent to use their verbal "wisdom" in his apologetic, lest the cross of Christ be made void (1 Cor. 1:17).

Paul rejected the assumptions of the philosophers in order that he might educate them in the truth of God. He did not attempt to find common beliefs which would serve as starting points for an uncommitted search for "whatever gods there may be." His hearers certainly did not recognize *commonness* with Paul's reasoning; they could not discern an echo of their own thinking in Paul's argumentation. Instead, they viewed Paul as bringing *strange, new* teaching to them (vv. 18-20). They apparently viewed Paul as proclaiming a new divine couple: "Jesus" (a masculine form that sounds like the greek *iasis*) and "Resurrection" (a feminine form), being the personified powers of "healing" and "restoration." These "strange deities" amounted to "new teaching" in the eyes of the Athenians. Accusing Paul of being a propagandist for new deities was an echo of the nearly identical charge brought against Socrates four and a half centuries earlier.[12] It surely turned out to be a more menacing accusation than the name "seed-picker." As introducing foreign gods, Paul could not simply be disdained; he was also a threat to Athenian well-being. And that is precisely why Paul ended up before the Areopagus council.

In the marketplace Paul had apologetically proclaimed the fundamental, apostolic *kerygma* which entered on Jesus and the resurrection (Acts 17:18; cf. Acts 4:2). This summed up God's decisive saving work in history for His people: Christ had been delivered up for their sins, but God raised Him for their *justification* (Rom. 4:25) and thereby constituted Him the Son of God *with power* (i.e. exalted Lord; Rom. 1:4). As mentioned previously, Paul's approach to those who were without the Scriptures was to challenge them to turn from their idolatry and serve the living God, whose *resurrected* Son would finally *judge* the world (cf. 1 Thess. 1:9-10). This was the burden of Paul's message at Athens.

> Paul was determined to know nothing among men save Jesus Christ and Him crucified....in His resurrection through the power of the Creator there stood before men the clearest evidence that could be given that they who would still continue to serve and worship the creature would at last be condemned by the Creator then become their Judge (Acts 17:31)....No one can be confronted with the fact of Christ and of His resurrection and fail to have his own conscience tell him that he is face to face with his Judge.[13]

It was specifically the aspect of Christ's resurrection in Paul's gospel that elicited a challenge from the philosophers. At this they hauled him before the Areopagus Council for an explanation and reasoned defense of the hope that was in him (cf. 1 Peter 1:3; 3:15).

Luke tells us that Paul was "brought before the Areopagus" (v.19). The *Areios pagos* literally means "'the hill of Ares" (or "Mars' hill"); however, his referent is not likely a geographical feature in the local surrounding of the agora. The *Council of the Areopagus* was a venerable commission of the ex-magistrates which took its name from the hill where it originally convened. In popular parlance its title was shortened simply to "the Areopagus," and in the first century it had transferred its location to the Stoa Basileios (or "Royal Portico") in the city marketplace—where the Platonic dialogues tell us that Euthyphro went to try his father for impiety and where Socrates had been tried for corrupting the youth with foreign deities. Apparently the Council convened on Mars' hill in Paul's day only for trying cases of homicide. That Paul "stood in the midst of the Areopagus" (v.22) and "went out from their midst" (v. 33) is much easier understood in terms of his appearance before the Council than his standing on the hill (cf. Acts 4:7).[14]

The Council was a small but powerful body (probably about thirty members) whose membership was taken from those who had formerly held offices in Athens which (due to the expenses involved) were open only to aristocratic Athenians. This Council was presently the dominating factor in Athenian politics, and it had a reputation far and wide. Cicero wrote that the Areopagus assembly governed the Athenian affairs of state. They exercised jurisdiction over matters of religion and morals, taking concern for teachers and public lecturers in Athens (and thus Cicero once induced the Areopagus to invite a peripatetic philosopher to lecture in Athens). A dispute exists over the question of whether the Areopagus had an educational subcommittee before which Paul likely would have appeared.[15] But one way or another, the Council would have found it necessary to keep order and exercise some control over lecturers in the agora. Since Paul was creating something of a disturbance, he was "brought before the Areopagus" for an explanation (even if not for a specific examination toward the issuance of a teaching license). The mention of "the Areopagus" is one of many indicators of Luke's accuracy as a historian. "According to Acts, therefore, just as Paul is brought before the *strategoi* at Philippi, the *politarchai* at Thessalonica, the *anthupatos* at Corinth, so at Athens he faces the Areopagus. The local name for the supreme authority is in each case different and accurate."[16]

Paul appeared before the Areopagus Council for a reason that probably lies somewhere between that of merely supplying requested information and that of answering to formal charges. After indicating the questions and requests addressed to Paul before the Areopagus, Luke seems to offer the motivation for this line of interrogation in verse 21—the proverbial curiosity of the Athenians. And yet the language used when Luke says in verse 19 that "they took hold of him" is more often than not in Acts used in the sense of *arresting* someone (cf. 16:19; 18:17; 21:30—although not always, as in 9:27, 23:19). We must remember that Luke wrote the book of Acts while Paul had been awaiting trial in Rome for two years (Acts 28:30-31). His hope regarding the Roman verdict was surely given expression in the closing words of his book—that Paul continued to preach Christ, "none forbidding him." An important theme pursued by Luke in the book of Acts is that Paul was continually appearing before a court, but never with a guilty verdict against him. Quite likely, in Acts 17 Paul is portrayed by Luke as *again* appearing before a court without sentencing. Had there been the legal formality of charges against Paul, it is inconceivable that Luke would not have mentioned them or the formal verdict at the end of the trial. Therefore, Paul's appearance before the Areopagus Council is best understood as an informal exploratory hearing for the purpose of determining whether formal charges ought to be formulated and pressed against him. Eventually none were.

In the same city which had tried Anaxagoras, Protagoras, and Socrates for introducing "new deities," Paul was under examination for setting forth "strange gods" (vv. 18-20). The kind of apologetic for the resurrection which he presented is a paradigm for all Christian apologists. It will soon be apparent that he recognized that the *fact* of the resurrection needed to be accepted and interpreted in a *wider philosophical* context, and that the unregenerate's *system* of thought had to be placed in *antithetic contrast* with that of the Christian. Although the philosophers had used disdainful name-calling while considering Paul in the marketplace (v. 18), verses 19-20 show them expressing themselves in more refined language before the Council. They politely requested *clarification* of a message which had been apparently incomprehensible to them. They asked to be made acquainted with Paul's strange new teaching and to have its meaning explained. Given their philosophical presuppositions and mindset, Paul's teaching could not even be integrated sufficiently into their think-

ing to be understood. This in itself reveals the underlying fact that a
conceptual paradigm clash had been taking place between them and Paul.
Given their own worldviews, the philosophers did not think that Paul's
outlook *made sense*. As Paul stood in the midst of the prestigious Council of the Areopagus, with a large audience gathered around from the
marketplace, he set himself for a defense of his faith. Let us turn to
examine his address itself.

Paul's Presuppositional Procedure

Acts 17:22-31 (American Standard Version)

(22) AND PAUL STOOD IN THE MIDST OF THE AREOPAGUS, AND SAID, YE
MEN OF ATHENS, IN ALL THINGS I PERCEIVE THAT YE ARE VERY RELI-
GIOUS (MARGIN: SOMEWHAT SUPERSTITIOUS).

(23) FOR AS I PASSED ALONG, AND OBSERVED THE OBJECTS OF YOUR WORSHIP,
I FOUND ALSO AN ALTAR WITH THIS INSCRIPTION, TO AN UN-
KNOWN GOD. WHAT THEREFORE YE WORSHIP IN IGNORANCE, THIS
I SET FORTH UNTO YOU.

(24) THE GOD THAT MADE THE WORLD AND ALL THINGS THEREIN, HE, BE-
ING LORD OF HEAVEN AND EARTH, DWELLETH NOT IN TEMPLES MADE
WITH HANDS;

(25) NEITHER IS HE SERVED BY MEN'S HANDS, AS THOUGH HE NEEDED ANY-
THING, SEEING HE HIMSELF GIVETH TO ALL LIFE, AND BREATH, AND ALL
THINGS;

(26) AND HE MADE OF ONE EVERY NATION OF MEN TO DWELL ON THE FACE
OF THE EARTH, HAVING DETERMINED THEIR APPOINTED SEASONS, AND
THE BOUNDS OF THEIR HABITATION;

(27) THAT THEY SHOULD SEEK GOD, IF HAPLY THEY MIGHT FEEL AFTER HIM
AND FIND HIM, THOUGH HE IS NOT FAR FROM EACH ONE OF US:

(28) FOR IN HIM WE LIVE, AND MOVE, AND HAVE OUR BEING; AS CERTAIN
EVEN OF YOUR OWN POETS HAVE SAID, FOR WE ARE ALSO HIS OFFSPRING.

(29) BEING THEN THE OFFSPRING OF GOD, WE OUGHT NOT TO THINK THAT
THE GODHEAD IS LIKE UNTO GOLD, OR SILVER, OR STONE, GRAVEN BY
ART AND DEVICE OF MAN.

(30) THE TIMES OF IGNORANCE THEREFORE GOD OVERLOOKED; BUT NOW
HE COMMANDETH MEN THAT THEY SHOULD ALL EVERYWHERE REPENT:

(31) INASMUCH AS HE HATH APPOINTED A DAY IN WHICH HE WILL JUDGE THE
WORLD IN RIGHTEOUSNESS BY THE MAN WHOM HE HATH ORDAINED;
WHEREOF HE HATH GIVEN ASSURANCE UNTO ALL MEN, IN THAT HE

HATH RAISED HIM FROM THE DEAD.

It must first be noted that Paul's manner of addressing his audience was *respectful* and gentle. The boldness of his apologetic did not become arrogance. Paul "stood" in the midst of the Council, which would have been the customary attitude of an orator. And he began his address formally, with a polite manner of expression: "You men of Athens." The *magna carta* of Christian apologetics, 1 Peter 3:15, reminds us that when we offer a reasoned defense of the hope within us, we must do so "with meekness and respect." Ridicule, anger, sarcasm, and name-calling are inappropriate weapons of apologetical defense. A Spirit-filled apologist will evidence the fruits of the Spirit in his approach to others.

Next we see that Paul's approach was to speak in terms of *basic philosophical perspectives*. The Athenians had specifically asked about the resurrection, but we have no hint that Paul replied by examining various alternative theories (e.g., Jesus merely swooned on the cross, the disciples stole the body, etc.) and then by countering them with various evidences (e.g., a weak victim of crucifixion could not have moved the stone; liars do not become martyrs; etc.) in order to conclude that "very probably" Jesus arose. No, nothing of the sort appears here. Instead, Paul laid the presuppositional groundwork for accepting the authoritative word from God, which was the source and context of the good news about Christ's resurrection. Van Til comments:

> It takes the fact of the resurrection to see its proper framework and it takes the framework to see the fact of the resurrection; the two are accepted on the authority of Scripture alone and by the regenerating work of the Spirit.[17]

Without the proper theological context, the resurrection would simply be a monstrosity or freak of nature, a surd resuscitation of a corpse. Such an *interpretation* would be the best that the Athenian philosophers could make of the fact. However, given the monism, or determinism, or materialism, or the philosophy of history entertained by the philosophers in Athens, they could intellectually find sufficient grounds, if they wished, for disputing even the *fact* of the resurrection. It would have been futile for Paul to argue about the facts, then, without challenging the unbelievers' *philosophy of fact.*[18]

Verses 24-31 of Acts 17 indicate Paul's recognition that between his hearers and himself two complete *systems of thought* were in conflict. Any alleged fact or particular evidence which was introduced into the discussion would be variously seen in the light of the differing systems of thought. Consequently, the Apostle's apologetic had to be suited to a philosophical critique of the unbeliever's perspective and a philosophical defense of the believer's position. He was called upon to conduct his apologetic with respect to *worldviews* which were in collision. The Athenians had to be challenged, not simply to add a bit more information (say, about a historical event) to their previous thinking, but to renounce their previous thoughts and undergo a thorough change of mind. They needed to be converted in their total outlook on life, man, the world, and God. Hence Paul reasoned with them in a presuppositional fashion.

The basic contours of a Biblically guided, presuppositional approach to apologetical reasoning can be sketched from scriptures outside of Acts 17. Such a summary will give us sensitivity and insight into Paul's argumentation before the Areopagus.

(1) Paul understood that the unbeliever's mindset and philosophy would be systemically contrary to that of the believer—that the two represent *in principle a clash of total attitude and basic presuppositions.* He taught in Ephesians 4:17-24 that the Gentiles "walk in the vanity of their mind, being darkened in their understanding" because of their "ignorance and hardened hearts," while a completely different epistemic condition characterizes the Christian, one who has been "renewed in the spirit of your mind" and has "learned Christ" (for "the truth is in Jesus"). The "wisdom of the world" evaluates God's wisdom as foolishness, while the believer understands that worldly wisdom "has been made foolish" (1 Cor. 1:17-25; 3:18-20). The basic commitments of the believer and unbeliever are fundamentally opposed to each other.

(2) Paul further understood that the basic commitments of the unbeliever produced only ignorance and foolishness, allowing an effective internal critique of his hostile worldview. The *ignorance of the non-Christian's presuppositions* should be exposed. Thus Paul refers to thought which opposes the faith as "vain babblings of knowledge falsely so called" (1 Tim. 6:20), and he insists that the wise disputers of this age have been made foolish and put to shame by those called "foolish" (1 Cor. 1:20, 27).

Unbelievers become "vain in their reasonings"; "professing themselves to be wise, they became fools" (Rom. 1:21, 22).

(3) By contrast, the Christian takes *revelational authority as his starting point and controlling factor* in all reasoning. In Colossians 2:3 Paul explains that "all the treasures of wisdom and knowledge" are deposited in Christ—in which case we must be on the alert against philosophy which is "not after Christ," lest it rob us of this epistemic treasure (v. 8). The Old Testament proverb had put it this way: "The fear of Jehovah is the beginning of knowledge, but fools despise wisdom and instruction" (Prov. 1:7). Accordingly, if the apologist is going to cast down "reasonings and every high thing exalted against the knowledge of God" he must first bring "every thought into captivity to the obedience of Christ" (2 Cor. 10:5), making Christ pre-eminent in *all* things (Col. 1:18). Upon the platform of God's revealed truth, the believer can authoritatively declare the riches of knowledge unto believers.

(4) Paul's writings also establish that, because all men have a clear knowledge of God from general revelation, the unbeliever's *suppression of the truth* results in *culpable ignorance.* Men have a natural and inescapable knowledge of God, for He has made it manifest unto them, making his divine nature perceived through the created order, so that all men are "without excuse" (Rom. 1:19-20). This knowledge is "suppressed in unrighteousness" (v. 18), placing men under the wrath of God, for "knowing God, they glorified Him not as God" (v. 21). The ignorance which characterizes unbelieving thought is something for which the unbeliever is morally responsible.

(5) Given the preceding conditions, the appropriate thing for the apologist to do is to set his worldview with its *scriptural presuppositions* and authority in *antithetical contrast* to the worldview(s) of the unbeliever, explaining that in principle the latter destroys the possibility of knowledge (that is, doing an internal critique of the system to demonstrate its foolishness and ignorance) and indicating how the Biblical perspective alone accounts for the knowledge which the unbeliever sinfully uses. By placing the two perspectives in contrast and showing "the impossibility of the contrary" to the Christian outlook, the apologist seeks to expose the unbeliever's suppression of his knowledge of God and thereby call him to *repentance,* a change in his mindset and convictions. Reasoning in this presuppositional manner—refusing to become intellec-

tually neutral and to argue on the unbeliever's autonomous grounds—
prevents having our "minds corrupted from the simplicity and purity
that is toward Christ," and counteracts the beguiling philosophy used by
the serpent to ensnare Eve (2 Cor. 11:3). In the face of the fool's challenges to the Christian faith, Paul would have believers meekly "correct
those who are opposing themselves"—setting Biblical instruction over
against the self-vitiating perspective of unbelief—and showing the need
for "repentance unto the knowledge of the truth" (2 Tim. 2:25).[19]

As we look further now at Paul's address before the Areopagus philosophers, we will find that his line of thought incorporated the preceding elements of Biblically presuppositional reasoning. He pursued a pattern of argument which was completely congruous with his other relevant New Testament teachings. They virtually dictated his method to
him.

The Unbeliever's Ignorance

As Paul began his Areopagus apologetic, he began by drawing attention to the *nature of man* as inherently a religious being (Acts 17:22; cf.
Rom. 1:19; 2:15). The term used to describe the Athenians in verse 22
(literally "fearers of the supernatural spirits") is sometimes translated "very
religious" and sometimes "somewhat superstitious." There is no satisfactory English equivalent. "Very religious" is too complimentary; Paul was
not prone to flattery, and according to Lucian, it was forbidden to use
compliments before the Areopagus in an effort to gain its goodwill. "Somewhat superstitious" is perhaps a bit too critical in thrust. Although the
term could sometimes be used among pagans as a compliment, it usually
denoted an excess of strange piety. Accordingly, in Acts 25:19 Festus
refers to Judaism, using this term as a mild reproach for its religiosity. It
is not beyond possibility that Paul cleverly chose this term precisely for
the sake of its ambiguity. His readers would wonder whether the good or
bad sense was being stressed by Paul, and Paul would be striking a double
blow: men cannot eradicate a religious impulse within themselves (as the
Athenians demonstrate), and yet this good impulse has been degraded by
rebellion against the living and true God (as the Athenians also demonstrate). Although men do not acknowledge it, they are aware of their
relation and accountability to the living and true God who created them.
But rather than come to terms with Him and His wrath against their sin

(cf. Rom. 1:18), they pervert the truth. And in this they become ignorant and foolish (Rom. 1:21-22).

Thus Paul could present his point by making an illustration of the altar dedicated "To an Unknown God." Paul testified that as he "observed" the Athenian "objects of worship" he found an altar with an appropriate inscription. The verb used of Paul's activity does not connote a mere looking at things, but a systematic inspection and purposeful scrutiny (the English term 'theorize' is cognate). Among their "objects of religious devotion'" (language referring to idol worship without any approbation) Paul finally found one which contained "a text for what he had to say."[20] Building upon the admission of the Athenians themselves, Paul could easily indict them for the ignorance of their worship—that is, any worship which is contrary to the word of God (cf. John 4:22). The Athenians had brought Paul before the Areopagus with a desire to "know" what they were missing in religious philosophy (vv. 19, 20), and Paul immediately points out that heretofore their worship was admittedly of the "unknown" (v. 23). Paul did not attempt to supplement or build upon a common foundation of natural theology with the Greek philosophers here. He began, rather, with their own expression of theological inadequacy and defectiveness. He underscored their *ignorance* and proceeded from that significant epistemological point.

The presence of altars "to unknown gods" in Athens was attested by writers such as Pausanias and Philostratus. According to Diogenes Laertius, such altars were erected to an anonymous source of blessing. For instance, once (ca. 550 B.C.), when a plague afflicted Athens without warning and could not be mitigated by medicine or sacrifice, Epimenides counseled the Athenians to set white and black sheep loose on the Areopagus, and then to erect altars wherever the sheep came to rest. Not knowing the specific source of the plague's elimination, the Athenians built various altars to *unknown* gods. This sort of thing was apparently common in the ancient world. The 1910 excavation at Pergamum unearthed evidence that a torchbearer who felt under some obligation to gods whose names were unknown to him expressed his gratitude by erecting an anonymous altar for them. Deissmann's conclusion bears repeating:

> In Greek antiquity cases were not altogether rare in which "anonymous" altars "to unknown gods" or "to the god whom

it may concern" were erected when people were convinced, for example after experiencing some deliverance, that a deity had been gracious to them, but were not certain of the deity's name.[21]

The Athenians had a number of such altars on Mars' hill alone. This was testimony to the Athenian conviction that they were lorded over by mysterious, *unknown* forces.

Yet these altars were also evidence that they assumed enough *knowledge* of these forces to worship them, and worship them in a particular manner. There was thus an element of subtle, internal critique in Paul's mention of the Athenian worship of that which they acknowledged as unknown (v. 23). Moreover, Paul was noting the basic schizophrenia in unbelieving thought when he described in the Athenians *both* an awareness of God (v. 22) and an ignorance of God (v. 23). The same condition is expounded in Romans 1:18-25. Berkouwer notes, "There is full agreement between Paul's characterization of heathendom as ignorant of God and his speech on the Areopagus. Ever with Paul, the call to faith is a matter of radical conversion from ignorance of God."[22] Knowing God, the unregenerate nevertheless suppresses the truth and follows a lie instead, thereby gaining a darkened mind. Commenting on our passage in Acts 17, Munck said:

> What follows reveals that God was unknown only because the Athenians had not wanted to know him. So Paul was not introducing foreign gods, but God who was both known, as this altar shows, and yet unknown.[23]

The unbeliever is fully responsible for his mental state, and this is a state of *culpable ignorance*. That explains why Paul issued a call for *repentance* to the Athenians (v. 30); their ignorant mindset was immoral.

The Authority of Revelational Knowledge

Having alluded to an altar to an unknown god, Paul said, "That which you worship, acknowledging openly your ignorance, *I proclaim* unto you." There are two crucial elements of his apologetic approach to be discerned here. Paul started with an emphasis upon his hearers' ignorance and from there went on to declare with authority the truth of God. Their *ignorance* was made to stand over against his unique *authority* and ability to expound the truth. Paul set forth Christianity as *alone* reasonable and true, and his *ultimate starting point* was the authority of Christ's revelation. It was not uncommon for Paul to stress that the Gentiles were ignorant, knowing not God. (e.g., 1 Cor. 1:20; Gal. 4:8; Eph. 4:18; 1 Thess. 4:5; 2 Thess. 1:8). In diametric contrast to them was the believer who possessed a knowledge of God (e.g., Gal. 4:9; Eph. 4:20). This antithesis was fundamental to Paul's thought, and it was clearly elaborated at Athens.

The Greek word for "proclaim" ("set forth") in verse 23 refers to a solemn declaration which is made with authority. For instance, in the Greek papyri it is used for an announcement of the appointment of one's legal representative.[24] It might seem that such an authoritative declaration by Paul would be appropriate only when he dealt with Jews who already accepted the scriptures; however, whether dealing with Jews or secular philosophers, Paul's epistemological platform remained the same, so that even in Athens he "proclaimed" the word of God. The verb is frequently used in Acts and the Pauline epistles for the apostolic proclamation of the gospel, which had direct divine authority (e.g., Acts 3:18; 1 Cor. 9:14; cf. Gal. 1:11-12). Therefore, we see that Paul, although ridiculed as a philosophical charlatan, presumed unique authority to provide the Athenian philosophers with that knowledge which they lacked about God. This was far from stressing common ideas and beliefs. How offensive the Pauline antithesis between their ignorance and his God-given authority must have been to them!

> They were sure that such a God as Paul preached did not and could not exist. They were therefore sure that Paul could not "declare" this God to them. No one could know such a God as Paul believed in.[25]

Paul aimed to show his audience that their *ignorance* would no longer be tolerated; instead, God *commanded* all men to undergo a radical *change of mind* (v. 30). From beginning to end the unbeliever's ignorance was stressed in Paul's apologetic, being set over against the revelational knowledge of God.

Culpable Suppression of the Truth

Paul reasoned on the basis of antithetical presuppositions, a different starting point and authority. He also stressed the *culpability* of his hearers for that ignorance which resulted from their unbelief. Natural *revelation* certainly played a part in his convicting them of this truth. However, there is no hint in Paul's words that this revelation had been handled properly or that it established a common *interpretation* between the believer and unbeliever. Rather, Paul's references to natural revelation were made for the very purpose of *indicting* the espoused beliefs of his audience.

His allusion to their religious nature has already been discussed. In addition, verses 26-27 show that Paul taught that God's providential government of history was calculated to bring men to Him; they should have known Him from His works. Paul's appeal to providence was conspicuous at Lystra as well (Acts 14:17). The goodness of God *should* lead men to repentance (cf. Rom. 2:4). Acts 17:27 indicates that God's providential governance of history should bring men to seek God, "if perhaps" they might feel after Him. The subordinate clause here expresses an unlikely contingency[26] The natural man's seeking and finding God cannot be taken for granted. Citing Psalm 14:2-3 in Romans 3:11-12, Paul clearly said: "There is none that seeks after God; they have all turned aside and together become unprofitable." Returning to Acts 17:27, even if the unregenerate should attempt to find God, he would at best "feel after" Him. This verb is the same as that used by Homer for the groping about of the blinded Cyclops. Plato used the word for amateur guess at the truth. Far from showing what Lightfoot thought was "a clear appreciation of the elements of truth contained in their philosophy"[27] at Athens, Paul taught that the eyes of the unbeliever had been blinded to the light of God's revelation. Pagans do not interpret natural revelation correctly, coming to the light of the truth here and there; they grope about in darkness. Hence Paul viewed men as blameworthy for not holding fast to the knowledge of God which came to them in creation and providence. The rebellious are left without an excuse due to God's general revelation (Rom. 1:19-23).

Paul's perspective in Acts 17 is quite evidently identical with that in

Romans 1. In both places he teaches that unbelievers have a knowledge of God which they suppress, thereby meriting condemnation; their salvation requires a radical conversion from the ignorance of heathendom. G. C. Berkouwer puts it this way:

> The antithesis looms large in every encounter with heathendom. It is directed, however, against the maligning that heathendom does to the revealed truth of God in nature and it calls for conversion to the revelation of God in Christ.[28]

So it is that Paul's appeals to general revelation function to point out the guilt of the unbeliever as he mishandles the truth of God. He is *responsible* because he possesses the truth, but he is *guilty* for what he does to the truth. *Both* aspects of the unbeliever's relation to natural revelation must be kept in mind. When evidence is found of the unbeliever's awareness of the truth of God's revelation around and within him, Paul uses it as an indicator of the unbeliever's culpability, and the apostle shows that it needs to be understood and interpreted in terms of the special revelation which is brought by Christ's commissioned representative. Where natural revelation plays a part in Christian apologetics, that revelation must be "read through the glasses" of special revelation.

In Acts 17:27, heathen philosophers are said at best to grope in darkness after God. This inept groping is not due to any deficiency in God or His revelation. The philosophers grope, "even though God is not far from each one of us." Verse 28 begins with the word, "for," and thereby offers a clarification or illustration of the statement that God is quite near at hand even for blinded pagan thinkers. The unbeliever's failure to find God and his acknowledged ignorance is not an innocent matter, and Paul demonstrates this by quoting two pagan poets. The strange idea that these quotations stand "as proof in the same way as biblical quotations in the other speeches of Acts"[29] is not only contrary to Paul's decided emphasis in his theology upon the unique authority of God's word, but it simply will not comport with the context of the Areopagus address wherein the groping, unrepentant ignorance of pagan religiosity is declared forcefully. Paul quotes the pagan writers to manifest their guilt. Since God is near at hand to all men, since His revelation impinges on them continually, they *cannot escape* a knowledge of their Creator and

Sustainer. They are without excuse for their perversion of the truth. Paul makes the point that *even* pagans, contrary to their spiritual disposition (1 Cor. 2:14), possess a knowledge of God which, though suppressed, renders them guilty before the Lord (Rom. 1:18ff.).

Paul supports this point before the Areopagus by showing that even pantheistic Stoics are aware of, and obliquely express, God's nearness and man's dependence upon Him. Epimenides the Cretan is quoted from a quatrain in an address to Zeus: "in him we live and move and have our being" (Acts 17:28a; interestingly, Paul quotes another line from this same quatrain in Titus 1:12). The phrase "in him" would have denoted in idiomatic Greek of the first century (especially in Jewish circles) the thought of "in his power" or "by him." This declaration—"By him we live..."—is not at all parallel to Paul's theology of the believer's mystical union with Christ, often expressed in terms of our being "in Christ." Rather, Acts 17:28 is closer to the teaching of Colossians 1:15-17, "in him were all things created...and in him all things consist." The stress falls on "man's absolute dependence on God for his existence,"[30] even though the original writing which Paul quoted had aimed to prove that Zeus was not dead from the fact that *men* live—the *order* of which thought is fully reversed in Paul's thinking (viz., men live because *God* lives). Paul's second quotation is introduced with the words, "as certain of your own poets have said." His use of the plural is further evidence of his educated familiarity with Greek thought, for as a matter of fact the statement which is quoted can be found in more than one writer. Paul quotes his fellow Cilician, Aratus, as saying "for we are also his offspring" (from the poem on "Natural Phenomena," which is also echoed in Cleanthes' "Hymn to Zeus"). Paul could agree to the formal statement that we are God's "offspring". However, he would certainly have said by way of qualification what the Stoics did not say, namely that we are children of God merely in a natural sense and not a supernatural sense (John 1:12), and even at that we are quite naturally "children of wrath" (Eph. 2:3). Yes, we can be called the offspring of God, but certainly *not* in the intended pantheistic sense of Aratus or Cleanthes! Knowing the historical and philosophical context in which Paul spoke, and noting the polemical thrusts of the Areopagus address, we cannot accept any interpreter's hasty pronouncement to the effect that Paul "cites these teachings with approval unqualified by allusion to a 'totally different frame of reference.'"[31] Those who make such remarks eventually are forced to acknowledge the qualification anyway: e.g., "Paul is not commending their Stoic doctrine," and he "did not reduce his categories to theirs."[32]

Berkouwer is correct when he says "There is no hint here of a point of contact in the sense of a preparation for grace, as though the Athenians were already on the way to true knowledge of God."[33] Paul was well enough informed to know, and able enough to read statements in context to see, that he did *not* agree with the *intended* meaning of these poets. He was certainly not saying that these philosophers had somehow arrived at unqualified, isolated, elements of the truth—that the Zeus of Stoic pantheism was a conceptual step toward the true God!

> This is to be explained only in connection with the fact that the heathen poets have distorted the truth of God.... Without this truth there would be no false religiousness. This should not be confused with the idea that false religion contains *elements* of the truth and gets its strength from those elements. This kind of quantitative analysis neglects the nature of the distortion carried on by false religion. Pseudo-religion witnesses to the truth of God in its apostasy.[34]

Within the ideological context of Stoicism and pantheism, of course, the declarations of the pagan philosophers about God were not true. And Paul was surely not committing the logical fallacy of equivocation by using pantheistically conceived premises to support a Biblically theistic conclusion. Rather, Paul appealed to the distorted teachings of the pagan authors as evidence that the process of theological distortion cannot fully rid men of their natural knowledge of God. Certain expressions of the pagans manifest this knowledge *as suppressed*. Within the philosophical context *espoused* by the ungodly writer, the expressions were put to a false use. Within the framework of God's revelation—a revelation clearly *received* by all men *but hindered* in unrighteousness, a revelation renewed in writing in the Scriptures possessed by Paul—these expressions properly expressed a truth of God. Paul did not utilize pagan ideas in his Areopagus address. He used pagan expressions to demonstrate that ungodly thinkers have not eradicated all idea, albeit suppressed and distorted, of the living and true God. F. F. Bruce remarks:

Epimenides and Aratus are not invoked as authorities in their own right; certain things which they said, however, can be understood as pointing to the knowledge of God. But the knowledge of God presented in the speech is not rationalistically conceived or established; it is the knowledge of God taught by Hebrew prophets and sages. It is rooted in the fear of God; it belongs to the same order as truth, goodness, and covenant-love; for lack of it men and women perish; in the coming day of God it will fill the earth 'as the waters cover the sea' (Is. 11:9). The 'delicately suited allusions' to Stoic and Epicurean tenets which have been discerned in the speech, like the quotations from pagan poets, have their place as points of contact with the audience, but they do not commit the speaker to acquiescence in the realm of ideas to which they originally belong.[35]

Paul demonstrated that even in their abuse of the truth pagans cannot avoid the truth of God; they must first *have* it in order that they might then distort it. As Ned B. Stonehouse observed,

The apostle Paul, reflecting upon their creaturehood, and upon their religious faith and practice, could discover within their pagan religiosity evidences that the pagan poets in the very act of suppressing and perverting the truth presupposed a measure of awareness of it.[36]

Their own statements unwittingly convicted the pagans of their knowledge of God, suppressed in unrighteousness. About the pagan quotations Van Til observes:

They could say this adventitiously only. That is, it would be in accord with what they deep down in their hearts knew to be true in spite of their systems. It was that truth which they sought to cover up by means of their professed systems, which enabled them to discover truth as philosophers and scientists.[37]

Men are engulfed by God's clear revelation; try as they may, the truth which they possess in their heart of hearts cannot be escaped, and inadvertently it comes to expression. They do not explicitly understand it properly; yet these expressions are a witness to their inward conviction and culpability. Consequently Paul could take advantage of pagan quotations, not as an agreed upon ground for erecting the message of the gospel, but as a basis for calling unbelievers to repentance for their flight from God. "Paul appealed to the heart of the natural man, whatever mask he might wear."[38]

Scriptural Presuppositions

In Acts 17:24-31 Paul's language is principally based on the Old Testament. There is little justification for the remark of Lake and Cadbury that this discourse used a secular style of speech, omitting quotations from the Old Testament.[39] Paul's utilization of Old Testament materials is rather conspicuous. For instance, we can clearly see Isaiah 42:5 coming to expression in Acts 17:24-25, as this comparison indicates:

> Thus saith God Jehovah, he that created the heavens and stretched them forth; he that spread abroad the earth and that which cometh out of it; he that giveth breath unto the people upon it...(Isaiah 42:5). The God that made the world and all thing therein, he, being Lord of heaven and earth...giveth to all life, and breath, and all things (Acts 17:24, 25).

In the Isaiah pericope, the prophet goes on to indicate that the Gentiles can be likened to men with eyes blinded by a dark dungeon (42:7), and in the Areopagus address Paul goes on to say that if men seek after God, it is as though they are groping in darkness (i.e., the sense for the Greek phrase "feel after Him," 17:27). Isaiah's development of thought continues on to the declaration that God's praise ought not to be given to graven images (42:8), while Paul's address advances to the statement that "we ought not to think that the Godhead is like unto gold, or silver, or stone, graven by the art and device of men (17:29). It surely seems as though the prophetic pattern of thought is in the back of the apostle's mind. F. F. Bruce correctly comments on Paul's method of argumentation before the Areopagus:

He does not argue from the sort of "first principles" which formed the basis of the various schools of Greek philosophy; his exposition and defense of his message are founded on the biblical revelation of God... Unlike some later apologists who followed in his steps, Paul does not cease to be fundamentally biblical in his approach to the Greeks, even when (as on this occasion) his biblical emphasis might appear to destroy his chances of success.[40]

Those who have been trained to think that the apologist must adjust his epistemological authority or method in terms of the mindset of his hearers as he finds them will find the Areopagus address quite surprising in this respect. Although Paul is addressing an audience which is not committed or even predisposed to the revealed Scriptures, namely educated Gentiles, his speech is nevertheless a *typically Jewish* polemic regarding God, idolatry, and judgment! Using Old Testament language and concepts, Paul declared that God is the Creator, a Spirit who does not reside in man-made houses (v. 24). God is self-sufficient, and all men are dependent upon Him (v. 25). He created all men from a common ancestor and is the Lord of history (v. 26). Paul continued to teach God's disapprobation for idolatry (v. 29), His demand for repentance (v. 30), and His appointment of a final day of judgment (v. 31). In these respects Paul did not say anything that an Old Testament prophet could not have addressed to the Jews. As the Lord Creator (cf. Isa. 42:5), God does not dwell in temples made by hand—the very same point spoken before the Jews by Stephen in his defense regarding statements about the Jerusalem temple which God himself commanded to be built (Acts 7:48). Both Paul and Stephen harkened back to the Old Testament, where it was taught that the heavens cannot contain God, and so neither could a man-made house (1 Kings 8:27; Isa. 66:l). And if God is not limited by a house erected by men, neither is He served by the sacrifices brought to such temples (Acts 17:25). Paul undoubtedly recalled the words of God through the Psalmist, "If I were hungry, I would not tell thee; For the world is mine, and the fullness thereof. Will I eat the flesh of bulls, or drink the blood of goats?" (Ps. 50:12-13). The Areopagus address stresses the fact that "life'" comes from God (v. 25), in whom "we live" (v. 28); such statements may have been subtle allusions to the etymology of the name of Zeus (*zao* in Greek, meaning 'to live')—the god exalted in the poetry of Aratus and Epimenides. The genuine Lord of life was Jehovah, the Creator, who in many ways was self-sufficient and very different from the Zeus of popular mythology or of pantheistic speculation. God has appointed the various seasons (or epochs) and boundaries of men (Acts 17:26)—even as the Psalmist wrote, "Thou hast set all the borders of the earth; Thou hast made summer and winter" (Ps. 74:17). Paul's mention of "appointed seasons" referred either to the regular seasons of the year (as in Acts 14:17, "fruitful seasons") or to the appointed periods for each nation's existence and prominence.[41] Either way, his doctrine was rooted in the Old Testament—the Noahic covenant (Gen. 8:22) or Daniel's interpretation of dreams (Dan. 2:36-45). Another point of contact between the Areopagus apologetic and the Old Testament is obvious in Acts 17:29. Paul indicated that nothing which is produced *by* man (i.e., any work of art) can be thought of as the producer *of* man. Here Paul's polemic is taken right out of the Old Testament prophets (e.g., Isa. 40:18-20). No idol can be likened to God or thought of as His image. God's image is found elsewhere, in the work of His own hands (cf. Gen. 1:27), and He thus prohibited the making of other pseudo-images of Himself ("Thou shalt not make unto thee a graven image...," Ex. 20:4). Paul's reasoning was steeped in God's special revelation.

Consistent with his teaching in the epistles, then, Paul remained on solid Christian ground when he disputed with the philosophers. He reasoned from the Scripture, thereby refuting any supposed dichotomy in his apologetic method between his approach to the Jews and his approach to the Gentiles. In any and all apologetic encounters Paul began and ended with God. "He was himself for no instant neutral."[42] "Like the biblical revelation itself, his speech begins with God the creator of all, continues with God the sustainer of all, and concludes with God the judge of all."[43] He had previously established his hearers' ignorance; so they were in no position to generate knowledgeable refutations of Paul's position. He had also indicated his authority to declare the truth; this was now reinforced by his appeal to the self-evidencing authority of God's revelation in the Old Testament Scriptures. Finally, he had established his audience's awareness and accountability to the truth of God in natural revelation. Paul now provides the interpretive context of special revelation to rectify the distorted handling of previous natural revelation and to supplement its teaching with the way of redemption.

Pressing the Antithesis

The themes of Paul's address in Acts 17 parallel those of Romans 1: creation, providence, man's dependence, man's sin, future judgment. Paul boldly sets the revelational perspective over against the themes of Athenian philosophy. The statements of Paul's Areopagus address could hardly have been better calculated to reflect Biblical theology while contradicting the doctrines of pagan philosophy. Paul did not appeal to Stoic doctrines in order to divide his audience (a ploy used in Acts 23:6).[44] Rather he philosophically offended both the Epicurean and Stoic philosophers in his audience, pressing teaching which was directly antithetical to their distinctives.

Against the monism of the philosophers, Paul taught that God had created all things (v. 24; cf. Ex. 20:11; Ps. 146:6; Isa 37:16; 42:5). This precluded the materialism of the Epicureans and the pantheism of the Stoics. Against naturalistic and immanentistic views Paul proclaimed supernatural transcendence. As his listeners looked upon the Parthenon, Paul declared that God does not dwell in temples made with hands (1 Kings 8:27; Isa 66:1-2).

God needs nothing from man; on the contrary man depends on God for everything (v. 25; cf. Ps. 50:9-12; Isa 42:5). The philosophers of Athens should thus do all things to God's glory—which is inclusive of bringing every thought captive to Him, and thereby renouncing their putative autonomy. Paul's teaching of the unity of the human race (v. 26a) was quite a blow to the Athenians' pride in their being indigenous to the soil of Attica, and it assaulted their felt superiority over "barbarians." Paul's insistence that God was not far from any would deflate the Stoic's pride in his elitist knowledge of God (v. 27b). Over against a uniform commitment to the concept of fate Paul set forth the Biblical doctrine of God's providence (v. 26b; cf. Deut. 32:8); God is not remote from or indifferent to the world of men.

Upon the legendary founding by Athena of the Areopagus court, Apollo had declared (according to Aeschylus): "When the dust drinks up a man's blood, Once he has died, there is no resurrection." However, the apostle Paul forcefully announced the resurrection of Jesus Christ, a fact which assures all men that He will judge the world at the consummation (Ps. 9:8; 96:13; 98:9; Dan. 7:13; John 5:27; Rom. 2:16)—a doctrine which contravened the Greek views of both cyclic and eternal history. The Epicureans were deceived to think that at death man's body simply decomposed, and that thus there was no fear of judgment; the resurrection refuted their ideas, just as it disproved the notion that the body is a disdainful prison. Throughout Paul's address the common skepticism about theological knowledge found in the philosophic schools was obviously challenged by Paul's pronounced authority and ability to openly proclaim the final truth about God.

Calling for Repentance and Change of Mindset

One can hardly avoid the conclusion that Paul was *not* seeking areas of agreement or common notions with his hearers. At every point he set his Biblical position in *antithetical contrast* to their philosophical beliefs, undermining their assumptions and exposing their ignorance. He did not seek to add further truths to a pagan foundation of elementary truth. Paul rather challenged the foundations of pagan philosophy and called the philosophers to full *repentance* (v. 30).

The new era which has commenced with the advent and ministry of Jesus Christ has put an end to God's historical overlooking of nations which lived in unbelief. At Lystra Paul declared that in past generations God "allowed all nations to walk in their own ways" (Acts 14:16), although now He was calling them to turn from their vanities to the living God (14:15). Previously, God had shown forbearance toward the sins of the Jews as well (cf. Rom. 3:25). However, with the advent of Christ, there has been a new beginning. Sins once committed in culpable ignorance have been made even *less* excusable by the redemptive realities of the gospel. Even in the past God's forbearance ought to have led men to repentance (Rom. 2:4). How much more, then, should men *now* respond to their guilt by repenting before God for their sins. The lenience of God demonstrates that His concentration of effort is toward the salvation rather than judgment of men (cf. John 3:17). This mercy and patience must not be spurned. Men everywhere are now *required* to repent. In Paul's perspective on redemptive history, he can simply say by way of summary: "*Now* is the acceptable time" (2 Cor. 6:2). As guilty as men had been in the past, God had passed over confrontation with them. Unlike in Israel, messengers had not come to upbraid the Gentiles and declare the punishment they deserved. God had "overlooked" (not "winked at"' with its inappropriate connotations) the former times of ignorance (Acts 17:30). Whereas in the past He had allowed the pagans to walk in their own ways, *now* with the perfect revelation which has come in Jesus Christ, God commands repentance (a "change of mind") of all men and sends messengers to them toward that end. Paul wanted the philosophers at Athens to not simply refine their thinking a bit further and add some missing information to it; but rather to abandon their presuppositions and have a complete change of mind, submitting to the clear and authoritative revelation of God. If they would not repent, it would be an indication of their love for *ignorance* and hatred of genuine knowledge.

Paul's appeal to them to repent was grounded not in autonomous argumentation but the presupposed authority of God's Son (v. 31), an authority for which there was none more ultimate in Paul's reasoning. Paul's hearers were told that they must repent, for God had appointed a day of final judgment; if the philosophers did not undergo a radical shift in their mindset and confess their sinfulness before God, they would have to face the wrath of God on the day of final accounting.

To whom would they have to give account? At this point Paul introduced the "Son of Man eschatology" of the gospels. The judgment would take place by a man (literally, a 'male') who had been ordained to this function by God. This man is the "Son of Man" mentioned in Daniel 7:13. In John 5:27, Christ spoke of himself, saying that the Father "gave him authority to execute judgment, because he is the Son of Man." After His resurrection Christ charged the apostles "to preach unto the people and to testify that this is He who is ordained of God to be the Judge of the living and the dead" (Acts 10:42). Paul declared this truth in his Areopagus apologetic, going on to indicate that God had given "assurance"' or proof of the fact that Christ would be mankind's final Judge. This proof was provided by the resurrection of Jesus Christ from the dead.

To be accurate, it is important for us to note that the resurrection was evidence in Paul's argumentation, it was *not* the conclusion of his argumentation. He was arguing, *not* for the resurrection, but for final judgment by Christ. The misleading *assumption* made by many popular evangelical apologists is that Paul here engaged in an attempted proof of the resurrection—although nothing of the sort is mentioned by Luke. Proof *by means* of the resurrection is mistakenly seen in verse 31 as proof *of* the resurrection.[45] Others know better than to read such an argument *into* the text and hold that detailed proof of the resurrection was *cut short* in Paul's address.[46] He *would* have proceeded to this line of reasoning, we are told, if he had not been interrupted by his mocking hearers. Once again, however, such an interpretation gains whatever plausibility it has with an interpreter in terms of preconceived notions, rather than in terms of textual support. F. F. Bruce remarks, "There is no ground for supposing that the ridicule with which some of his hearers received his reference to Jesus' rising from the dead seriously curtailed the speech he intended to make."[47] Haenchen says, "There is no hint that Paul is interrupted"; the speech as it appears in Acts 17 "is inherently quite complete."[48] Paul proclaimed that Christ had been appointed the final Judge of mankind, as His resurrection from the dead evidenced. The Apostle did not supply an empirical argument for the resurrection, but argued theologically from the fact of the resurrection to the final judgment. For Paul, even in apologetical disputes before unbelieving philosophers, there was no authority more ultimate than that of Christ. This epistemological attitude was most appropriate in light of the fact that Christ would be the ultimate Judge of man's every thought and belief.

The Outcome of Paul's Apologetic

Acts 17:32-34 (American Standard Version)

(32) NOW WHEN THEY HEARD OF THE RESURRECTION OF THE DEAD, SOME MOCKED; BUT OTHERS SAID, WE WILL HEAR THEE CONCERNING THIS YET AGAIN.

(33) THUS PAUL WENT OUT FROM AMONG THEM.

(34) BUT CERTAIN MEN CLAVE UNTO HIM, AND BELIEVED: AMONG WHOM ALSO WAS DIONYSIUS THE AREOPAGITE, AND A WOMAN NAMED DAMARIS, AND OTHERS WITH THEM.

Had Paul spoken of the immortality of the soul, his message might have appeared plausible to at least some of the philosophers in his audience. However all disdained the idea of the resuscitation of a corpse. When Paul concluded his discourse with reference to the resurrection of

Christ, such an apparent absurdity led some hearers to "sneer" in open mockery of Paul. There is some question as to what should be made of another reaction mentioned by Luke—namely, that some said they would hear Paul again on this matter. This may have been a polite procrastination serving as a brush-off,[49] an indication that this segment of the audience was confused or bewildered with the message,[50] or evidence that some wistfully hoped that Paul's proclamation might prove to be true.[51] One way or another, it should not have been thought impossible by anybody in Paul's audience that God could raise the dead (cf. Acts 26:8), but as long as this philosophical assumption controlled their thinking, the philosophers would never be induced to accept the fact of the resurrection or allow it to make a difference in their outlook.

Until the Holy Spirit regenerates the sinner and brings him to repentance, his presuppositions will remain unaltered. And as long as the unbeliever's presuppositions are unchanged a proper acceptance and understanding of the good news of Christ's historical resurrection will be impossible. The Athenian philosophers had originally asked Paul for an account of his doctrine of resurrection. After his reasoned defense of the hope within him and his challenge to the philosopher's presuppositions, a few were turned around in their thinking. But many refused to correct their presuppositions, so that when Paul concluded with Christ's resurrection they ridiculed and mocked.

Acceptance of the facts is governed by one's most ultimate assumptions, as Paul was well aware. Paul began his apologetic with God and His revelation; he concluded his apologetic with God and His revelation. The Athenian philosophers began their dispute with Paul in an attitude of cynical unbelief about Christ's resurrection; they concluded the dispute in cynical unbelief about Christ's resurrection. However, Paul knew and demonstrated that the "closed system" of the philosophers was a matter of dialectical pseudo-wisdom and ignorance. Their view that God dwelt in impenetrable mystery undermined their detailed teaching about Him. Their view that historical eventuation was a matter of irrational fate was contravened by their conviction that all things are mechanistically determined, and so on. In their "wisdom" they had become utterly ignorant of the ultimate truth.

Paul knew that the explanation of their hostility to God's revelation (even though they evidenced an inability to escape its forcefulness) was to be found in their desire to exercise control over God (e.g., v. 29) and to avoid facing up to the fact of their deserved punishment before the judgment seat of God (v. 30). They secretly hoped that ignorance would be bliss, and so preferred darkness to light (John 3:19-20). So Paul "went out from among them" (v. 33)—a statement which expresses nothing about his apologetic being cut short, and which gives no evidence that Paul was somehow disappointed with his effort. Such thoughts must be read into the verse.

The minds of the Athenian philosophers could not be changed simply by appealing to a few disputed, particular facts, for their philosophical presuppositions determined what they would make of the facts. Nor could their minds be altered by reasoning with them on the basis of their own fundamental assumptions; to make common cause with their philosophy would simply have been to confirm their commitment to it. Their minds could be changed only by challenging their whole way of thought with the completely different worldview of the gospel, calling them to renounce the inherent foolishness of their own philosophical perspectives and to repent for their suppression of the truth about God.

Such a complete mental revolution, allowing for a well-grounded and philosophically defensible knowledge of the truth, can be accomplished by the grace of God (cf. 2 Tim. 2:25). Thus Luke informs us that as Paul left the Areopagus meeting, "certain men clave unto him and believed" (v. 34). There is a note of triumph in Luke's observation that some within Paul's audience became believers as a result of his apologetic presentation. He mentions conspicuously that a member of the Areopagus Counsel, Dionysius, became a Christian, as well as a woman who was well enough known to be mentioned by name, Damaris. These were but some converts "among others." Ecclesiastical tradition dating from around 170 A.D. says that Dionysius was appointed by Paul as the first elder in Athens. (In the fifth century certain pseudepigraphical works of a neoplatonic character made use of his name.) However Luke himself mentions no church having been planted in Athens, as we would have expected an educated Gentile to mention if a church had been started in Athens. Indeed, a family residing in Corinth was taken by Paul as the ecclesiastical "firstfruits of Achaia" (1 Cor. 16:15). Apparently no church was immediately developed in the city of Athens, even though patristic writers (especially Origen) mention a church being in Athens—eventually getting under way sometime after Paul's ministry there, so it seems. The earliest post-apostolic apologists, Quadratus and Aristides, wrote during the time of Emperor Hadrian, and both were from Athens. However we choose to reconstruct the ecclesiastical history of the city, it is plain that Paul's work there was not futile. By God's grace it did see success, and his apologetic method can be a guide and goad for us today. Would that we had the boldness in a proud university setting, enjoying the highest level of culture of the day, to proclaim clearly to the learned philosophers, with their great minds, that they are in fact ignorant idolaters who must repent in light of the coming judgment by God's resurrected Son.

Observations in Retrospect

(1) Paul's Areopagus address in Acts 17 has been found to set forth a classic and exemplary encounter between Christian commitment and secular thinking—between "Jerusalem and Athens." The Apostle's apologetical method for reasoning with educated unbelievers who did not acknowledge scriptural authority turns out to be a suitable pattern for our defending the faith today.

(2) Judging from Paul's treatment of the Athenian philosophers, he was not prepared to dismiss their learning, but neither would he let it exercise corrective control over his Christian perspective. The two realms of thought were obviously dealing with common questions, but Paul did not work to integrate apparently supportive elements from pagan philosophy into his system of Christian thought. Because of the truth-distorting and ignorance-engendering character of unbelieving thought, Paul's challenge was that *all reasoning* be placed within the presuppositional context of revelational truth and Christian commitment. The relation "Athens" should sustain to "Jerusalem" was one of necessary dependence.

(3) Rather than trying to construct a natural theology upon the philosophical platform of his opponents—assimilating autonomous thought wherever possible—Paul's approach was to accentuate the antithesis between himself and the philosophers. He never assumed a neutral stance, knowing that the natural theology of the Athenian philosophers was inherently a natural idolatry. He could not argue from their unbelieving premises to Biblical conclusions without equivocation in understanding. Thus his own distinctive outlook was throughout placed over against the

philosophical commitments of his hearers.

(4) Nothing remotely similar to what is called in our day the historical argument for Christ's resurrection plays a part in Paul's reasoning with the philosophers. The declaration of Christ's historical resurrection was crucial, of course, to his presentation. However he did not argue for it independently on empirical grounds as a brute historical—yet miraculous—event, given then an apostolic interpretation. Argumentation about a particular fact would not force a shift in the unbeliever's presuppositional framework of thought. Paul's concern was with this basic and controlling perspective or web of central convictions by which the particulars of history would be weighed and interpreted.

(5) In pursuing the presuppositional antithesis between Christian commitment and secular philosophy, Paul consistently took as his ultimate authority Christ and God's word—not independent speculation and reasoning, not allegedly indisputable eyeball facts of experience, not the satisfaction or peace felt within his heart. God's revelational truth—learned through his senses, understood with his mind, comforting his heart, and providing the context for all life and thought—was his self-evidencing starting point. It was the presuppositional platform for authoritatively declaring the truth, and it was presented as the sole reasonable option for men to choose.

(6) Paul's appeal was to the inescapable knowledge of God which all men have in virtue of being God's image and in virtue of His revelation through nature and history. A point of contact could be found even in pagan philosophers due to their inalienable religious nature. Paul indicated that unbelievers are conspicuously guilty for distorting and suppressing the truth of God.

(7) In motivation and direction Paul's argumentation with the Athenian philosophers was presuppositional. He set two fundamental worldviews in contrast, exhibiting the ignorance which results from the unbeliever's commitments, and presenting the precondition of all knowledge—God's revelation—as the only reasonable alternative. His aim was to effect an *overall* change in outlook and mindset, to call the unbeliever

to repentance, by following the two-fold procedure of internally critiquing the unbeliever's position and presenting the necessity of the Scripture's truth. Through it all, it should also be observed, Paul remained yet earnest. His manner was one of humble boldness.

Notes:

[1] F.F. Bruce, *The Defence of the Gospel in the New Testament* (Grand Rapids: Wm. B. Eerdmans, 1959), p.18.

[2] E.g., H. Conzelmann, "The Address of Paul on the Areopagus," *Studies in Luke-Acts*, ed. L. E. Keck and J. L. Martyn (Nashville: Abingdon, 1966), pp. 217ff. A. Schweitzer, *The Mysticism of Paul the Apostle* (New York: H. Holt, 1931), pp. 6ff.

[3] Johannes Munck, *The Anchor Bible: The Acts of the Apostles*, revised by W. F. Albright and C. S. Mann (Garden City, New York: Doubleday & Co., 1967), p. 173; cf. Adolf Harnack, *The Mission and Expansion of Christianity* (New York: Harper and Brothers, 1961), p. 383.

[4] Kirsopp Lake and Henry J. Cadbury, *The Acts of the Apostles*, vol. 4 (Translation and Commentary) in *The Beginnings of Christianity*, Part 1, ed. F. J. Roakes Jackson and Kirsopp Lake (Grand Rapids: Baker Book House, 1965 [1932]), pp. 208-209.

[5] Ernst Haenchen, *The Acts of the Apostles, a Commentary* (Philadelphia: Westminster Press, 1971 [German, 1965]), pp. 528, 529.

[6] E.g., W. M. Ramsay, *St. Paul the Traveller and the Roman Citizen* (New York: G. P. Putnam's Sons, 1896), p. 252; cf. P. Vielhauer, "On the 'Paulinism' of Acts," *Studies in Luke-Acts*, ed. Keck and Martyn, pp. 36-37.

[7] Ned B. Stonehouse, *Paul Before the Areopagus and Other New Testament Studies* (Grand Rapids: Wm. B. Eerdmans, 1957), pp. 9-10.

[8] Martin Dielius, *Studies in the Acts of the Apostles* (New York: Charles Scribner's Sons, 1956), p. 79.

[9] Bertil Gartner, *The Areopagus Speech and Natural Revelation* (Uppsala: C. W. K. Gleerup, 1955), p. 52.

[10] For further details on the philosophical schools of the Hellenic and Roman periods the reader can consult with profit the standard historical studies of Guthrie, Brehier, and Copleston.

[11] Cf. Oscar Broneer, "Athens: City of Idol Worship," *The Biblical Archaeologist* 21 (February, 1958):4-6.

[12] For a comparison of the apologetical methods of Socrates and Paul see G. L. Bahnsen, "Socrates or Christ: The Reformation of Christian Apologetics," in *Foundations of Christian Scholarship*, ed. Gary North (Vallecito, CA: Ross House Books, 1976).

[13] Cornelius Van Til, *Paul at Athens* (Phillipsburg, New Jersey: L. J. Grotenhuis, n.d.), pp. 2, 3.

[14] Contrary to Haenchen, *Acts Commentary*, pp. 518-519, 520.

[15] For the affirmative position see Gartner, *Areopagus Speech*, pp. 64-65; for the negative see Haenchen, *Acts Commentary*, p. 519.

[16] Lake and Cadbury, *Acts of the Apostles*, p. 213.

[17] Van Til, *Paul at Athens*, p. 14.

[18] Cornelius Van Til, *A Christian Theory of Knowledge* (Nutley, New Jersey: Presbyterian and Reformed, 1969), p. 293.

[19] For further discussion of the presuppositional method, refer to the earlier chapters of this book.

[20] F. F. Bruce, *Commentary on the Book of Acts*, in the New International Commentary on the New Testament (Grand Rapids: Wm. B. Eerdmans, 1955), p. 356.

[21] Adolf Deissman, *Paul: A Study in Social and Religious History* (London: Hodder and Stroughton, 1926), pp. 287-291.

[22] G. C. Berkouwer, *General Revelation* (Grand Rapids: Wm. B. Eerdmans, 1955), p. 145.

[23] Munck, *Anchor Bible: Acts*, p. 171.

[24] J. H. Moulton and George Milligan, *The Vocabulary of the Greek New Testament* (Grand Rapids: Wm. B. Eerdmans, 1950), p. 324.

[25] Van Til, *Paul at Athens*, p. 5.

[26] Henry Alford, *The Greek New Testament* (Boston: Lee and Shepherd Publishers, 1872), 2:198.

[27] J. B. Lightfoot, "St. Paul and Seneca," *St. Paul's Epistle to the Phillipians* (Grand Rapids: Zondervan Publishing House, 1953), p. 304.

[28] Berkouwer, *General Revelation*, p. 145.

[29] Haenchen, *Acts Commentary*, p. 525.

[30] Gartner, *Areopagus Speech*, p. 188.

[31] Gordon R. Lewis, "Mission to the Athenians" part IV, Seminary Study Series (Denver: Conservative Baptist Theological Seminary, November, 1964), p. 7; cf. pp. 1, 6, 8, and part III, p. 5.

[32] Ibid., part III, p. 2; part IV, p. 6.

[33] Berkouwer, *General Revelation*, p. 143.

[34] Ibid., p. 144.

[35] F. F. Bruce, "Paul and the Athenians," *The Expository Times* 88 (October, 1976): 11.

[36] Stonehouse, *Paul Before the Areopagus*, p. 30.

[37] Van Til, *Paul at Athens*, p. 12.

[38] Ibid., p. 2.

[39] Lake and Cadbury, *Acts of the Apostles*, p. 209.

[40] F. F. Bruce, *The Defense of the Gospel in the New Testament*, pp. 38, 46-47.

[41] Compare Gartner, *Areopagus Speech*, pp. 147-152, with Haenchen, *Acts Commentary*, p. 523.

[42] Berkouwer, *General Revelation*, pp. 142-143.

[43] F. F. Bruce, "*Paul and the Athenians*," p. 9.

[44] Contrary to E. M. Blaiklock, *The Acts of the Apostles, An Historical Commentary*, in the Tyndale New Testament Commentaries, ed. R. V. G. Tasker (Grand Rapids: Wm. B. Eerdmans, 1959), pp. 140-141.

[45] E.g., R. C. Sproul, tape "Paul at Mars' Hill," in the series Exegetical Bible

Studies: Acts (Pennsylvania: Ligonier Valley Study Center), tape AX-13.

[46] E.g., Blaiklock, *Acts, Historical Commentary*, p. 142; Everett F. Harrison, *Acts: The Expanding Church* (Chicago: Moody Press, 1975), p. 272.

[47] F. F. Bruce, *Book of Acts*, p. 362.

[48] Haenchen, *Acts Commentary*, p. 526.

[49] Harrison, *Acts*, p. 273.

[50] Lake and Cadbury, *Acts of the Apostles*, p. 219.

[51] J. S. Steward, *A Faith to Proclaim* (New York: Charles Scribner's Sons, 1953), p. 117.

Scripture Index

Index

A

academic: 5, 182
Academy, the: 241
accountability: 254
Acropolis: 245
Adam: 173
Aeschylus: 223, 266
afterlife: 177, 207
agnostic: 8, 9, 65, 103, 159
agnosticism: 9, 11, 15
agora: 246
Albright, W. F.: 149
always ready: 115, 151
Anaxagoras: 249
Angeles, Peter: 193
anonymous: 255
anti-materialist: 241
Antiochus of Ascalon: 241
Antipater of Tarsus: 240
antitheism: 170
antithesis: 7, 8, 23, 39, 77, 84, 124, 128, 257, 259, 266, 272, 273
antithetical: 67, 253, 258, 266, 267
Apollo: 266
apologetic: 59, 69, 72, 74, 83, 85, 96, 128, 240, 246, 249, 251, 254, 256, 265, 270
  encounter: 104
  method: 88
  procedure: 64, 77
  strategy: 63, 67, 239
  success: 65, 83, 85, 88, 89, 95, 100

apologetics: 3, 5, 7, 9, 16, 51, 55, 63, 64, 65, 71, 72, 74, 75, 103, 109, 111, 115, 118, 120, 123, 126, 130, 133, 140, 141, 151, 163. *See also* Defense of the Faith
apologist: 3, 33, 60, 62, 64, 68, 72, 73, 75, 78, 80, 85, 88, 91, 95, 96, 99, 100, 103, 112, 118, 127, 138, 141, 148, 157, 194, 196, 228, 235, 253, 264, 268
Aratus: 243, 260, 262, 265
arbitrary: 138, 141, 170, 186, 193, 196
Arcesilaus: 241
Areios pagos: 248
Areopagus: 223, 238, 239, 240, 245, 247, 252, 254, 255, 260, 261, 263, 264, 266, 271, 272
argument: 5, 7, 32, 33, 63, 68, 111, 129, 130
argument chains: 72
argumentation: 41, 55, 67, 68, 70, 71, 73, 74, 77, 91, 93, 105, 133
argumentative: 129
Aristides: 272
Aristotle: 133, 135, 241
Arminianism: 229
arrogant: 111, 129, 251
assumptions: 4, 7, 13, 17, 24, 55, 67, 68, 77, 79, 84, 88, 95, 105, 119, 121, 136,

140, 141, 198, 246, 267, 268, 270, 271
atheism: 149
atheistic: 57
atheists: 103
Athena: 245, 266
Athenodorus the Stoic: 241
Athens: 196, 235, 236, 237, 238, 240, 241, 242, 243, 244, 246, 255, 257, 258, 266, 268, 271, 272
atomism: 153, 241
atomistic: 55
attitude: 4, 64
Augustine: 20
authority: 16, 17, 24, 25, 50, 57, 63, 65, 68, 69, 72, 73, 74, 79, 89, 99, 101, 105, 112, 113, 142, 151, 173, 174, 198, 199, 200, 212, 235, 236, 237, 253, 257, 259, 264, 265, 267, 268, 272
  God's: 16, 17, 24, 25
  self-attesting: 23, 25–26
autonomous: 47, 48, 51, 56, 57, 64, 83, 85, 87, 88, 92, 96, 97, 99, 100, 101, 154, 157, 158, 201, 230, 231, 254, 268, 272
autonomy: 16, 20, 24, 39, 46, 49, 51, 52, 56, 57, 65, 84, 93, 95, 106, 114, 221, 266
Ayer, A. J.: 211

B

Bacchus: 245